NEW GAME+

The Geek's Guide to Love, Sex, & Dating

HARRIS O'MALLEY

CONTENTS

Author's Note   v

1. The Secret Origin of Dr. NerdLove   1

2. Adjust Your Attitude, Fix Your Dating Life   8

3. Women Love Assholes (And Other Dating Myths)   26

4. How to Be the Most Interesting Man in the World   41

5. How to Be More Attractive in 5 Easy Steps   76

6. How to Talk to Women   116

7. How to Build Attraction   162

8. The Attraction Plan   196

9. Dating for Dummies   247

10. I Got Her Home... Now What? A Guide to What Comes Next   282

11. Dating Pitfalls   313

12.   After Completion   341

      Further Resources   345
      About the Author   347

AUTHOR'S NOTE

Before you get started on your journey to building a new and better life, I wanted to give you some tips on how to get the most out of this book. It'll be tempting to leap around from section to section, focusing on specific sections. This will actually end up slowing your progress.

Dating is a holistic activity and this book is written to reflect this. Most dating issues don't stem from a lack of skill, but from deeply held negative attitudes and beliefs – either about yourself or other people. My system helps you rebuild yourself from the inside out, focusing on your inner self before moving on to your exterior; skipping around means you run the risk of trying to treat the symptoms of your dating dilemmas rather than the underlying causes.

And while this *is* written for heterosexual men looking for romantic or sexual relationships, all of the advice herein can still apply on many levels for queer and platonic relationships.

CHAPTER 1.

THE SECRET ORIGIN OF DR. NERDLOVE

I want to make this clear from the very start: no matter how bad you are at dating... I was worse than you. I've made just about every single mistake possible. I've stewed in the bitter resentment that only a socially awkward geek with absolutely no facility with women can know. I watched girls I'd harbored not-so-secret crushes on hook up with jocks and assholes who would go out of their way to flaunt their success in front of me. I was the prototypical geek: bookish and unathletic, with the sort of skin tone that can only be achieved by bathing in the cathode ray glow of the TV while playing hours of Super Nintendo.

Most importantly, I had little sense of style or how to relate to girls. In fact, it seemed as though I'd carefully structured my life so as to make sex disappear. While everyone else was into sports, the high-school social scene, and who was hooking up with whom, I was into video games, comic books and anime. I didn't lack a sense of style so much as turn myself into a singularity from which no fashion sense could escape. I owned a Three Wolf Moon shirt. I was the proud owner of a silk – not rayon, but honest-to-God silk – shirt from Hot Topic with anime characters from X/1999 emblazoned on it. And I thought it was cooler than a penguin's ass in ice cream.

My idea of flirting involved following the girl I liked like a lost puppy. I spent so much time in the Friend Zone that I could declare it my primary residence and run for political office there. There was not a single part of my life that didn't seem to be built to ensure that I would never see a woman naked in person.

Plus, I was surrounded by people who outclassed me in every way possible, which didn't help the continual crotch-kicks of my life. Most of my close friends were all naturally socially gifted. My brother was a jock. One of my oldest, dearest friends looked like the love-child of Hugh Grant and Rob Lowe and attracted women the way that cheese attracts mice. And then there was me: "The One Who Wasn't Good With Girls." I was a Geek with a capital-G, pathetic, sexless and doomed to a life of permanent virginity and being "like a brother" to every girl I ever lusted after.

Naturally, I believed in the Dating Binary; either you were good with girls or you weren't... and there was simply no way to change this. Even attempting to try was guaranteed to mark you as a pathetic loser trying to rise above his station.

By the time I graduated from college, I had been in exactly one relationship, which turned so toxic that I ended up in therapy. For years after that break-up, I stumbled from one pathetic attempt at getting a girlfriend to another until the night it all changed for me. The night I had my Batman moment.

It was the night of my brother's wedding and I had

developed a massive crush on one of the guests. Unfortunately, she had also caught the eye of my friend Miles – the aforementioned Hugh Grant/Rob Lowe love-child. Full of young lust and a determination to win, Miles and I went head to head over her... and I lost. And because the universe was powered by my tears, Miles happened to have the room next to mine. So as I sat there, listening to them, crying and masturbating while using my tears as lube, I resolved that this would never happen to me again. I demanded a sign, a sign from the universe...

(...by which I mean I googled "How to get girls"...)

...and I got my answer.

Where Bruce Wayne found inspiration from a bat crashing through his window, I found inspiration in a review of Neil Strauss' "The Game – Penetrating The Secret Society of Pick-Up Artists." It was the first time that anyone ever explained that dating is a skill that even a geek like me could learn! I raised my fists to the sky and said, "Yes, I shall become... a pick-up artist!"

I took to pick-up with the zeal of the newly converted. I changed my hair, tossed out my old wardrobe and started to rebuild my life from the ground up. After having spent so long believing that sex was something that happened to other people, I was determined that, by God, I was going to be the player I never thought I could be. I dove into the Austin bar and club scene like Templeton the Rat chowing down at the garbage smorgasbord that was the county fair... and it made me *fucking miserable.*

I was getting laid like a bandit to be sure, but I wasn't happy at all. I was spending time in bars I hated surrounded by people I loathed, paying too much for beer, choking on cigarette smoke – all in the name of getting my dick wet. Everything about my life became about pick-up. The majority of my social circle were my wingmen and fellow PUAs in town. Almost every conversation I had inevitably revolved back to the topic of pick-up. I was out three or four nights a week. I came home reeking of smoke, stale beer and a miasma of cologne and AXE body spray, with my head pounding and my ears ringing. If I scored that night, then I was on the top of the world... but if I didn't, I was dragging the tattered remains of my ego home with me feeling lower than a snake's balls in a drainage ditch.

And the less said about how I was treating women, the better. Women were targets. They were gatekeepers, withholding access to the sex I wanted so I had to cajole or persuade them into giving it up. They were just about anything except actual people and so I treated them abominably.

It was only when I stepped away from the community that I started to recognize the problem and was able to fix things. I wasn't just having sex because I'm a sexual person and it was part of who I was; I was using sex as validation. The more sex I had, the better a person I must be. When you're getting your validation from sex and using other people as a yardstick to measure your success, you're going to end up in a dark and unpleasant place.

This wasn't the answer; it was only a stepping stone along the way.

You see, the reason why guys respond to pick-up artistry is that there is so little worthwhile information out there for men who want to get better at dating. The traditional advice – "women want a nice guy," "just be yourself," and "you'll find love when you're not looking" – is worse than useless. It actually retards a person's chances at finding love or sex by teaching them all of the wrong lessons. Pick-up, on the other hand, promises you results and gives you concrete ideas about what to do. It takes something that seems arcane and mysterious and makes it relatable. Even better, if you're a nerd, it turns social interaction into a formula. It demystifies everything and – even better – gives you specific things to say and do with pre-canned material, a "progression model," even an idea of what you should be doing when – here's when you touch her, here's when you should kiss her, here's when you should take her back to your room. If that seems kind of sketchy… that's because it is. But when you're an awkward nerd who treats Ducky like his patron saint, being able to treat meeting women like running a raid on the Lich King is incredibly appealing. It's a frame of reference you can understand: Okay, she's thrown up her bitch-shield, you need to use a neg to bring it down, then apply kino to bring up her buying temperature.

But the problem is that this is a Band-Aid at best. It's Dumbo's misogynistic magic feather, convincing you that if you create this false persona and use these pre-scripted routines and canned material, you can achieve success. Not only does it teach you to treat women as the enemy, but it means you're not addressing your real issues. Hell, you're not even living your own life; you're papering over it with somebody else's idea of what women like.

I left the pick-up scene because frankly I didn't like what it was turning me into. But at the same time, I had to admit that I learned a lot. And just between you, me and everyone else who bought this book… I was loving getting laid. So it became my mission to figure out how to take what I'd learned and turn it into something positive. I wanted to work out how to meet and attract women without the toxic mindset that turns sex into a competition and how you can find the relationship you want while still being your authentic self instead of a persona.

And so I attacked the question with the laser-like focus that only nerds and religious zealots can apply. I studied every book I could get my hands on about influence, social dynamics, sex, grooming, and interpersonal relationships. I had to unlearn everything I knew about meeting women, to sort out the gold from the dross, and relearn it with these new ideals in mind. My personal life took a dive, which nearly sent me into the depths of despair... but then it started to come back, rising like an especially geeky phoenix from the ashes.

At the time, I was also a member of a geek-interest podcast, the League of Extremely Ordinary Gentlemen. One fateful evening, we did a Valentine's Day episode entitled "The League Versus Our Evil Exes" dedicated to answering our listener's questions. As the resident man-about-town, I took the lead by sharing my perspective and what I'd learned over the years.

That was the night Dr. NerdLove was born.

It's been a crazy ride since then. A podcast episode and a nickname given in jest turned into a blog – www.doctornerdlove.com – which took off like wildfire. Since then, I've been dispensing advice via blog and podcast to an audience of hundreds of thousands and have been featured in podcasts, blogs, newspapers, magazines and on television shows around the world.

And now, I want to give you something that I wish I'd had all those long years ago. I want to help you avoid the mistakes I made and skip the heartache and frustration that I went through as I tried to learn how to get better at dating. In short: I want to give you the instruction manual that I wish I'd had when I was twelve, when I was eighteen, when I was twenty-one. I want to teach you how to build the life you've always wanted and finally find the dating success you've always dreamed of.

Strap yourselves in. It's going to be an amazing ride.

(Remember: Dr. NerdLove is not a real doctor.)

CHAPTER 2.

ADJUST YOUR ATTITUDE, FIX YOUR DATING LIFE

HOW YOUR MENTALITY AFFECTS YOUR DATING LIFE

I'm going to let you in on a secret. In fact, this is something most dating gurus and relationship experts won't tell you: dating isn't as hard as you're making it out to be. In fact, most of the time when you're having problems with dating... the answer is usually that you're standing in your own goddamned way.

Now, before you get upset over my having told you that your biggest dating issue is, well, you, let me explain.

You see, I've been where you are. I've been the guy who couldn't get a girlfriend to save his life. I've been the Nice GuyTM who was "just like a brother" to the girl I had a crush on. I've been the "eww, not even if we were the last two people on Earth." I've been the creeper and the bitter, resentful single guy. But underpinning the vast majority of my dating issues was simply me. More specifically, it was my attitude. It was the way I viewed myself and – critically – the way I viewed the world around me. One of the hardest things I had to learn over the years is how many of my dating "problems" were entirely in my head. I was my own worst enemy... just like you are yours.

As long as you believe that you're undatable, that women only go for "other guys" or that you've been uniquely fucked over by the universe, you *will* be. You can't improve – and you won't improve – until you believe you can. The stronger your belief in your ability to change and improve, in your very basic desirability, the better you will be at dating. I'll be the first to admit that this sounds like some Eckhart Tolle/*Think and Grow Rich*/*The Secret* bullshit that promises you that you'll eventually sleep with Scarlett Johansson just because you really, *really* want to[1]... but it's completely true.

You see, the key to dating success isn't amazing good looks or the gift of gab. In fact, dating success is 80% attitude and 20% skill. A lot of the supposed "secrets" to dating – whether it's pre-canned material from the pick-up artist scene to dating/lifestyle makeovers to private sessions with dating coaches – are the romantic equivalent of Dumbo's magic feather. They're not actually doing as much as you think they are; more often than not, all any of it is doing is allowing you to believe that improvement is possible. It's a way of shutting up the jerk-voice in your brain that keeps telling you that you're worthless, that there's nothing anybody can do to help you and that you've been branded unfuckable. You believe you've finally found this magic bullet that is going to change everything for you, but like every Saturday morning cartoon has been telling you, the ability was in you all along...

---

1. Because trust me, if that worked, I'd have gotten there *years* ago...

… just, y'know, if you'd get out of your own damn way. Don't get me wrong: this isn't just about embracing tired clichés about "it's what's inside that counts," nor am I saying that dating doesn't require practice and the development of certain skill-sets. But as long as you hold on to the self-limiting beliefs, you can be the sharpest-dressed man in the world with perfect hair and teeth, dropping bon-mots like M&Ms from the hands of a man with no fingers and still be without a date on Friday night. Not only will you be driving people away, you'll never even notice the ones who are all but holding up illuminated billboards about how much they want to see you naked.

So before we get into issues like "how to start a conversation" or "how to get her home with you," let's start with your core and work our way outwards.

IDENTITY AND THE POWER OF LABELS

There's no dating advice I hate more than "just be yourself." Not only is it a cliché that gets handed out like received wisdom every time the subject of dating comes up, it's often one of the first things that people throw at me when I try to help them. I tell people constantly: if you're doing the same thing over and over again, you're going to get the same results over and over again. Something needs to change. And there will be people who inevitably insist that change is wrong, that you should "be yourself" no matter what. It's a truism that's stated repeatedly in books, television shows and movies that the people who change themselves for other people are weak-willed or too eager to please others and we should steadfastly "just be ourselves" no matter what.

Which is why I always have to ask: Being yourself. How's that working out for you so far?

It's an unfortunate truth that sometimes the "you" that is presented to the world isn't exactly the most attractive version that you could be putting forward. This is not to say that it's a matter of winning the genetic lottery for facial symmetry or embracing the Paleo diet and performing two hundred crunches every morning. Humans are complex, layered beings and attractiveness is more than just a matter of physical looks. You can have Jake Gyllenhaal's face and Ryan Reynolds' abs and still find out the hard way that Saturday night is the loneliest night of the week because you're a negative asshole that people can't stand to be around.

Similarly, if you've decided that your concept of "yourself" is someone who's incapable of getting a girlfriend... well, you're going to be right. Your self-concept – your identity – is a composite. It's the amalgamation of who you spend time with and how you see yourself. As you grow and mature, you have more control over your definition. Your label. Your *identity*. And labels are *powerful*. They're your filter with the world, describing how you see and interpret the world around you... and *how the world sees you*.

There was a famous psychological study in the '60s about the power of labels. A group of students were given a series of tests and were divided into two groups: ones who were labeled as "gifted" or "academic bloomers" and "normal kids." They were put into different classes and the teachers were informed whether their students were "gifted" or "average." In reality, the labels were actually completely arbitrary and assigned to each child at random... but at the end of the year, the children who were labeled as "gifted" outperformed the students who were labeled as "normal." The difference was in how the teachers responded to the students based on the label.

Nerds and geeks are a classic example of people who've absorbed somebody else's definition into their own identity. We *still* identify geeks as hopeless neckbearded virgins a la *The Simpson's* Comic Book Guy or socially clueless *Big Bang Theory*-esque Aspergers cases who'd rather argue the finer points of whether the Enterprise could outrace the Millennium Falcon.[2] They're outcasts and losers, destined to never see a woman naked in person...

And yet, geek culture is pop culture. If you look at the top-grossing movies of all time, you have *Avatar, Star Wars, The Avengers, Star Wars Episode 1, The Dark Knight, The Dark Knight Rises, Shrek 2* and *E.T. The Extra-Terrestrial.* The only non-geek property in the top 10 is *Titanic.* Expand the list to the top 25 and it's all geek properties until you hit *Passion of the Christ.* On television, *The Walking Dead, Orphan Black, Doctor Who, Supernatural, Arrow* and *Game of Thrones* are among the most beloved series while *The Big Bang Theory* is one of the highest-rated sitcoms of all time. Despite all this, geeks and nerds buy into the idea that they're unlovable outcasts because of their interests... interests that are apparently shared *by the rest of the goddamn world.*

But geeks and nerds have absorbed this definition and

2. Incidentally, the Millennium Falcon is *much* faster than the Enterprise. The Falcon is able to travel from the Outer Rim to the center of the galaxy in approximately less than a week. The Enterprise, on the other hand, takes three days to get to the nearest *star*...

made "dateless loser" an intrinsic part of their identity – many even go so far as to *romanticize* their status as social outcasts. And as a result: the world treats them that way.

Tell somebody that a person is a nerd and they will respond to that person differently than if you tell them that they were popular in school. Both of those identities carry different expectations and they will color people's perceptions. This applies even to the labels you give yourself, consciously or unconsciously.

To give a personal example: when I was growing up, I had a tight group of friends. As is often the case in such groups, we all had our roles. One of us was "The Good One." Another was "The Troublemaker." My twin brother was "The Athletic One," while our friend Miles – the man who ultimately triggered my personal transformation – was "The Natural." I wanted to be like Miles in the worst way, but I was continually edged out, overshadowed by Miles' natural easy charm and my brother's athleticism and looks. I was awkward, solitary and bookish. I was uncomfortable expressing myself, *especially* around women I was attracted to... and as a result, every time I tried to talk or flirt with a girl, I'd fuck up in the most epic ways. Because of my clumsiness and various relationship disasters, I was labeled "The One Who Wasn't Good With Girls." This was a label that followed me through high school and even well into college – a place where nobody knew who the hell I was, a place where I was free to completely re-invent myself. Why?

Because I had passively accepted that label as part of my self-concept. I had allowed myself to be defined as "The One Who Was Not Good With Girls." It became part of who I was. Even when I had dates or a girlfriend, that identity remained a core part of me and I lived in dread anticipation of when the universe would remember that I was undatable and everything would fall apart again.

It wasn't until years later that I realized what I had done. I had taken a label, someone else's idea of who I was, and absorbed it into my self-concept. And by doing so, I directly affected not only how I saw myself, but how the *world* saw me.

When I saw myself as "The One Who Wasn't Good With Girls," it colored every interaction I had. I missed out on women blatantly hitting on me because I couldn't possibly believe that they could possibly want me; clearly I was misunderstanding. I read entire volumes into every minute gesture. Every unanswered text or instant message was a sign that she was avoiding me, not that she couldn't get to her phone or was otherwise occupied. I constantly expected to get rejected or dumped, and every "Let's Just Be Friends" speech was further confirmation that women just didn't like me. I was ignoring positive signals, over-emphasizing the negative ones and generally wrapping my identity of "The One Who Wasn't Good With Girls" around me like armor. My identity meant that I was *locked* into place, that there was simply nothing to be done.

Not surprisingly, I felt like I spent more time in the Friend Zone than Peyton Manning does in the end zone.

The only way this could change is if I were to willingly give up my label and build myself a new identity, one that allowed me to grow and improve, rather than keeping the one that said "this is how you are forever."

The problem is that negativity is damned hard to change...

NEGATIVITY IS A SELF-FULFILLING PROPHECY

Raise your hand if you've ever thought something like this:

"Women don't like me because I'm too _____"

"Only _____ people get what they want."

"If I do _____, people will figure out I'm a fake."

"There's no point in _____, it'll never work anyway."

Any of this sound familiar? They do to me. I've been thinking them for most of my life.

These are what are known as "self-limiting beliefs." They're the voice of self-doubt. These are what your jerk-brain whispers when you dream of trying to improve your dating life. And they're incredibly insidious, because they're self-fulfilling prophecies. When you believe that no woman could like you, you will *make* it come true... even though you don't *want* to.

Your beliefs affect how you see the world. Just as your identity is your filter, the beliefs associated with that identity control how you interpret the world around you, and, more importantly, how you *react* to it. People who see themselves as lucky tend to be happier, more positive people because the world inevitably works out the way they hope. This has nothing to do with luck, though, and everything to do with how they interact with the world. Because they *believe* they're lucky, they're on the lookout for opportunities to *be* lucky. When something comes up – a man looking for a job happens to hear that a position's opened up at his friend's company, for example – they're in a better position to take advantage of it. Meanwhile, somebody who believes they're unlucky will miss that same opportunity because they don't believe it could work out for them. They're focused inward, paying more attention to their own misery rather than focusing outward and looking for opportunities to prove themselves.

Similarly, somebody who believes that they're attractive to women will be on the lookout for signs of interest. He carries himself with confidence, looks people in the eye and smiles at women he finds appealing. He's making a point of noticing people and being noticed. He'll see that cute redhead giving him the come-hither stare and respond by introducing himself because he was actively looking for it. He believed it would be out there and so he seeks it out. At the other end of the spectrum, somebody who believes that he *isn't* desirable or that women don't like him will do the opposite. He folds in on himself, afraid to take up space. He won't look people in the eye because he's afraid to be that assertive and he certainly isn't going to approach anyone for fear of rejection. His body language conveys the attitude "I know you don't like me; I don't really like me either," and he's focused on passing by as invisibly as possible for fear that people will realize he's there and mock him. He'll never see that same cute redhead giving him the eye because he doesn't believe it's *possible* for someone to like him. If he did see it, he would have any number of rationalizations as to why it couldn't possibly be that she was interested: she was looking at someone behind him, she was actually registering disgust, or he just plain imagined it.

People with self-limiting beliefs tend to have what's known as a "scarcity" mentality: the belief that a particular resource – in this case, attractive, available women – is in incredibly limited supply. Someone with a scarcity mentality believes that because there are so few women out there, each time they get rejected they're one step closer to *never* finding love and they're that much more likely to die alone, unloved and unmourned. And as with other self-limiting beliefs, it's self-reinforcing. Just as someone who believes women couldn't possibly like him will ignore signs of interest and repel them with his attitude, somebody with a scarcity mentality will chase off potential relationships because of his fears. Since he's so afraid that he'll never find someone like her again, he may over-invest in the relationship, committing too quickly. He may act profoundly needy, constantly texting her and messaging her over Facebook and Twitter. Or he may demand constant reassurance that everything is all right and that yes, she really *is* interested in dating him. As a result, he snatches defeat from the jaws of victory. His behavior ends up driving her away and reinforcing the idea that he's never going to find a love like that again. When he *does* meet somebody else, the cycle repeats itself and he watches his hopes of "maybe this one will work out" disappear in a puff of sandalwood and loneliness.

THE COMMODITY MODEL OF SEX

It doesn't help that, all too often, these negative beliefs are bolstered by seeing women as "the enemy." Too many men – especially men who've been exposed to the pick-up community – have an antagonistic view of sex and relationships. They approach women with the idea that they've been pre-rejected. In order to persuade a woman to date them or to sleep with them, they have to jump through hoops and overcome trials in order to be deemed worthy of Mario being allowed to go down the Warp Pipe of Love. It puts men and women on an antagonistic footing from the get-go... and it makes sex that much harder to attain for *both* parties.

One of the oldest and most pernicious double standards when it comes to male/female relationships is how the culture encourages us to view sex. Men are lionized for the sex they have while women are told their value is measured by the sex they *don't* have. A man with a hundred partners is a stud; a woman with a hundred partners is a slut at best, actively deranged at worst. This dichotomy gets bolstered by the popular idea that women don't *want* sex as much as men do; since men presumably desire sex more, then it stands to reason[3] that women control access to it. They, in effect, are the gatekeepers setting the market price for sex. Men, if they want access, need to either meet her price or go without. Of course, men are taught that they're supposed to get sex as cheaply as possible – for *free*, if they can get away with it – and a man who pays market price (or more...) is a loser and an idiot. Meanwhile, since women are devalued for the sex they have, they're supposed to set the market price suitably high, the ideal price being a diamond ring and a marriage proposal, according to conservative circles. A woman who sells sex too cheaply or too readily is a slut because she devalues sex for *every* woman since she's flooding the market. It's the commodity model of sex, banging as capitalism, with everyone's nethers being stroked by the invisible hand of the free market.

3. For suitably small definitions of "reason"...

There are so many problems with this attitude towards sexual relations that they could fill a book of their own... but the most relevant is that it turns sex into a zero-sum game. Perpetuating the belief that women a) don't like sex and b) are supposed to hold off for as long as possible before "giving it up" teaches men that sex is something that they are supposed to get *at all costs*. All is fair in love and war (and love *is* war, apparently) so men are justified in begging, cajoling, deceiving or coercing women into "giving it up." Of course, it's a no-win situation for women; if they have sex (especially for below the metaphorical market price), they're excoriated as sluts. If they don't, they're insulted for being prudes. No matter which way they turn, it's a losing proposition for them. Small wonder then, that women would be less interested in sex, especially casual sex...

But believe me, they want sex. In fact, studies conducted by Dr. Meredith Chivers at Queen's University in Ontario, found that women had a greater capacity for sexual desire and arousal than men do. Similarly, Professor Terry Conley of the University of Michigan found that, contrary to popular belief, women were *very* interested in casual sex... provided they thought the sex would be worth it. After all, what was the point of risking their personal safety and social opprobrium if all they were going to get out of it was a lousy lay?

Coming into an interaction with a woman, especially if you're hoping to get a date out of it, with the assumption that you're in a battle of wills is an excellent way to turn a woman off. It tells women that you see them as the competition instead of a partner and sends the message that, not only do you not respect them, but that quite frankly, the sex is going to *suck*.

Better instead to approach sex as a collaboration rather than a competition. It's a negotiation towards the fulfillment of mutual interests, not "what is the bare minimum I have to offer in order to get what I want from you?" It tells women that you're conscientious of their safety and their pleasure as well as your own. And more importantly, it changes how you communicate with them – you're not coming from a place of bitterness, resentment or fear, which makes you *much* more attractive.

ABSORB WHAT IS USEFUL. DISCARD WHAT IS NOT.

Now, having talked about all of these negative attitudes and why they hinder you, the question becomes: how do we fix them?

It's a difficult process. Most of us have lived with these self-limiting beliefs for years, if not for a lifetime. They become habitual, part of the background radiation of our day-to-day lives, wearing a groove in our brains. Trying to shift them can be incredibly difficult because our brains respond more strongly to negativity; we pay more attention and give more credence to the negative. It's a psychological effect known as the negativity bias. Much like with our sense of fear, the negativity bias is an evolutionary development meant to keep us alive; being more highly attuned to negative feelings meant that we're better able detect and react to danger. Unfortunately, what was necessary to keep us alive back in the days of saber-toothed cats, dire wolves and cave bears doesn't play well with our capacity for abstract reasoning; what used to be a survival technique is the same thing that makes it harder for us to dismiss the feeling of failure. Negative thoughts and self-limiting beliefs affect us five times more than positive ones. This ratio causes an interference effect – it's harder to appreciate the positives of something when there's a negative associated with it as well.

This is why negative opinions and thoughts seem so much more "valid" than positive ones – your brain pays more attention to them and gives them more statistical weight. It's why negative thought patterns are so hard to banish and self-limiting beliefs are so hard to shake. But it *can* be done. It just takes time and effort to literally retrain your thought patterns. And the first thing you need to do is come to grips with the "why" of your attitude and self-limiting beliefs.

I want you to do a couple of exercises. The first is very simple: you're going to practice positivity. I know this sounds a little woo-woo, but stick with me. You see, negativity is a *habit*. To break out of it, you have to retrain your brain and how you see everything. So you'll practice positivity. You spend seven consecutive days consciously not thinking anything negative about anyone. You think positively about yourself, about your life, everything. You look for the things to be grateful for, the things that make life worth living, no matter how minor. You actively compliment yourself. If you think even *one* negative thought, then you're back to day one. The point of this exercise is to make you aware of your thought patterns and to retrain yourself out of reflexive negativity. It's part of how you learn to believe in yourself and your ability to improve. It sounds like it's really fluffy-bunny New Age bullshit but trust me, it *works*.

The other task is slightly more in-depth. I want you to

write down the answers (write by hand as this accesses a different part of your brain than typing on a keyboard) to two simple questions:

1. What is it about dating that scares you?
2. *Why* does it scare you?

Don't just give one-word answers. I want you to write detailed answers. If you're afraid of rejection, then what is it about rejection that scares you? Is it the fear of humiliation? Is it the scarcity mentality? Do you struggle with feelings of being unworthy of love? Do you believe that only other people can date? Do you *want* to approach women but you keep gaming out every possible worst-case scenario? How does that happen? What are your specific triggers?

The reason why I'm asking you to do this is because your negative attitude and self-limiting beliefs are based on emotions, not facts. Humans are very bad about knowing why we feel the way we do. We simply feel the emotion and rationalize the explanation after the fact. The "reasons" are simply how we justify feeling the emotion in the first place. Your fear of rejection isn't because of careful study of data; it's born of that time Becky Kartheiser laughed when you told her you liked Manasa in Pre-Algebra and said there was no way she would ever like a ginger like you.

Er, not that this happened...

Once you've managed to identify the roots of these beliefs, it's easier to confront them and overcome them. It makes you better able to recognize the cognitive biases we use to justify our feelings. It allows you to challenge every negative belief and attitude you have. You test it.

You push at it over and over again. Every time a doubt or a limiting belief bubbles up in your mind, you ask yourself: "Is this useful?" If it gives you a way to get closer to your goal, then it's useful; hold on to it. If it's *not* useful, if it holds you back, you discard it. For example, saying that "women only date X guys" isn't useful; it's a way of excusing your failures. It keeps you from progressing. Discard it. Recognizing that you're bad at identifying signs of interest is useful; it's something concrete you can improve upon. Not liking how you look can be useful as long as you recognize the ways you can improve. Believing that you're just "too ugly" isn't useful. Failing can be useful... as long as you learn from it. Blaming yourself or using it as a way to confirm your self-limiting beliefs is not useful. The commodity model of sex is not useful; making women your opponent encourages them to put their guard up and to not trust you. Embracing a collaborative model of sex *is* useful.

And the least useful thing you can do is to "try." Either you succeed or you fail. "Try" is the way you excuse yourself for half-assing it. It's the ego-protector that says, "That failure didn't count because I tried." Accept that you failed, examine why you failed and then do it again. If you fail again, then fail *better*. Do. Or do not. There is no try.

Here's the thing about limiting beliefs: they're an excuse. They're lies. They are why you say you can't when what you really mean is that you *choose not to*. You may believe that you're too short or too fat or too whatever for women to find you attractive, therefore you don't bother approaching women, but you frame it as "you can't approach them because..." The truth is that you don't want to risk rejection therefore you choose not to. That self-limiting belief is how you explain that you don't want to do something you're afraid of.

And hey, fair's fair. Nobody likes getting rejected. It hurts! If you don't want to get rejected, nobody says you have to. But you have to be honest enough to admit the truth: you can't find a relationship not because you're X, but because you don't want to risk rejection. If you wanted it badly enough, you'd be out there taking it on the chin, wiping the dirt off and trying again. You'd be saying, "Damn right I can do this."

And therein lies the key. If you want something, you have to work towards it. You have to accept the pain and the stress, the emotional ups and downs, the disappointments, the frustrations and the time, and that means choosing to improve. You have to embrace that it may be harder for you than for others. To pick a semi-random example, taller guys have an advantage over shorter guys when it comes to finding relationships, but short guys do find them. They may get lucky off the bat and find somebody who digs them for who they are – or even digs short guys – or have to work a bit more than taller guys. It sucks, but it's life. Either you accept that it's part of the price of entry or you get off the ride. Both are equally valid options, but you have to admit that either the rewards are worth the risks or that you're not willing to put the work in.

If you want to fix your dating life, you're going to have to do things that you find uncomfortable, even painful. "It's too much trouble," "It's too hard" and "I don't have the time" are excuses, the voice of self-limiting beliefs holding on for dear life. You can and will find the internal strength to power through your doubts and insecurities.

I had to willingly subject myself to things I dreaded; I

had to make myself emotionally vulnerable and submit myself for rejection by women I was attracted to. I had to face up to having what others call "approach anxiety" and muscle my way through it even as my heart was pounding and my head began to swim. I had to be willing to approach and be rejected hundreds of times in order to pinpoint what I was doing wrong and fine tune what actually worked. And you can do it too.

Change is hard. Change is scary. Change can be painful. But to quote a wise man: "Without pain, without sacrifice, we have nothing. What you're feeling isn't pain, it's premature enlightenment."

CHAPTER 3.

WOMEN LOVE ASSHOLES (AND OTHER DATING MYTHS)

STOP ME IF ANY OF THIS SOUNDS FAMILIAR...

In the last chapter, we talked about self-limiting beliefs. In this chapter, I want to talk about some of the toxic myths that we buy into that make our dating lives so much harder.

Stop me if this sounds familiar:

Back in the bad old days, I was a huge believer in what I called "The Platonic Friend Back Door Gambit." I was so terrified of rejection that whenever I was interested in a woman, I'd do everything I could to wedge myself into her life. I'd be her best friend in the world. I'd be the one to bring her soup and cold meds when she was sick; I'd be the shoulder to cry on when her boyfriend was being an asshole. Of course, as I was holding her and patting her back in a "there-there" manner, I was also trying to hide my throbbingly painful erection because, well, the girl I wanted was clinging to me and boobs were still things that only existed after ten o'clock on Cinemax.

There was one incident from college I remember

extremely well. Her name was Elysa[1] and I thought she was perfect.

Of course, at the time, "perfect" meant "first girl on campus who was actually nice to me," but I wasn't going to be picky. She had red-gold hair, deep brown eyes, a nose adorably dusted with freckles and a body to make Gandhi cry... And, by God, I was going to make her mine come hell or high water.

But I couldn't just tell her I was interested and ask her out. Oh no. I'd lost track of how many times I'd confessed my feelings to a girl and been shot down in flames like a TIE Fighter pilot in need of LASIK surgery. The potential that she might return my feelings hung in the air like a soap bubble; actually trying to do anything about it would be like poking it with a stick, and I couldn't risk that.

So instead I decided to be her best friend; if movies had taught me anything, it was that she would eventually wake up and realize that everything she'd been looking for was right beside her the entire time!

And so I set out to integrate myself into her life. I would go out of my way to hang out near her classes, so that we could "just happen" to run into each other and go spend time in the Student Union. I took her to see *Se7en* just because she had a crush on Brad Pitt. When she was feeling down, I bought her flowers – even going so far as to look up Victorian flower code, in hopes of sending subliminal messages via the Perk Up Bouquet.

The fact that I was acting like a stalker was lost on me. If the movies had taught me anything, it was that everything was forgivable if it was done in the name of love.

1. Names and identifying features have been changed to protect the guilty... namely, me.

When I wasn't with her, my days were consumed with trying to figure out whether or not she was starting to fall for me. I would spend every night – the ones where I wasn't looking for free online porn, anyway – going over every single thing she said like it was the Zapruder film. I was examining every word, gesture and nuance for even the slightest shred of evidence that she was starting to see me as more than a friend. Everything she did had secret meaning. Did she agree to go to an impromptu dinner with me? That meant something. Did she leave her hand on my shoulder for just a microsecond longer than she normally would? Clearly it was a sign that she was weakening! *Stay on target... stay on target...*

Now to be sure, I could have moved on to other women, ones who might have actually returned my affections, but what would be the point? I was in LOVE. She was The One. Nobody was as perfect as she was. As far as I was concerned, cartoon animals showed up to clean her house while she sang and danced in a pastel pastoral wonderland. This was destiny! Surely, once I won her heart, this would be a love for the ages!!!

It worked out about as well as you might expect. Which is to say, in tears, self-pity, reams of bad poetry and my friends being forced to nurse me through yet another self-inflicted heartbreak.

I knew I wasn't the only one who was suffering through this either. There were literally dozens (this was in the early days of the World Wide Web, remember) of badly coded websites where similarly afflicted nerds were pouring their hearts out to strangers about the cruelty of women and the pain of the Platonic Friend. Oh, how we all cringed at our love interest saying, "If only I could meet a nice guy like you" while crying about how her asshole boyfriend kept treating her like dirt.

The problem of course, was that we all focused on the word "nice."

You see, I had fallen victim to one of the classic Nerd Dating Blunders: I had convinced myself that women liked "nice" guys.

And so I set out to be the ultimate Nice Guy™.

THE TROUBLE WITH NICE GUYS™

"But women say they want to date a nice guy! I'm nice! Why won't they date me?" I hear you cry.

Well... because honestly? Odds are you're not really nice. You're "Nice."

Let's talk about the so-called Nice Guy for a second. A Nice Guy is the one who is running around with the girl, taking her shopping, buying her gifts, taking her out to dinner. He's the one who spends all of his time and effort on his crush and gets absolutely nowhere. He goes out of his way to do nice things for his "friend," earns her trust and her confidence, provides a shoulder to cry on and an ear to listen with.

This would be all well and good if he were being a genuine friend to her.

He is not.

You see, all of this is done not with the desire to support his friend, but to ingratiate himself to her. His friendship comes with an unspoken obligation that the things he does for her entitle him to a reward later on down the line.

But the Nice Guy doesn't see it this way. In his mind, by

acting like her friend – doing her favors, spending time with her, giving her emotional support at times when her real boyfriend is acting like a raging asshole – he's engaging in an especially grind-y MMO quest line. He's collecting the requisite number of boar asses; when she breaks up with her boyfriend at the end of the quest, he can finally redeem all of those hard-earned boar-asses for a girlfriend... or at least one night of vulnerability-induced sex and an incredibly awkward morning after full of regrets and Jägermeister-flavored vomit.

All this would be bad enough if she were the only person he was lying to.

Unfortunately, she isn't. Y'see, the Nice Guy is also lying to himself.

Check any of the many "I've been friend-zoned" or Nice Guy rants on Facebook or Reddit – no, seriously, go ahead. I'll wait – and you'll see a recurring pattern: "She doesn't want a nice guy, she only wants those assholes who treat her badly. She needs to be dating me, I actually respect her!"

No, son. No, you really don't.

The Nice Guy has usually bought into the lies that he's peddling: that he's really being a good friend to her, that he respects her in ways her asshole boyfriends don't, that his love for her is a purer, more deserving love than anyone else she might know. Except of course he isn't, he doesn't, and it isn't. A true friend doesn't make his relationship with a person conditional to the idea that someday that person is obligated to fall in love (or a reasonable facsimile thereof) with him. Friends don't hatch Machiavellian schemes to persuade girls to love them. Friends don't think that if you feed enough kindness tokens into the machine, you'll eventually be rewarded with hours of mind-blowing sex.

Moreover, he continues to lie to himself because, quite frankly, most Nice Guys know how their lust-object feels about them. Now to be fair, confessing your love for someone can be absurdly intimidating; after all, you are deliberately making yourself vulnerable to rejection. However, the Nice Guy may dress his hesitancy up as a failure of courage, but deep down he knows exactly why he's not going to say anything: because as soon as he does, the illusion is ruined. All of the Nice Guy Points™ he's accumulated drain away along with the fantasy that he might wear her down to the point that she would give in and he would be forced to acknowledge the ugly truth that it's just never going to happen. At this point, the Nice Guy has two options: continue to hang around knowing that he never stands a chance, or to run away.

Small wonder most Nice Guys choose to run away and complain about it on their social networks instead.

Let's be honest: you're not a nice guy. You're not even really her friend.

But for the sake of argument, let's say that you're trying to be a nice guy, not a Nice Guy. You're still doing yourself a disservice, because you're not listening to what women are actually saying. Straight talk: when a girl says she wishes she could meet a nice guy, what she's really saying is "I wish I could meet a guy who isn't a complete dickbag but also actually excites me."

Notice that last part? That part about excitement? That's the key.

Nice guys are passive.

Nice guys are clingy.

Nice guys are predictable.

Nice guys are boring.

Unfortunately, we tend to assume that if women don't like nice guys (as opposed to Nice Guys), they must like assholes instead.

THE MYTH OF THE "ALPHA MALE"

If there is one thing that men, especially nerdier, geekier men – men more prone to be Nice Guys and White Knights[2] – will complain about when it comes to their dating problems, it's that women don't like "nice" men. No, the millions of men who heard "I wish I could meet a nice guy like you" one time too many turned around and assumed that the path of the "bad boy" was the way to win women's hearts and loins.

There is no dating cliché older or more lingering than the appeal of the "bad boy." If you were to listen in on men's conversations about women and dating, you would think that assholes have some sort of mystical, mesmeric power over women. That douchebaggery and Abercrombie and Fitch clothing combine into an alchemical formula that leads to getting more ass than a man in a car chase who plows through an ass cart and crashes through a plate ass window. To pick a historical example, poet and known rake Lord Byron was famously "mad, bad and dangerous to know." Between the drinking, the narcissism, the substance abuse, the squandering of his money and his chronic inability to keep it in his pants, Byron was like lousy boyfriend Yahtzee... Hell, the man's

2. Men who want to "save" women from themselves. We'll talk the danger of being a White Knight in Chapter 10.

sexual scandals eventually caused him to flee England, never to return.

And yet, if you were to ask women – and believe me, I have – it's all bullshit. Just because women don't necessarily want timid Nice Guys with their senses of entitlement and passive-aggressive tendencies doesn't mean that they want some jerkwad who patronizes them, insults them and generally treats them like crap. There isn't a woman out there who is sitting around thinking "I wish I could find a guy with great abs who would call me a bitch, belittle my hopes and dreams, isolate me from my friends and cheat on me repeatedly."

So why do people think "bad boys" are the only ones that can rev a woman's engine? Well, there are a number of theories.

One of the most common tropes that gets brought up is the idea of evolutionary psychology and the theory of "alpha males." In the primate world, the alpha male is the dominant ape in the group who stands at the top of the hierarchy by dint of his fitness and aggression. These are all favorable factors which influence his potential to survive in a harsh environment long enough to reproduce, which means that his children are also more likely to survive to pass on their genes in turn. This makes them primo breeding material in the eyes of Ms. Ape and all of her friends.

Because of the way ape sociology works, the alpha male has sexual access to all of the females in the group. The apes below him in the hierarchy, the betas, do not. The alpha keeps his position via intimidation and furious violence. Betas who piss off the alpha (for example, by trying to bone one of the females on the sly) do so at their own risk. Because humans are descended from apes, many people try to understand our behavioral patterns by looking to our evolutionary ancestors, trying to rationalize human mating behavior – explaining who is going to shack up with whom – by examining chimpanzee mating behavior and looking for parallels. Other people, exhibiting a poor understanding of both the evolutionary and psychological aspects of evolutionary psychology, make the leap that because chimpanzees organize themselves into alphas and betas, it only makes sense that humans do as well.

When the idea of alpha/beta relationships is translated onto human mating patterns (humans, after all, are basically hairless apes, according to many), the idea is that women are naturally attracted to alpha males – dominant, powerful, high-status men – while disdaining the weaker, less dominant betas. When women do decide to hook up with a beta – so the theory goes – it's a matter of convenience and materialism. She's trading sex for material support when, secretly in her heart of hearts, she yearns for a high-status, big, hairy-chested manly man to come and bang the ever-loving shit out of her so she can upgrade and ditch the beta.

Too bad it's also bullshit.

Ignoring the misunderstanding of ape sociology (chimpanzee females mate with beta males all the time… they just wait until the alpha's back is turned), humans aren't chimpanzees. There are three mammals that have sex outside of estrus: humans, dolphins and bonobos ("pygmy chimpanzees"). Chimpanzees only have sex for reproduction and only when the females are in heat. Humans have sex for any number of reasons at any damn time: for pleasure, because we're bored, because we make poor decisions, out of a sense of obligation… sometimes simply because it's Tuesday and why the hell not?

But hey, labeling behavior as "alpha" and "beta" sounds like a simple, easily digestible solution to solving the world's dating problems, right? Why face the complicated bundle of issues that is human sexuality and social behavior when you can just provide an answer that fits on a bumper sticker?

Well, because it doesn't actually work. To start with: the reason why the dominant chimpanzee gets to breed with most of the females is because he straight-up tries to *murder* any other male he catches trying to mate with "his" females. It has nothing to do with the females being "naturally" attracted to the alpha. It turns out that "I will find you and I will kill you" is an amazing cockblock strategy.

But why let the realities of animal behavior get in the way? It's all metaphorical, right? Unfortunately, when you take a bunch of people with a shaky grasp on evolutionary psychology who try to apply the concept of alpha status onto the convoluted morass that is human sexuality and sell it as advice, you end up with the vague idea that being alpha means being "dominant" or "socially superior." Just how this so-called dominance is supposed to manifest is, in itself, a subject of great contention amongst the sages of the dating world. Some will tell you that it's all about being aloof, proving you don't need or care about her as much as she needs or cares about you. Some will tell you that it's about staring down or squeezing out the other men around the woman you're interested in. Some will say that it's about keeping her insecure about the state of the relationship and always having to please you.

In other words… you're supposed to act like an asshole.

Now spread that idea amongst frustrated men who are angry about the fact that the women they like are dating jerks. As they moan and commiserate about how unfair life is, they'll all agree that women prefer to date assholes instead of Nice Guys like them, which provides all the confirmation they need. After all, if their friends are noticing this too, *surely* this means that there's something to it, right?

Well, there's a reason why the plural of "anecdote" isn't "data."

And don't call me Shirley.

THE APPEAL OF BAD BOYS

Humans are complex beasties, sexually. There's a hell of a lot going on sexually under the hood that we're not even vaguely aware of or able to control on a conscious level. These are all things that lead up to answering the question "Will I fuck this person or not?" and very little of it is bound up by biology. What goes on between our thighs tends to have a lot to do with what's going on between our ears.

It's true that men and women with certain negative personality traits seem to be more popular. We all remember the Queen Bee at the top of the high-school pecking order, enforcing her will through manipulation and cruelty. Similarly, it seemed as though the douchiest of jocks were inevitably the Big Men on Campus. We can't stand them... so why does everyone seem to love these assholes?

Well, it turns out that three personality traits known as the "dark triad" are actually associated with being able to enhance a person's physical attractiveness. The so-called dark triad consists of three separate but overlapping personality traits perceived as having similar underlying commonalities:

- Narcissism– defined as an overly developed sense of self-worth and entitlement matched with intense egotism.

- Machiavellianism – defined by the person's reliance on manipulation to get what he or she desires without regard for others as well as a cynical dismissal of morality as being "for other people."

- Psychopathy – a loaded term; it doesn't refer to a violent maniac, but to someone defined by reckless thrill-seeking, selfishness, lack of remorse and affect and a certain level of superficial charm.

Scientists have known for a while that narcissism, for example, actually directly correlates with initial popularity. Please note very carefully that I said *initial* popularity. We'll be coming back to this.

A study conducted in 2010 by Mitja Back and Boris Egloff of Johannes Gutenberg-University of Mainz found that – upon first meeting them – people thought that narcissistic individuals were "flashier," "more confident" and more immediately likable. What made things interesting is a new study, conducted in 2012 by Nick Holtzman and Michael Strube of Washington University in St. Louis, which found that individuals whose personality types conformed to the dark triad were perceived to be more physically attractive than people who didn't have these personality aspects.

To test this idea, Holtzman and Strube invited 111

college students to participate in a study. The students – more women than men – were photographed in their usual clothes, then given gray, featureless sweatsuits to change into. Anyone wearing makeup was asked to remove it, while anyone with long hair was asked to pull it into a ponytail. The idea was to take as neutral and natural a photo of the participants as possible as a control. Students were asked to answer a questionnaire and rate themselves on a personality scale. To help counterbalance any errors introduced by self-reporting, Strube and Holtzman also interviewed acquaintances of the subjects about their personalities. From these results, the subjects were rated and scored with regard to dark triad personality types.

The photos of the subjects – both the dressed up and neutral shots – were then shown to strangers, who were asked to rate them in terms of physical attractiveness. Those who scored higher on the dark triad were consistently found to be more attractive by strangers than those who rated lower… but only when they were dressed up. When all of the subjects were wearing the sweatsuits and showing their more natural look, the influence of the dark triad personality type disappeared.

As it turns out, those individuals who rank higher on the dark triad scale are better at presenting themselves and knowing how to make themselves look good. Just as with the earlier narcissism study, those with "darker" personality traits are better able to cultivate their sense of style. They tend to wear edgier, more stylish clothes that make them stand out more, sport a more fashionable hairstyle, use more confident body language and smile more often. In short: they know how to make a better first impression than other people do. By knowing how to display themselves to their best advantage, they make themselves look more attractive. By doing so, they take advantage of a phenomenon known as the "halo effect": because they are perceived as being more physically attractive, we automatically assume that they're also better people – kinder, smarter, more trustworthy, etc.

(Don't worry, we'll be covering how you can make this transformation yourself in Chapter 6.)

One thing to keep in mind is that the Black-Etjoff study found is that people with dark triad personalities – assholes – may make great initial impressions but lousy long-term ones. In fact, their personal popularity tends to drop the more people get to know the real person behind the flash and smoke.

It's almost impossible to keep the charade up for very long. Inevitably people will begin seeing the man behind the mask and start realizing that he's actually pretty damn repulsive. Moreover, while assholes are able to get the girl, they can rarely keep her. Their relationships are like a bad B movie: short, monotonous, and full of tedious drama punctuated by fights, screaming and the occasional Sharknado.

So that's the science behind the appeal of bad boys. The other problem with Nice Guys is their behavior. They're so focused on being "nice" that they don't connect with the women they're attracted to. Of course, when they decide to turn over a new leaf and start being jerks, they miss the point entirely. After all, it's not that treating women like dirt is so incredibly sexy that it makes panties melt away like sugar in the rain. Those frustrated Nice Guys™ never realize what it is about assholes that women like so much; all they're doing is emulating the surface qualities of an asshole instead.

As a result, like a Pacific Islander cargo cult that thinks that building an ersatz airstrip will lead to goodies raining from the skies, they try to dress like the people they claim to hate, wandering around in ripped jeans, too-tight graphic print tees or polo shirts with the collar popped, or trucker hats and a sneer. They talk a big game that they could never hope to pull off. They think that they're being bad boys, but they're coming off like a poodle pretending to be a pit bull.

So the question you want to ask yourself *isn't* "How can I be a bad boy?" It's "How do I become the sort of man women actually *want?*"

Well, I'm glad you asked.

CHAPTER 4.

HOW TO BE THE MOST INTERESTING MAN IN THE WORLD

THE MOST ATTRACTIVE PART OF A MAN

As a rule of thumb, there are two ways to be good with women, in as much as "good" means getting dates and getting laid. The first is to become a master manipulator and use a combination of social pressure, compliance escalation and other psychological tricks based off high-pressure sales techniques in order to get your way. Many pick-up artist schools are based upon these techniques. They teach young, poorly socialized men how to be wanna-be Svengalis and unleash them upon the club scene with memorized routines for every possible occasion and outcome. And in fairness, this does work – on a very specific type of woman. I have known many people who were proficient manipulators who would target women with low self-esteem and who had poor boundaries and essentially treat them like customers at a sleazy used-car lot.

I call this path the Dark Side. I should know; I travelled it myself for quite some time. For someone who spent his life believing that sex was something that happened to other people, the idea of magically having sex on tap was compelling. But as the wise man once said: "Stronger? No, no, no. Quicker, easier, more seductive the Dark Side is."

And it doesn't come without a price. It's a horrible way to treat other people, and it eats away at your own soul. You are, for all intents and purposes, trying to cover up your *real* personality with a persona and subsuming your authentic self into somebody else's creation. Most of the people I've known with a shred of conscience who followed this path inevitably had psychological breakdowns. You can only go through life never having a *genuine* interaction with anyone for so long before you hit the wall, and the results are never pretty.

The other path is to become a better, more confident, charismatic and more interesting person.

Over the years, I've gotten to know many people who were amazingly skilled with women. Some of them were pure naturals. Others were people like me, who learned how to improve their social skills over time. Some of them were blessed with classic good looks or had enviable careers. Others were overweight and out of shape, while some were balding; in fact, to put it charitably, several of them were regularly punching above their weight class. They were average dudes who still managed to date incredibly smart, sexy women. But one thing that they all had in common was that everybody liked them. They were *fun*. They knew how to make people feel good. They were genuine, interesting people with stories to share and a genuine interest in getting to know the people they talked to. They made friends wherever they went. Complete strangers were charmed by these guys within minutes of meeting them.

It's incredibly obvious when you think about it: we instinctively like people who make us feel good. The better they make us feel, the more we like them. This is what's known as the Reward Theory of Attraction – we are attracted to people whose presence or behavior makes us feel appreciated and liked. When the feeling of pleasure at a person's presence in our lives outweighs the costs[1], then we prioritize that relationship over others. The brain increases the production of dopamine and norepinephrine, which light up the brain's pleasure and reward centers. We associate the pleasure with the person; as a result, we want to spend more time in their presence. We become addicted to them.

Think about it. How awesome would it be to walk into a room and know everyone's *excited* to see you? Imagine what it would be like knowing that women are eager to talk to you because they know you tell the best stories. Pretty sweet, right?

But being fun isn't just about putting on a performance and telling some jokes until they laugh their panties off. It's a holistic part of dating. People who are fun are genuinely interesting. They're great conversationalists. They know how to charm people. They have confidence. They know how to work a room. They know how to make people feel good about themselves, rather than sucking all the energy out of the room like an emotional vampire.

Sounds amazing, doesn't it?

Let's look at how you can put this all together and transform your life from the humdrum to the amazing.

---

1. For example: the guy who's hilarious... as long as you're not the target of his jokes. Or the person who's full of crazy energy but inevitably ends up starting a fight or getting you thrown out of the party.

LEARNING TO BE INTERESTING

Interested is Interesting

One of the first rules of being a more interesting, charismatic person is to care about other people. We are all our own favorite topics; in fact, studies have found that talking about ourselves actually triggers the same pleasure centers in our brains that light up when we eat our favorite foods. One of the most common qualities of interesting, compelling people is that they show interest in what other people have to say. Tom Cruise is one of the most famous examples of someone who understands how to be charming. Reportedly, one of his gifts is that he can make anyone feel as if they're the most fascinating person in the room, no matter who they are or what they do.

The easiest way to make people feel as though you're interested in them is to be an active listener. Most of us are bad listeners; we're not paying attention to what other people are saying so much as waiting for our turn to talk. Someone who's an active listener, on the other hand, is not only paying attention but demonstrates their interest by actively taking part in the conversation. To start with, you want to give simple signs that you're listening: "Uh huh," "Yeah," "Interesting."

Next, simply ask questions about what the other person just said – sometimes even paraphrasing what they told you in your own words. For example, if someone had just told you about taking scuba diving lessons while on vacation, you might respond with "You've been scuba diving? That's amazing, I've always wanted to try that. Did it feel weird to not have to hold your breath underwater?" This shows that not only are you listening, but that you *understand*. You can also use their stories to springboard to other topics by saying things like, "Oh, that's cool... have you ever done X or Y too?"

Expand Your Horizons

Most people live quiet, unadventurous lives. Day in and day out they eat the same foods, watch the same TV shows, read the same books, buy the same groceries and drive the same route to work. Every day looks more or less the same as the last as the days blur into months and years pass in the blink of an eye. We coast along on autopilot, so caught up in the rut that is our lives that we barely notice the world around us

Doesn't sound terribly interesting, does it?

When we get caught up in ruts, our brains functionally go on automatic; they don't bother processing the data around us and instead just fill in what we expect to see. We *literally* no longer see the real world around us. Shocking yourself out of that rut is one of the best ways to re-engage with the world around you; suddenly, you're able to pick up on information you never realized was there because you've gotten so used to seeing it. Forcing yourself out of a rut lets you see the world as though you're encountering it for the first time. It's a great way to jump-start your intellectual curiosity and discover new interests. It encourages you to take an active role in your own life. After all, when you find your own life exciting, it's easier to relate to others' lives too. Think of it as leveraging confirmation bias in your favor. Have you ever noticed that when you buy a new gadget or smartphone, you suddenly see it everywhere? When you live a more interesting life, you'll find other people are living interesting lives as well.

So once a week, try something you've never done before. It can be as simple as taking a new route to work or eating in a new (non-chain) restaurant, or as active as learning to cook a new cuisine you've had before – the more out of your usual experience, the better. Watch a movie that's utterly different from your favorite genre. Read a new book, especially non-fiction, just for the hell of it. Listen to a new genre of music. If you like rock, try old-school rhythm and blues or jazz. If you're into country, try some bluegrass or swing. These little changes can lead to large discoveries and open up new worlds to you.

And while you're at it, take this as an opportunity to refine your tastes a little. If you're a beer drinker who sticks to Miller or Budweiser, try an IPA or a Hefeweizen. If you like the occasional shot of Jack Daniels, attend a Scotch or bourbon tasting. If you like chocolate, try an artisanal chocolate bar – especially one with a high cocoa count or unusual ingredients like chili powder. Instead of getting take-out Chinese, try Indonesian or Javanese. Eat at an Ethiopian restaurant instead of the usual diner. The point isn't to become a foodie or cultural snob; it's simply to experience a wider array of flavors, textures and sensations and introduce yourself into a wider world.

Pursue Your Passions

One of the most important parts of being interesting is having passion – simply loving something because you think it's awesome, without fear of judgment or looking foolish. The vast majority of people have no passion in their lives; their existence is a senseless trudge from the cradle to the grave with very little thought given to anything that isn't necessary for keeping body and soul together. Having passions gives you an opportunity to express yourself and to indulge in something simply for the pure joy of it. They're ways of decompressing after a long week and to inject some much-needed relief from the day-to-day grind.

Interesting people have things that give them the desire to get out of bed and attack the day because they're so excited to indulge them. Maybe your passion is photography, playing a musical instrument or acting in local plays. Maybe it's collecting vintage comicbooks or taking part in the rockabilly community. Simply having a passion in your life helps you stand out from the crowd whose daily life is "wake up, go to work, come home, go to bed" and gives you something to talk about.

And if you *are* one of those people who has no passion in your life? Then it's time to start finding things that really *speak* to you. It may take time. You may have to experiment with different activities or pursuits, just to see whether they speak to you. It may help to reconnect with the things you loved as a child, or to try some of the things your friends enjoy.

One thing you *shouldn't* do is put limits on yourself about what you may or may not like. Don't worry about whether something is "cool" or not; cool isn't the point, *passion* is.

Plus: pursuing your passions is a *great* way to meet women with similar interests.

Collect Experiences

Interesting people have stories to tell... but that doesn't do you any good if you don't *have* any stories, does it?

One of the keys to being interesting is to be living an interesting life. If you're living a bland life, you're going to be a more drab, less interesting person, same as everyone else out there. Standing out from the crowd means that you have to do things differently.

In fact, an interesting lifestyle is a key component to attraction. Study after study has found that being exciting beats being pleasant. Couples who engage in exciting activities – things that actively raise one's heart rate such as social dancing, hiking and the like – were consistently happier and more in love with one another than couples who preferred blander activities. The familiar and the expected, while perfectly enjoyable, simply aren't exciting or really all that interesting.

To live a more interesting life, you need to be willing to put yourself out there and take chances, especially if you're the sort of person who normally plays it safe. The most interesting people make a point of collecting new experiences and trying new things, if only because it'll give them something to talk about afterwards. Just as you should shake up your daily life in order to get out of a rut, you should pursue opportunities to go on adventures and experience the unfamiliar and unexpected. It doesn't need to be expensive or even incredibly unusual – it just has to be *new to you*.

So get out of your comfort zone. Take a surfing lesson or two. Watch some classic foreign films in a genre you've never tried before. Climb mountains or rappel down walls. Find a Makerspace or the local DIY community and learn how to build things. Go hiking in the forest or take a class at the local community college. Go on roadtrips with no particular aim or goal. Jump up on stage and sing karaoke with a live band, even though you may not be able to carry a note with both hands and a bucket. Take a chance and start that business you've always dreamed of running.

The worst regrets we have are when we look back at all the things we *didn't* do. Collecting experiences means that you're living a fuller, more interesting life – one that other people will want to be part of.

Remember, when in doubt, err on the side of having a new story to tell. And speaking of that:

Know How to Tell Stories

It doesn't do you any good to have stories to tell if you don't know how to tell them in ways that makes people want to *listen* to them. There's an art to storytelling, and knowing how to sell an experience will help keep people riveted.

To start with: know the ending before you start. A good story is like a joke –everything is a lead-up to the punchline. The last thing you want to hear is "So then what happened?" as it means that you didn't stick the landing. Any story you tell should prompt an emotional response from your audience: a laugh, an "awwww" or admiration. These are all positive emotional reactions – ones that they'll associate with *you*.

Next, use an effective transition to start the story. There's phrasal lead in, where you say, "Hey, that reminds me of this time…" "Wow, that's like when I…" "Check this out..." or "The funniest thing happened..." There's also the cold read of the person you're talking to, where you use them as the transition: "You remind me of my buddy So-And-So. Actually, it's funny, I was hanging out with So-And-So yesterday when..." Then there's the observational transition, where you use someone else as a springboard into your story.

Then you want to set the hook. The hook is what grabs their attention and makes the listener perk their ears up. You want the hook to be as close to the beginning of your story as possible because it sets up the tension of how the story ends. If you take too long to set the hook, then nobody will notice it. Let's say that you're telling the story of something crazy that happened while you were on vacation:

Yeah, the last time we went on vacation, we went on this photo safari in Tanzania. It was kinda awesome; I mean, you're running around in the savannah in this open-top car, just, like, right there in the middle of it. The thing is, being so close to all the animals can be kinda risky. At one point, this elephant decided it didn't like us, so it chased us all the way down a hill. It was trying to kill us, y'know?

This is an example of a poorly set hook. You've lost your audience's attention before you've gotten to the fact that you were staring down a two-ton pachyderm trying to stomp you into paste. Here's how you properly set the hook:

"Last time I went on vacation, I nearly got killed by a rampaging elephant."[2]

Boom. Now you've got the audience's attention.

You also want to have characters. Characters will make

2. True story, by the way.

or break your story. The dullest story in the world can be enlivened by the proper use of characters. "I went to the store, I got caught in traffic, I saw a homeless guy on the corner, I had a fight with my girlfriend over the phone because I was late for dinner" is a boring story in and of itself. Now let's say that the homeless man you saw on the corner was actually a balding, bearded cross-dresser wearing Daisy Dukes, high heels, a crop top and a tiara, and he's actually trying to help by directing traffic.[3] Suddenly it's much more interesting. Characters make the most mundane stories fascinating. One of my favorite stories to tell is about the time I was at my favorite bar with my girlfriend when a dude walks in, hits on my girl, grouses at the bartender, hits on another girl at the bar and eventually leaves.

Except the guy? He's a male escort/porn star clown.[4]

Check in with your audience on occasion. Check-ins are little phrases you use to help keep people's attention on you. "You know what I mean?" "You know what that's like, right?" "No, seriously, check this out." "Can you believe that?" And keep those stories *short*. Brevity is the soul of wit and taking too long to get to the point just bores your audience.

And don't forget: practice counts for everything. Take time to tell your stories in the mirror. Learn how to find the proper pace of the story; not too fast, not too slow.

---

3. Also a true story. Leslie Cochran was an Austin legend and we all miss him.
4. Yes, this really happened. Keep Austin weird, folks.

Being interesting is only part of being a more attractive, appealing person. You can live a life of high adventure, but it's not going to do you any good if you're an insufferable asshole. Of course, this tends to be many people's default setting. It certainly doesn't help when we have so many popular characters from television and movies telling us that the best way to be beloved by millions is to be a complete shit to everyone you know. *The Avengers'* Loki, *The Big Bang Theory's* Sheldon, *Sherlock's* titular Sherlock Holmes and Dr. House are sardonic, arrogant asshats. We love them because we love to watch them putting fools in their place and unleashing their superior intellect and rapier wit upon the deserving. In fact, they're usually saying the things we *wish* we could say and looking cool while doing it. The thing we never stop to consider is that we like them because we're at a step removed from them; we're watching from the outside, where we can see that, yes, these people are idiots and deserve every single delicious moment of their tongue-lashing. We never stop for a second to think what it would be like for *us* to be on the receiving end of that treatment.

There's a *reason* why Sherlock Holmes doesn't have any friends besides John Watson – because he's a cold, closed-off son of a bitch. He's the guy who would insult you for trying to talk to him at a party because you're taking up time he could be putting to greater use... like considering which brand of toilet paper to buy. Women go nuts for Loki because Tom Hiddleston is pretty and has a knack for witty repartee. But he's the classic asshole boyfriend who will charm you for what he wants and then promptly turn around and insult you for letting him trick you in the first place.[5] The brooding, sardonic loner type makes for great fictional characters, but in real life they're insufferable pricks.

Charming, charismatic people are exactly the opposite of that. They're the ones who draw you in and make you feel amazing about yourself. Idris Elba is an example of someone who exudes warmth; he seems like someone who'd be the coolest motherfucker in the room, but he's eager to hear what *you* have to say. Similarly, Ryan Gosling is someone who gives you the impression that he'd love to have a beer with you and talk about loving B movie classics in a completely unironic way. Bill Clinton may be an incredibly divisive political figure, but anyone who's met him in person – even his most dedicated haters – will tell you that when he turns on the thousand-watt smile and envelops your hand in that bear-hug he calls a handshake, you can't help but *like* the guy.

In geek fiction, we have our charming rogues too. Han Solo may present himself as a self-involved jackass, but he's also funny, engaging and fiercely loyal. Tony Stark has his prickly side, but he's also a caring and giving person at his core that draws us in even when he's acting like a snarky teenager.

If you want to be the person who lights up the room when he enters and leave people feeling like you're the coolest guy they've ever met, then you have to learn how to build rapport with them. When you master these skills, you'll be able to network like other people breathe and

5. However, he *does* get cool points for working "mewling quim" into a sentence without sounding like a pretentious ass.

leave people wishing they could bottle your charm and sell it on the black market.

Develop Your Presence

One thing that charismatic people have in common is that they have presence and warmth. They make you feel like not only do they like you, but they *understand* you and are riveted by what you have to say.

The first step is incredibly simple, yet so many people fail to do it: give a genuine smile. Too many guys try to pull the solemn brooding look and just end up looking vaguely annoyed. A warm and inviting smile makes you look friendlier and more approachable – and in a nice bit of biofeedback, makes you *feel* happier and friendlier.

Next is to have open body language. Your arms should be at your sides or angled slightly away from your body. Your arms and legs should be uncrossed. Crossing your arms sends the message that you're closed off and you're trying to keep people from reaching you. One of the most common ways that people inadvertently close off their bodies is when they're carrying drinks; they hold them across their torso like a shield. Putting anything between you and the person you're talking to is going to create an ersatz barrier, making it harder for others to feel as though they can connect with you.

The final and most important way of using presence is simply to give someone your full attention. This means not being distracted by the people around you – unless you're *both* making a point of people-watching – or letting the TV at the bar drag your eyes away. While she's talking, make a point of showing that you're paying attention; those active listening skills I mentioned earlier help reinforce that you *want* to know what she has to say.

Mirror Other People for a Charisma Boost

Another key to building rapport is to emphasize similarities. Contrary to what Paula Abdul taught us in the 90s, opposites *don't* attract. In fact, we instinctively prefer people who are similar to us. Humans are tribal creatures and we tend to divide the world into "us" and "not us"; when we meet new people, we look for subtle signs as to whether this person is of the same "tribe." The more similarities we find, the more we define them as "like us." If you want to show somebody that yes, you *are* like them – or that they're like you – then one of the keys is to reflect how they see themselves.

The first key to building rapport is to show that you're on their wavelength by matching their energy – the level of enthusiasm and intensity that they're exhibiting. If they're laid back, you want to be low-key, otherwise you might come off like an over-enthusiastic puppy. If they're excited and bubbly, then you want to up your energy level to be around the same level, otherwise you can seem like you're trying to drag them down. When your energy levels clash, you end up irritating each other. For a practical example, think about the morning people you know. If you're like me and are only barely human before your morning coffee, somebody who hops out of bed at 6 AM totally refreshed and ready to high-five the world will inspire you to try to set them on fire with the power of your hate. Their energy level is night-and-day different from yours, and it's profoundly irritating; you may love them with all your heart, but right then you're contemplating how to hide their corpse.

Of course, this doesn't mean that you're stuck at their level forever. Have you ever known somebody whose energy was contagious? The trick is that they match the other person's energy level and then subtly adjust their own; the more interested the other person is, the more they'll adjust their *own* energy levels in order to maintain the rapport. This is known as "mirroring and leading," which is a powerful technique for getting people to open up to you. In fact, it's incredibly useful combined with the next tip: to subtly mirror their body language.

One of the surest signs that we're interested in somebody is that we'll unconsciously start to mimic their body language. If they take a sip of their drink, we may do so as well. If they shift their weight to one foot, we'll do the same. We may start using similar language or tone of voice. This is called "synchronization," where we mirror people in order to increase the feeling of "this person is similar to me." The cool thing is that we can do this deliberately. Just as you're matching their energy level, you want to match their body language. If they've angled their body in a particular direction, point yours in the same direction. If they're putting their weight on one foot, shift yours to the same foot. If they're leaning back, settle back into your seat.

As the two of you become more in sync, you can then start to lead a little; by adjusting your body, they will start to mirror you in turn. Lean forward to show interest in what they have to say and they'll be more likely to lean forward themselves. Open up your body language and visibly relax, and they are more likely to as well. Angle your body towards them and they'll shift their position to match yours.

Just remember: this is supposed to be *subtle*. These are supposed to be natural adjustments, not "Man in the Mirror" acting exercises.

Find Commonalities and Build Emotional Connections

The next key to being charming is to build rapport by finding commonalities with the person you're talking to. Charming people have the ability to make us feel as though we've known them forever, even if we've only just met them thirty minutes ago. They bring an easy sense of familiarity and intimacy that we don't often feel with other people, especially with people we've only just met, but it feels so natural that we never think about it. In fact, one researcher found that it was possible to build an incredibly intense emotional connection – one stronger than even some long-term friendships – in the span of an hour. Those little things you have in common are a critical part of feeling connected to someone. That feeling that somebody just gets you on a primal level, that they can speak to some specific aspect of who you are, is incredibly powerful.

The trick to finding commonalities is asking questions and finding ways to relate to the answers. Ask them something about themselves, then use those answers as a springboard for more questions, ones designed to get at deeper, more probing truths. As they answer, watch for points of commonality, areas where your experiences intersect, or where you have interests in common. When you find them, take time to point them out; share your own thoughts and exploits before moving on to asking about another topic.

One of the easiest ways to do this is through the Question Game[6], where you take turns asking meaningful questions of one another. You may ask shallow questions like "What's your favorite book of all time" or more probing ones like "What would a perfect day look like to you"? They may sound cheesy... but they're the ones that elicit the emotional truths and help forge those surprisingly deep and intimate connections that make us feel so close to someone we've just met.

So you may want to ask something like "What would you do if you could do anything with no chance of failure?" or even just sharing an embarrassing – but amusing – incident in your life. The key is that you want to convey a hint of vulnerability; being charming means letting others feel as though they're getting and insight into you that few other people get.

Funny is Sexy

The most charming, charismatic people out there have excellent senses of humor. Some are droll and witty, others are self-deprecating, while yet others are brash, even borderline offensive... and we love them for it. Brad Pitt, for all of his pretty-boy good looks, has a remarkable sense of comedic timing. His best roles are often the ones where he's playing against type and relying on his comedic chops rather than his symmetrical facial features.

---

6. This is actually one of my favorite games to play on a first date or when I'm meeting someone at a party. I'll go into more detail in Chapter 8.

Any time you read a poll about what women find attractive in men, a sense of humor consistently ranks in the top five – frequently at number one. It's not terribly surprising; it ties directly into the Reward Theory of Attraction. Laughter produces endorphins that go straight to the pleasure centers of your brain and relieves physical tension and stress in the muscles, making you feel more relaxed. If you're able to make a woman laugh, you're able to make her feel good, and she'll associate feeling good with being with *you*.

Moreover, there's a correlation between a sense of humor and practical and social intelligence. After all, most humor is ultimately intellectual in nature. Puns – the lowest form of humor – are all about wordplay. Pratfalls and even lowbrow humor like fart jokes require a strong sense of comedic timing and a juxtaposition of the unexpected (and inappropriate) against what's considered socially appropriate. In addition, understanding the proper time and place for different *kinds* of humor is a sign of someone who's highly socially calibrated. They know how to read a room or an individual and correctly gauge what is or isn't going to be funny in that instance.

This is why you can't just tell knock-knock jokes as a way into somebody's pants. It's about knowing when and *how* to use humor. Someone who tells jokes all the time becomes tedious; it feels less like they're having a conversation with someone so much as putting on a performance. Similarly, someone who consistently makes ill-timed or inappropriate jokes comes off as an asshole rather than charming and delightful.

The line between someone being charmingly funny and trying too hard – or worse, being painfully unfunny –

is a very thin one that requires careful social calibration. Many forms of flirting and banter, for example, walk the line between being funny and being mean. If you are the sort of person who likes a more antagonistic form of flirting, then you need to be able to clearly signal that while you may say things that are teasing or even appear mean on the surface, it's intended to be playful and fun. It's about verbal sparring rather than insulting or offending the other person. Cocky-funny "jokes" and negging[7], on the other hand, are designed to insult the other person and demonstrate your supposed superiority. This is neither attractive, nor particularly charming. Even offensive or uncomfortable humor has its place – one of the sex-gettingest men I know can say the most shockingly outrageous things and have the entire room eating out of his hand – but you have to be a social surgeon in order to do this without coming across like a shithead who has watched too much *Tosh 2.0*.

To be sure, not everybody can be a laugh riot, but understanding how to get women to laugh makes you much more charismatic. If you're not a naturally gifted comedian, you should immerse yourself in things that *are* funny. Watch comedians, read books that make you laugh and pay attention to comedy websites like Cracked, Dorkly, College Humor and FunnyOrDie. Watch how people you find funny play with words and expectations and study the rhythm of how they tell their stories or have unique turns of phrases. You don't want to *copy* them

---

7. Negging is a term invented by Pick-Up Artists for using left-handed compliments and outright insults as a way to prove that you're of equal or greater social status as the woman you're hitting on. Theoretically, it shows that you're not intimidated by them. In practice, it's supposed to hurt their self-esteem and make them crave your approval. "You're not hot enough to act like this" is a classic example of a neg.

so much as simply give yourself a broad reference base. Some of it will click with you and some of it won't. Some you will understand and some will seem like a mystery. But the more you're exposed to, the more you will be able to put together when the time comes.

HOW TO BUILD YOUR CONFIDENCE

Straight talk time: confidence is sexy.

Someone who lacks confidence, even if he looks like a GQ cover model, is going to be considerably less attractive than someone who doesn't have perfect facial features but *does* have abundant self-esteem. This isn't just some feel-good bullshit; confidence actually alters how other people see you. In a study published by the *International Journal of Cosmetic Science*, researchers found that raising men's confidence – in this case, via the placebo effect triggered by giving men a new cologne – made them visibly more attractive as rated by a panel of women who viewed them on video. Their facial structure was less important than their body language, posture and behavior.

The problem is that "just be more confident" is useless advice. It's like telling somebody that flying is easy; they just have to throw themselves at the ground and miss. Confidence isn't something that's acquired, but rather something that is developed over time. Unfortunately, it can be something of a catch-22: if you don't have confidence in the first place, it's hard to develop it. In fact, the less confident you are to start with, the easier it is to *lose* what you already have.

So how do you break this vicious cycle?

Fake It 'Til You Make It

The easiest way to jumpstart your confidence is simply to pretend that you're *already* confident. You literally trick your brain into thinking you're more confident than you are, which actually gives you genuine feelings of confidence. As much as we believe that the brain rules the body, it turns out that the opposite is true.

In the '70s and '80s, psychologists discovered that adopting the physical posture of an emotional state will actually trick your brain into thinking that it's actually experiencing that emotion. People who force themselves to smile – a real smile, one that reaches the eyes – find themselves actually feeling happier. Men who slouch and keep their eyes downcast will feel more ashamed. Men who act confident will *feel* more confident. It's known as "embodied cognition," and it's a great way to trick yourself into being more confident... even if you aren't.

One of the quickest and easiest ways for an immediate confidence boost is to adopt what's known as a "power pose" for a few minutes before doing something that you find stressful or intimidating. Certain poses model specific attitudes and beliefs and cause the brain to respond in kind; your brain notices that your body is performing behavior that corresponds with confidence and then decides that yes, you are, in fact feeling confident. When we feel powerful, we feel confident... so you want to stand or sit in ways that say "power." Stand with your feet shoulder-width apart, pull your shoulders back to puff out your chest and put your fists on your hips like a superhero. You might feel a bit self-conscious at first, but it's hard to ignore the feeling of power that comes from it. If you're sitting, prop your feet up on a table and lean back. Lace your fingers behind your head and point your elbows outward. It's another very powerful pose; you're sitting like you're the boss, giving orders to your subordinates. Let that feeling of power flow through you and fill you with confidence. Two or three minutes and a little bit of privacy is all you need to jumpstart your confidence.

Next, fix your posture. A straight back is a confident pose; a curved one is a questioning or doubting pose. We'll be talking more about body language in the next chapter, but for now, imagine an invisible thread attached to the crown of your head that's pulling you gently upwards, pulling your spine straight and leaving your head level. Let your arms dangle loosely at your sides, let your knees bend slightly, and keep your feet approximately shoulder-width apart, with your weight evenly distributed between them. Pull your shoulders back, but not so far that you're standing at attention; you're aiming for confident not "I just got out of the military."

Then, slow down your movements and relax your limbs. Quick and jerky gestures make you look and feel nervous and panicky. You want to move with smooth deliberation and purpose and you can't do that when your muscles are tense. You also want to control your breathing; inhale slowly, hold it, then exhale slowly. This will help slow your heart rate and ease the jitters of nervousness. It's *literally* impossible to be nervous when you keep your heart rate down and your breathing even. Speak slower and more deliberately; we tend to speed up when we're excited or nervous, so speaking slower forces you to calm down.

It can also help to watch what confident people do and learn to model their behavior. Watch interviews with George Clooney and you'll see what confidence looks like. The man simply oozes self-assurance. Watch his body language; his shoulders are back, his back is straight and his head is level.[8] He moves deliberately. He makes strong, lingering eye contact with whomever he's talking to, he speaks with low, measured tones and he has that large, toothy grin. Watching Clooney, you will see a man who looks as though that no matter what's going on, he's not just secure in his own awesomeness, but that he's having the time of his life.

Physical actions can also help short circuit the mental side of low confidence. Scientists have found that questioning your doubts actually decreases them. When we apply positive reinforcement to a thought or feeling – nodding along in agreement to somebody's lecture, for example, we validate it and solidify its effects. So when we apply positive reinforcement to a negative thought, we make that thought stronger and more present in our minds. Similarly, if we apply negative reinforcement of a positive thought, like shaking our head over the idea that we're going to get that barista's phone number, we decrease our certainty and confidence. However, negative reinforcement of a negative thought actually decreases the uncertainty and lack of confidence. Like an AI trying to divide by zero, negatively reinforcing a negative thought actually induces a paradox in our unconscious minds, making us less certain about the

8. ...especially after Steven Soderbergh made him ditch that head-bobble he used to do.

negativity... leaving us feeling more confident. The reason why our doubts have so much validity is because we trust them. But by deliberately applying negative reinforcement – questioning our doubts, shaking our head at the visions of failure – we're actually able to weaken their hold on us.

Take the Little Victories to Earn the Big Ones

The most common mistake people make that ruins their confidence is that they set their sights too high and try to take on too much at once. We assume that we should be able to do the impossible right off the bat, and we can't, so then we just *suck*. I see this all the time in people who are trying to get better at dating: they're so used to being "The One Who Isn't Good With Girls" that they focus like lasers on the end result (getting any woman they want). But all this does is make every night's practice an exercise in frustration and misery and serves to highlight just how far away the goal still is. Holding yourself to insane standards – being able to run a marathon when you've never run a mile or taking girls home every night when you're barely able to hold a conversation with your classmates – is a great way to set yourself up for failure. The goal is just so far beyond your current abilities that it's practically impossible. With that kind of unrealistic goal, when you do fail, it just reinforces the narrative that you're a loser and invalidates the progress you *do* make.

What you want to do is focus on incremental improvement, collecting the smaller victories and achievable goals. It can be as simple as "stay in a conversation with a woman for fifteen minutes," "get one phone number" or "run five laps slightly faster than I did last week." They don't have to be epic feats of skill, but they do have to be actual challenges... just so long as they are attainable ones. Reaching those small victories proves that you're making quantifiable progress. Keeping a journal can help you track your progress and provide you with a visual record of just how far you've come.

Is it as sexy as going from zero to hero in a four-minute training montage while "Eye of the Tiger" is jamming in the background? No, but it *does* bring you another step closer to your goal. And, more importantly, you get the satisfaction of having bested yet one more challenge, which helps boost your confidence enough to take on the next challenge, and the one after that.

That's how confidence is built.

Embrace Failure

There's a quote from Thomas Edison that I live by: "I have not failed. I have merely found 10,000 ways that don't work."

We have a tendency to look at failure as a personal flaw, that by failing at something we *ourselves* are failures. It's one of the insidious ways that we actually sabotage our confidence: we let failure override everything else about us. We act as though we need to do everything perfectly, as though the littlest screw-up is going to lead to our being Force-choked by Darth Vader.

But failure is often the best thing that can happen to you... as long as you know how to *use* it. Our successes, especially our early ones, are actually misleading. It's harder to learn from success because often you're not able to see all of the factors that lead to your triumph. Did something succeed because of pure random chance, or because you did everything right? Failure, on the other hand, has specific causes. It's in failure that we find the flaws and the places that need improvement. How can you improve if you don't know whether the problem was a lack of skill, a deeper personal issue, or even just plain bad luck? Failure, put simply, is how we *learn* to succeed. Why do we fall? So we can learn how to get back up again.

Back in the early days of my transformation, one bad rejection was all it would take to absolutely sink my night. This would devastate my confidence for the entire evening; every other approach I'd make that night would be colored by the idea that I was a failure and I was only going to get rejected again. Not surprisingly, I'd do horribly for the rest of the evening, which would just make me feel worse and worse until I would finally call it quits and go home pissed at the world and myself. It might take days before I could bring myself to go out and try again.

When failure is something we fear or dread, it takes up significant real estate in our heads and it starts to affect everything we do... especially when we associate failure with our own self-worth. We become less concerned with succeeding than we are with not failing. That, in turn, makes us less likely to actually succeed. It's the centipede's dilemma: we get so overcome with thinking about all the ways things can screw up that we can't do things that were otherwise second nature to us. The more you fear failure, the more likely you are to choke when the pressure is on.

But when you embrace failure, it can be liberating.

Failing at something simply means that something didn't work out, and then you know to do it differently next time. It's not easy; you have to consciously reframe the situation and remind yourself that failing is how you learn. But over time, it becomes natural, even instinctual. In the end, you learn to fear failure less and respond to in a positive fashion – which is a mark of confidence.

Fear + Survival = Confidence

You need to face your fears.

Fear is the mind killer. Fear is the little death. Fear holds you back. And you need to learn to be stronger than your fears. When you confront your fears and survive, you will start to master them, and with mastery comes self-confidence.

It's understandable to fear rejection or humiliation; romantic rejection *hurts*. But as scary as it is, rejection isn't going to kill you. At the end of the day, whether getting rejected by someone you're attracted to hurts or not is ultimately up to you. With enough experience and exposure, you'll start to learn that how it affects you is determined by your attitude. Rejection can destroy you or it can be something that you learn from.

Fear can be a tool. It can be used to motivate you. Use your fear as a signal; when you feel intimidated or afraid of approaching someone, use that as a sign that you need to go up to her if only to prove to yourself that you can beat this. Through exposure and repetition, you will begin to understand that what you fear is the product of your own mind. Your fear of rejection is really tying your self-worth to her reaction. By giving her that much power over your self-image, you're taking the locus of control of your life and handing it to someone else.

Once you begin to understand that rejection is nothing to be fear, you'll start to relax around women. Relaxing around women will make you feel more self-assured and more in the moment. Just as important, by decoupling your fear of rejection from your self-worth, you'll be able to actually enjoy talking to these amazing women, even when it doesn't necessarily go exactly where you want it to.

Every time you confront your fears, they lose the ability to control you. Every time you let that fear wash over you and push through it, you'll feel the sense of accomplishment that comes with conquering a challenge. Every time you beat your fear, you'll feel your sense of ease and confidence grow.

FINDING YOUR SWAGGER

Let's go back to some of the most compelling figures in genre fiction. Whether you're thinking of Peter Venkman, Mal Reynolds, James Bond or Stacker Pentacost, they have one thing in common: that certain "swagger" that other men don't. It's that ineffable quality that we see in ridiculously confident men, the ones who always look as though they're saying, "I'm sorry, I can't hear you over how awesome I am."

It's that extra bit of confidence that almost – but not quite – borders on arrogance, that willingness to push the boundaries that helps separate the Nice Guys™ from the players... and it's unspeakably appealing. A hot guy with no confidence is *less* attractive than a plain guy with the right attitude.

So how do you find your swagger? By adopting the traits that makes these characters so riveting.

Be a Challenge

One of the kinks of human psychology is that we want things that we can't have and we value the things that we had to work for more than the things that just fell into our laps.

For example: Hollywood is always awash in stories of the rakes and ladykillers amongst the celebrities – the ones who never seem to settle down but move from relationship to relationship, cutting a wide swath through the female celebrities like a hot knife through butter. Whether it was Jack Nicholson and Warren Beatty in the 70s, Colin Farrell in the 90s or George Clooney in the last twenty years, every time they were seen in the presence of yet another lady, all of the gossip would be focused on "Is she the one? Is she going to be the one to finally tame him?"

This is part of what makes the bad boy we talked about earlier seem so appealing. He has attitude to spare. He has no problem being sarcastic or giving the hottest girl shit. He'll tease her mercilessly or bust her balls. He loves to play hard to get. He has no problem walking away if he needs to.

Most other men, on the other hand, are easy. There's no real challenge to them. They're so afraid of ruining what they see as their one chance that they wouldn't dream of sassing a woman back; after all, what if she got upset?

Too many guys think that the way to a woman's heart and/or panties is to be kind and obliging to the point of excess, running to and fro like puppies, wagging their tails in the hopes of getting a treat. Why would a woman be interested in someone who acted like that?

The takeaway here is that you need to not be a doormat, constantly saying "yes," always hanging around and dancing in attendance on her every wish. It all ties back to the idea of the push-pull dynamic. You don't want to be an asshole, so you actually treat her with respect and consideration, but at the same time, you also don't treat her like a princess or put her on a pedestal. Bantering and teasing (as covered in Chapter 12) help establish that you're not just a pushover and you're not going to follow her around like an imprinted gosling.

Be Honest

There's a saying I love: "Telling the truth means never having to remember what you said the night before." Being honest about yourself and your intentions makes things simpler in the long run. Part of what makes Nice Guys™ unappealing is that they're liars; they're pretending to be something they're not in order to get what they want. It's a sign to the world that they don't believe in themselves enough to be straightforward – instead they have to present a false face because they want to try to avoid getting rejected.

Ask yourself this question: can you imagine Bond feeling like he can't just tell someone he wants them? How about Tony Stark? When you're interested in someone, make it clear that you're interested in them and why:

you want to date them, you want to sleep with them, you're looking for a romantic relationship. Being honest about your intentions cuts through the confusion and the bullshit. It means nobody ever has to wonder what's really going on ("Was this a date? I don't know if this was a date" or "I can't tell if he's looking to date me or just to sleep with me"). It simplifies your life immensely.

Be Assertive

Men with swagger are a little bit selfish; they're more than willing to give their interests a priority. As a result, when they see something they want, they go for it. They aren't wringing their hands over the possibility of rejection because every moment they spend thinking about it is one that they aren't using to get the girl in the first place.

Too many men are risk averse and fear being rejected. They don't want to take the chance that they'll make a move and ruin everything, not when they could live in the vague hope that "maybe she'll realize how awesome I am and learn to love me."

Interesting, charming men, men who are good with women, aren't following women around, hoping for crumbs of approval or looking for the slightest hint that there is a chance that she likes them. They assume that it's a foregone conclusion and make their move accordingly. If she doesn't like him? Well, hell, there are more women out there; time to move on and find someone better. This sort of abundance mentality keeps them from being completely hung up on the idea that they have one shot and one shot only before resigning themselves to never knowing love ever again. If he gets rejected... well, who gives a damn? Rejection rolls off his back and he rolls on to the next girl. You know what that looks like?

That looks like confidence.

And – say it with me now – confidence is sexy.

The trick is that there's a difference between being a pushy jerk and being confident. The appeal in being assertive isn't about badgering people, it's in demonstrating the confidence to go out and approach women rather than waiting for them to do all of the heavy lifting. It's in being secure enough not to let rejection shatter your self-esteem into pieces.

Being willing to take risks means that you are more likely to find someone who likes you than the guy who's so afraid of rejection that he can only make his move when he's 110% assured of success... and possibly not even then.

Be Self Validating

Confident men don't base their self-worth on what other people think of them. As far as he is concerned, he's the shit, baby. He's the hottest thing jumping out of the coffee pot. He's money. He's money and he knows he's money. If a girl rejects him, she's clearly just not right for him. Maybe she just broke up with someone. Or maybe she's just blind. The reasons don't matter, it just all comes down to "I'm awesome and if she couldn't see it, there's something wrong with her."

Confident men, men with swagger, don't need validation from other people. They get all they need from themselves.

One problem nerds frequently have is that they often

look to others for validation. They frequently come from a background of being ostracized and bullied. They're told over and over again that they're losers and freaks; as a result, they tend to look for outside sources that justify who they are and give them meaning. This is part of why geek guys often fetishize geek girls; if he can land that hot girl with the Doctor Who tattoos and the shrine to Joss Whedon, it's proof that he is cool because he's a geek. This fetishization goes beyond wanting to connect with someone who shares his interests and becomes about using her as a prop. The girl isn't a person so much as a trophy that he can point to and say, "See? SEE?"

This need for external validation manifests itself in the way that men without confidence respond to other people; they come across as needy and clingy. They're basing their self-esteem on the opinions of others and that's ultimately a losing game. It's giving away control of your life and making it impossible to actually improve or even appreciate your own life.

The confident man? He doesn't need to prove anything to anybody. He's not going to have his ego crushed if his girlfriend argues with him or gets angry. He keeps his self-esteem high, and this attitude makes him more attractive to women. You need to learn not to put your self-esteem and value into the hands of other people and instead find that Zen state where you don't need the approval of others to feel good about yourself. Relying on others to validate you makes you needy, which is the Anti-Sex Equation; there's nothing attractive about someone who needs constant reassurance and approval from others. When you know what you're worth – and you're worth a lot – then you're much sexier.

Strike the Balance

Let's return for a moment to the learning how to be The Most Interesting Man in the World. The great thing about being an interesting charismatic man is that there isn't one way to act. Being interesting doesn't mean being a bore. Being confident doesn't mean being a jerk. Being nice doesn't mean being "nice" (or NiceTM).

There are many men out there who are known for being some of the sweetest, kindest guys... yet are also confident and assertive. Joseph Gordon-Levitt isn't anyone's idea of a macho shithead with a cock where his brain should be, yet he's a modern day sex symbol. Ryan Gosling and Andrew Garfield have hordes of female admirers without acting like bro-tastic entitled jerks. There's nothing wrong with being nice. The problem is being a Nice Guy™. So quit trying to be "nice" and treating women like the prize you win for collecting enough Proof of Nice Guy™ coupons. Take those aspects of the bad boy that girls find so appealing and learn how to incorporate them without becoming the sort of overcompensating jackass that they're associated with.

Finding your swagger means walking the line between "nice" and "100% a dick."

You can be a challenge to women while still being incredibly sweet on occasion. You can have a little of that bad boy edge without being an ass.

Be a lot more confident. Be a little harder to pin down. Be a lot more aggressive.

Don't be a Nice Guy™.

Be a *good* guy. An *interesting* guy.

CHAPTER 5.

HOW TO BE MORE ATTRACTIVE IN 5 EASY STEPS

THE DIFFERENCE BETWEEN "GOOD LOOKING" AND "ATTRACTIVE"

One of the never-ending debates that arise when you're talking about men's dating issues is how much looks count when it comes to attraction. On the one hand, you have people who will insist that the *only* guys who can get dates are the six-foot Adonises with abs like damn. On the other hand, you will have people who insist that women are far less visually oriented than men and that character and personality count for more.

Of course, then those guys are promptly given wedgies and called wimps.

Here's the truth: looks are very important. They're also very unimportant.

Confused? It's understandable. The reason why this debate keeps raging on without end is because people are continually mistaking "good looks" for being attractive. There are very few standards for what's considered to be good looking. The only qualities that are widely considered to be good looking tend to be based around outward signs of physical health: facial symmetry, clear skin, strong teeth, shiny hair, and a v-shaped torso in men with a 1.0 waist-to-hip ratio and a .7 hip-to-waist ratio in women. The rest tends to be the result of personal preference and external influences. It's hard to overestimate how much media affects our tastes in looks; people exposed to mainstream media (such as through Internet access) tend to prefer slimmer women and more macho men while those with less exposure tend to prefer more feminine men and more zaftig women.

Now let's be clear up front: there's no question that traditional good looks help in life. Humans are psychologically predisposed to be more positively inclined toward people who are physically attractive; a cognitive bias known as the "halo effect" influences people's judgments and impressions about a person based purely on their physical appearance. A person who is blessed with physical good looks will frequently have a leg up in the world because people unconsciously assume them to be smarter, kinder and more moral.

However, the definition of what women consider to be good looking varies wildly. Studies have shown that while men tend to have a consensus on what they consider hot, women's tastes vary far more. Men tend to think that all women go for Chris Hemsworth's god-like build and leonine mane of hair when women may be far more likely to scream for Joseph Gordon-Levitt's more wiry frame, Chiwetel Ejiofor's gap-toothed smile or Matt Smith's fivehead.

Not everybody can be good looking. The only way to change your facial features involves expensive, insanely painful surgeries that may very well make things worse.

Being *attractive*, on the other hand, is an entirely different beast. *Every* man can be attractive. Attraction is about the whole person, not just his physical features. To give a concrete example: Serge Gainsbourg was nobody's idea of a male model. Quite frankly, he looked like the love-child of Steve Buscemi and Droopy Dog. However, he got more famous ass[1] than a drunk man with a stolen credit card at a celebrity donkey auction. He may not have been good looking, but he was *attractive as hell*.

Cold hard truth time: people judge you by your appearance. There is no getting around this. When you're dressed like a slob in a stained t-shirt and baggy jeans with a scraggly beard and a fedora, people are going to make snap judgments about you, and they *won't* be pretty. You may have a beautiful soul, but your external self is helping to ensure that nobody is going to get close enough to find out. If you want to be attractive, you're going to have to invest in yourself and put the effort in.

You can't change your looks, but you *can* change your appearance. Following these steps will make drastic changes to how attractive you are – in many cases, almost overnight.

FOOD AND FITNESS

Garbage in, Garbage Out

The first critical step in changing your appearance is to change your diet. If you're shoveling garbage into your system, you will pay a penalty for it – not just in terms of your health, but in the way you look and feel. Don't get

---

1. His wives and lovers included Brigitte Bardot, Jane Birkin, Catherine Denevue and Vanessa Paradis, among others.

me wrong: this isn't about being fat, it's about your health and the way eating the wrong foods affect your looks. You are literally what you eat and shitty food is going to make you look like shit – it screws up your skin, your hair and body… not to mention the effects of all that salt and processed food on your internal organs and circulatory system. The excess salt, sugar and preservatives in processed foods damage our skin's elasticity and shine while causing us to retain water, making us look older, tired and puffy. The nutritional void of snack foods and sodas leave our hair dull and brittle; in fact, some scientists suggest that a poor diet can lead to thinning hair or even hair loss.

Moreover, *many* of the foods we love – the ones that we say make life worth living – also screw with our emotions. The sugar from soda metabolizes in our bodies so quickly that as soon as the sugar rush wears off, our mood plummets almost immediately. The omega-6 fats in chips and snacks like Cheetos block our bodies from metabolizing omega-3 fatty acids, which are important for brain function and mood regulation.

Now I'll be the first to tell you: this is an area I struggle with. My addiction to Diet Dr. Pepper is legendary and I will quite cheerfully eat damn near anything if you deep fat fry it. It doesn't help that food companies have spent billions of dollars not only on making processed foods as addictive as heroin, but on how to hook us at as early an age as possible. Anyone who's tried to quit diet soda will tell you just how much of a nightmare it can be. But even minor changes to your diet can produce major results. Start simple and small and build up; trying to go cold turkey is only going to ruin your efforts and sabotage any progress you make.

Drink More Water

Changing your drinking habits is, hands down, the easiest and best thing you can possibly do for yourself. Most of us simply aren't drinking enough water – we tend to substitute soda, sports drinks and energy drinks instead. On a purely physical level, drinking more water flushes toxins out of your system and helps refresh and hydrate your skin, giving it a healthy glow. Dehydration leads to dizziness and fatigue, so hydration improves your physical performance and decreases joint pain by keeping your cartilage hydrated. Dehydration affects your mood as well; you end up with nagging headaches and disorientation and grogginess.

Switching to water *also* helps control your weight. Sodas, energy drinks and even most fruit juices are liquid calorie and sugar bombs. If you have to have fruit juice, try to stick to freshly squeezed, organic juice; your morning glass of Tropicana is more chemicals and added sugar than actual juice. And don't just switch to diet sodas. Aspartame actually makes you consume more, since your body isn't getting the calories it was expecting with the sweetness. Tea and coffee are okay in moderation; teas have a number of healthy antioxidants while the caffeine in coffee is a natural performance enhancer. Just keep it to one to two cups per day. As an added bonus: cutting down on the total amount of coffee you drink daily means that the caffeine will start affecting you more.

Eat Clean

The next best thing you can do for your body is to eat "clean" – that is, to eat as few processed foods as humanly possible. If your meal involves ingredients that either you can't pronounce or find on their own in a grocery store, you don't want to be putting it in your body. This includes trying to avoid high-fructose corn syrup as best you can. It's difficult – the stuff is in literally almost *everything* these days – but the difference in how you will feel makes it worth the effort.

The best adjustment you can make to your diet is to eat more fruits and green leafy vegetables. These will supply the lion's share of your nutrients and you're almost certainly not eating enough of them. They're also going to be your major source of fiber – another thing that you're almost certainly not getting enough of. Higher levels of insoluble fiber help fill you up as well as assist in clearing up certain gastric issues that crop up in our modern diets. If at all possible, eat it fresh and preferably organic. I realize that this isn't always possible; lots of us live in areas where fresh produce is scarce and "organic" translates to "out of my price range." Canned or frozen veggies are almost as good, just make sure that they don't have added sugar or sodium.

You *need* lean protein and amino acids – they're important not only for muscle building, but also for hair and skin luster. Your best sources are chicken, turkey, lean cuts of beef and fish. If you're vegetarian or vegan, I advise hemp protein, almonds, walnuts, pecans, quinoa and black beans. You also want to eat plenty of sources of healthy fats –especially salmon, avocados, nuts and peanut butter.

Cut out the hidden calories from fatty cream-based sauces, salad dressings and spreads as much as possible. All of these are sources of bad fats that you often overlook when you're considering trying to eat better. It doesn't help to eat more broccoli if you're going to drown it in ranch dressing first.

Limit your consumption of simple carbs – potatoes, white bread, pasta and white rice – when you can. Complex carbs – sprouted grain breads, brown rice, sweet potatoes, green leafy veggies, legumes, apples, pears, mangos – have nutrients and fiber that offset the bump to your glucose levels and they're far better for you.

A healthier diet will make you feel like a new man. You'll have more energy, you'll feel more positive, and your immune system will be boosted, and you'll look better too.

Cheat Sparingly

I'll be the first to tell you that cookies are fucking awesome and I loves me some french fries in ranch dressing. Giving yourself a day off once a week can help you not lose your goddamn monkey mind as you try to eat better.

Find Your Cardio (And Lift Some Weights While You're at It)

Being active is incredibly important. Humans are simply not built for the sedentary lifestyle that most of us lead these days. We're built to move and remaining seated all day, every day is slowly killing us. You need some form of cardiovascular exercise to keep your circulatory and respiratory systems in shape, not to mention to avoid issues like diabetes and osteoporosis. Cardiovascular exercise is also an incredible mood-enhancer and antidepressant. Exercise promotes the production of endorphins which make you realize that you may feel like pounded shit but, by God, it's the kind of pain that makes you realize that you feel more *alive* than you've felt in a long goddamn time.

This doesn't mean that you need to go to the gym and hit the elliptical machines five times a week or run 5ks every day. Not everybody has it in them to get up at 5 AM and go running, and, let's be honest, the treadmill is goddamn *boring*. You need to find some form of physical activity – something that elevates your heart rate for at least thirty minutes – that you enjoy. It might be a daily pick-up basketball game. It might be an amateur dodgeball league. You might want to find a parkour gym, join a dojo or take swing dancing lessons. It can also help to give yourself a goal to work towards, by signing up for a Mud Run or a Zombie 5k race for example.

You also want to seriously consider adding weight lifting to your exercise regimen. The health benefits are immense – building muscle actually speeds up your metabolism and helps you burn more calories – and toning up goes a long way to making you look good. If you've got the money, I recommend working with a trainer for a couple of weeks; they can help you develop an exercise routine that will help you reach your goals and teach you how to lift properly and avoid injuring yourself.

It's important to note: just because you're eating right and exercising doesn't mean that you'll magically become a *Men's Health* cover model. You're restricted by your genetics and build; not everybody is going to have those perfect-looking six-pack abs no matter how much they work out. In addition, those shirtless dudes you see in ads, on covers and in the movies don't live the same lifestyle you do. Their job is literally to look good; their day-to-day life is entirely structured around the exercise routines and meals that it takes to look like that. You simply don't have the same time to commit that they do. And that's *before* people add human growth hormone, dehydration, lighting tricks, makeup and Photoshop.

The point of changing your diet and adding the exercise is to fix your overall health and sense of well-being. Being healthy is a greater component of being attractive than having a specific body type. Women love a *wide* variety of bodies from the lean to the husky. There are women out there who like big, burly, hairy men and others who love the heroin-skinny guys. It's more important to learn to accept and love your build for what it is, instead of trying to force yourself to live up to a physical ideal that you literally cannot match.

THE POWER OF GROOMING

One of those key steps to better physical attractiveness is to embrace proper grooming and hygiene.

This is where a lot of guys fall down. Most guys have absolutely no idea how to take care of their skin. In fact, many of us roll our eyes at the seemingly complicated and occult skin-care rituals that our mothers, sisters, girlfriends and wives go through. All of those bottles, tubes and pots of strange-smelling liquids, unguents, powders and creams which have to be applied just so in a very specific order at different times of day make it seem more like alchemy than helping to even out their skin tone and prevent blemishes.

Men don't need all that crap. Soap and water, some shampoo, a little shaving cream and some aftershave if you're feeling fancy and we're all good, right? Right. Except: women's skin looks so much *better* than ours. It's softer, more supple, clearer and brighter. Meanwhile, we're watching all those wrinkles, blotches, blackheads, and beard-rash pile up on our shiny, shiny faces and wondering why nobody wants to get into our personal space.

Trust me: all those good-looking asshats who are getting the women you wish *you* could hook up with? They're taking care of their personal grooming. If you want to get in the race, you need to do so as well.

Take Care of Your Face

Let's be logical here: women are going to be looking at your face. You want your face to look good. Not taking care of your skin detracts from that. Proper skin care will make you look younger, more alert and more attractive. The problem is that most guys do it wrong.

To start with: stop washing your face with bar soap. This actually dries your skin and makes things worse. You want a gentle, fragrance-free facial cleanser – one that works for all skin types – and to use it on a daily basis. Some advocate using it just before bed so you don't grind all the crap on your face into your pillow and let it soak back into you overnight. Others make using their cleanser as part of their morning routine. Ideally, you also want to use a toner after your cleanser. It helps clean out the pores and cuts, getting rid of excess oil and sebum, leaving you with clearer, more even skin. If you're having regular acne problems, a toner with salicylic acid will go a long way towards healing current breakouts and preventing new ones.

Follow up the cleanser and toner with a moisturizer, especially one that has sun protection in it. The moisturizer helps hydrate your skin and fill out wrinkles while the sunscreen prevents damage from UV rays that make your skin look like leather and give you skin cancer in the process.

At least once a week, use an exfoliating scrub. A good granular scrub strips away all of the dead skin and debris, clears out the pores and helps brighten and smooth out your skin. It also will help prevent blackheads and keep the ones you *do* have from becoming Vesuvius-like eruptions.

Also: learn to corral your unwanted hair. Get a decent pair of tweezers and attack your eyebrows and any ear and nose hair. Keeping bushy eyebrows under control (especially if you tend towards a unibrow) will work wonders for improving your look and confidence, and you don't want anyone getting in close to notice stray nose or ear hairs. Just make sure to follow the natural arc of your brows; you don't want to give yourself a permanent look of dull surprise. YouTube has a number of excellent tutorials about how to tweeze and shape your brows.

...”And what is that smell?!”

Next, it's time to deal with your odor problem. Nothing is going to make sex disappear faster than a guy who smells bad. Bad breath is an obvious starting point and you need to keep it under control. Besides basic brushing and flossing, you want to be careful what you actually put *in* your mouth. Coffee and other acidic beverages – including soda – lower the pH balance in your mouth, causing bacteria to grow that release sulfurous compounds and make your breath reek. If you're doing a high-protein, low-carb diet, you have to be particularly careful; if you eat less than 100 grams of carbohydrates daily, you risk going into ketosis which makes your breath smell like nail polish remover (amongst other things).

Gum and mouthwash can help with bad breath, but ultimately all they're doing is masking a smell; your bad breath *will* come through eventually. The best cure is simply to rinse with water after eating or drinking. Water helps restore the pH balance of your mouth and swishing it around will help dislodge particles of food stuck in your teeth.

You also want to deal with your body odor. Buy a decent deodorant; the cheap stuff from the drugstore is okay, but most of them are going to wear out in the middle of the day *and* leave an ugly residue on your clothes. This is one area where you do better to shell out for one of the pricier brands. Check the men's section of your local department store or Sephora.

And speaking of body odor... here's the one thing that's going to *really* make you stand out: know how to use cologne *properly*. Almost every woman out there has complained about how men simply do not know how to wear cologne – they tend to *bathe* in the stuff until you can smell them from a block away. Getting close to them is like being tear-gassed with Drakkar Noir and Calvin Klein, which is not something that's going to lead to her going back to your place at the end of the night. The key to wearing cologne is subtlety. First: find a scent that actually *works* with you; colognes are going to interact with your body's chemistry which will change how they smell. Don't just get a sample on a stick: spray it on your wrist and walk around for a bit to let it evaporate. This will give you an idea of how it's going to smell on *you*, rather than in the bottle. When you apply it, you want to be incredibly sparing – one spritz, two at the most. A woman shouldn't be able to smell your cologne until she's close enough to kiss you. Any more than that and you've used too much.

(Here's a secret tip from my personal bag o' tricks: forgo cologne entirely and go for essential oils from your local health-food store or Amazon. Dab a drop or two on your throat and wrists and head out the door. Trust me, whenever I've worn a scent like Nemat amber or vanilla musk, I've had total strangers come up to tell me how nice I smell…)

Get That Cool Haircut

Never underestimate the power of an amazing haircut. A proper cut and style is more than just trimming off a couple of inches every month. A skilled barber or stylist can completely transform how you look, using your hair to balance out your features, shape your face and head and even show off some of your personality.

The first step is deciding whether you want to go to a barber or a stylist. Barbers tend to be a little cheaper than stylists and, in traditional shops at least, tend to not require appointments. Usually, you can show up and wait until there's a free chair. Most of the time, the haircut you get from a barbershop is going to be on the simpler side. It'll be clean and easy to maintain, but you're rarely going to find someone who can give you the most stylish or terribly complicated cut. On the other hand, many barbers – especially in larger, more metropolitan cities – are your best bet if you're looking for a more retro, rockabilly or punk look.

A stylist tends to cost more, but they offer more services and more styling options. Stylists will be more familiar with the latest fashions and trends in men's hair and able to help out if you're looking for something slightly more complicated than just a quick trim. A stylist will usually have a quick consultation with you to help figure out not just what you want, but what works best with your features and hair type.

Either way: do *not* go to SuperCuts or the place in the mall. Sorry, but this is one of those times when you get what you pay for. A cheap haircut is almost always a *lousy* haircut.

The next step is to know what you want. Most guys go in with only vague ideas of the look they're trying to achieve and have no idea how to communicate it; as a result, they come out with a cut that may or may not look like what they were hoping for. If you want to avoid this then you need to do what women do and bring a picture. Find a photo of the hairstyle you like – ideally featuring someone who has hair similar to yours – and rip it out of the magazine, print it out or save it to your smartphone. You may feel awkward, but trust me: your stylist will appreciate it. It makes things much easier for both of you. Just be willing to be flexible; a good barber will be taking your head and face shape, hair thickness and texture into account. Not everybody is going to be able to pull off the same style. Certain hairstyles don't go well with certain face shapes or hair textures, no matter how badly you want it to work.

One thing to keep in mind: if you have thinning, receding hair or you're balding, a good haircut is even more critical. Yes, losing your hair may well be proof of God's hate, but a good stylist knows how to make it work for you. Many short hairstyles work well with high foreheads, and a close crop not only minimizes the appearance of bald spots but can help provide the illusion of volume. Another option is to simply adopt the shaved look; it's a very masculine – even aggressive – style and many women especially love to run their fingers (and other parts) over a freshly shaved scalp. If you have a nicely shaped skull – one that's fairly symmetrical with few dents or bumps – then grab some clippers and shave it to the skin. Remember: bald equals bad-ass; just look at Avery Brooks, Michael Clarke Duncan, Bruce Willis, Yul Brenner, Jason Statham or Charles Dance.

Manage Your Facial Hair

Facial hair is frequently God's gift to men. When grown and shaped properly, it's an incredibly versatile way to highlight certain features and draw attention away from others, visually reshaping your face. Carefully maintained stubble, for example, can make your face appear thinner by creating contrast and shadow. It can also enhance your cheekbones and give you a more masculine profile.

If you have a weak jawline, you can get some much-needed definition with a neatly trimmed beard. If you have a wide face, a Van Dyke help provides visual separation. Similarly, a goatee will help fill out a weak chin; letting it grow a little at the bottom helps fill in the space and lend some much-needed symmetry. A short beard can shape and define your jawline and provide visual contrast between your jaw and neck, slimming down your facial profile.

(Notice very carefully that I said "beard," not "chin-strap." Nobody likes the chinstrap. It makes you look like you've been trying to find a drummer for your Creed cover band, and nobody wants that.)

Different facial hairstyles work better with different shapes and sizes. Do a little research if you're considering one; find a celebrity or model who has a face shape similar to yours and see what works on them. Celebs have stylists dedicated to making them look good... and there's no reason why you shouldn't blatantly steal their expertise.

If you're going to grow a full beard, you need to keep it trimmed and shaped. The dreaded neckbeard gets mocked for good reason: it looks sloppy and immature. You want to shape your beard around your jawline, giving it a gentle curve towards your ear and straight down from your sideburns. And while we're at it: it's mandatory that you shampoo and condition your beard regularly. Not only do you not want to have to deal with chin-dandruff (a real thing), but conditioning it keeps it soft, luxuriant and much less likely to cause beard-burn on any prospective make out partners. Nobody wants to feel like their face is getting scraped off during sloppy make outs.

Handle Your Body Hair

In one of the cruelest ironies the universe has ever devised, while men tend to lose hair from their heads, we often end up with far more than we want everywhere else.

Of course, it's worth keeping in mind: acceptable levels of body hair are a matter of fashion. It wasn't that long ago that having a luxurious thicket of body hair was the height of masculine beauty. The current fashion, however is towards more of an almost complete removal of all body hair. Yes, all of it. There are even some adventurous souls who go for the "Boy-zillian," a concept that makes most men curl up on themselves in sympathetic agony. Personally, I think many body types simply look weird without hair, but as with a lot of issues, it comes down to personal preference and many men would prefer to be less hirsute... especially if they have a particularly hairy back.

The first option is simply to manscape by using a hair clipper designed specifically for body hair to trim your man-fur to acceptable levels. As a general rule, it's better to leave the chest hair longer, while trimming the hair on your upper arms, stomach and sides short. The contrast will make your chest look larger and slim down your torso. Of course, unless you are exceptionally flexible or have an especially indulgent roommate, the odds are that you won't be able to reach your back. There is the odd trimmer with an extra long handle for reaching the impossible-to-access parts of your anatomy but you're probably going to end up with random patches that you simply couldn't reach.

It's worth noting that you may want to consider trimming your public hair as well. Not only does it make your junk seem bigger, but many women appreciate a man who keeps things neat and tidy. You don't want to trim it down to porn-star or prepubescent levels – just tame the thicket somewhat.

The next option is professional hair removal via waxing or sugaring. This is performed by a licensed aesthetician at a salon and has the benefit of keeping the hair off from anywhere between three to six weeks. Of course, the problem is that it can *hurt like a motherfucker*. The famous chest-waxing scene from *The 40 Year Old Virgin* may be exaggerated... but not by much. It's also fairly pricy; sessions run from $60-$80 depending on what you're trying to wax, and if you're not diligent with the aftercare, waxing can lead to painful and unsightly ingrown hairs as it grows back in.

Laser hair removal offers a more permanent solution – the pulses actually kill the follicle and prevent future growth – but it too has its limitations. To start with, it's expensive, with treatments costing upwards of $400 a session, and takes at least five or six sessions to permanently inhibit hair growth. It's also incredibly painful – akin to having rubber bands snapped on your skin a thousand times a second – and doesn't work on many hair/skin combinations. If you have pale skin and light colored hair, you're basically out of luck.

Keep in mind, though, that there are many, *many* women (and men) who love a hairy, burly man. Just because you're not seeing fuzzy dudes on the cover of GQ doesn't mean that there isn't a woman out there waiting to find the bear of her dreams. They're far more common than you'd think.

BUILDING A COOL WARDROBE

The way you dress directly affects how people see you. Dress like a slob, people will assume you're a slob. If you want to be more attractive, you need to dress attractively. The problem is that so many men seem to perpetually misunderstand the power that a very simple upgrade in wardrobe can bring you. Clothes are an outward extension of your identity. Clothes are the first thing people will notice about you, and that will color their first impressions of you. The right outfit – or the wrong one, for that matter – can completely change you.

Know How Your Clothes Are Supposed to Fit

There are three factors that will ultimately decide how your clothes look on you: material, quality and fit. Of these, fit is the most important. Material and quality make a difference, but fit will *transform* you. A $200 suit from Banana Republic or Express that fits you properly will look far better than a $4000 Armani that's sagging in the seat, puddling at your ankles and drooping off your shoulders. Even if you're not in absolutely perfect shape, you want to wear clothes that actually *fit* your body; wearing things that are too big or too loose doesn't actually hide your flaws; instead, they make you look sloppy and unkempt.

Most men wear clothes that are a size (or two) too big. Clothes that fit properly are supposed to conform to the shape of your body. Most clothes – especially anything that you might wear to work or on a date – are not supposed to be so loose that you could play a pick-up game of basketball while wearing them. Loose-fitting clothes are great for relaxing, working around the house or playing sports. Clothes that fit the way they're supposed to will actually support you.

Here's how clothes are *supposed* to fit you:

- A shirt's shoulder seam should sit at your shoulder joint. If it goes any further, it's too big and looks like it's falling off of you. Cuffs on a dress shirt should not reach past your wrist. In a short-sleeved shirt, the sleeve should stop mid-bicep. *Any* shirt, casual or formal, should fit close to your torso without too much material on the sides. A buttoned shirt should fit snugly around your chest without looking stretched. If the buttons are pulling – especially as you move your arms – or you look like you're about to Hulk out of it, then it's too small. If it balloons out when tucked into your pants, it's too big. If a shirt is meant to be worn untucked, it will have a square hem and come to the level of your belt. If it's meant to be worn tucked in, it will reach down to your seat, and it will look sloppy if you wear it untucked.

- A dress shirt's collar should be loose enough so that you can slip two fingers into the neck without effort. Any tighter and you risk actually pinching your carotid artery. Any looser and you look like you're wearing the Cone of Shame.

- Blazers, jackets and sports coats should also have shoulder seams that sit at the shoulder joint. The sleeves should stop around three-fourths of an inch from the back of your hand, allowing just a little cuff to show.

- Pants are meant to sit at your natural waist,at or up to three fingers below your navel. If your pants sag below this point without a belt holding them up, they're too big. Pant legs should be slim, not too wide or too tight. Wide pants will make you look like you have sausages for legs. Unless you're heroin-thin, avoid skinny pants.

- Jeans should feel snug. They'll loosen up as you wear them, so you want a pair that fits slightly tighter in the waist, thighs and seat than you're used to.

- The bottom of your pants leg should sit just at your shoes. Some dress pants will have what is known as a "break," where the pants crease into a natural fold from resting on the top of the shoes. A "medium" break is traditional – a shallow crease with the back of the pants coming down to midway between the top of the back of the shoe and the sole. A full break is more daring as it creates a very deep crease and brings the back of the pants leg to just above the sole of the shoe. No break is considered to be more retro – think *Mad Men* – and is often a feature of tailored Italian suits. Jeans should have a very slight break. No pants should have more than one crease; if they do, they are too large.

Something to keep in mind is that you should never underestimate the value of a tailor, especially if you have a hard time finding clothes that fit. Your best option is to buy clothes that fit around your widest parts – your neck, your chest, your waist, what-have-you – and have the rest altered to fit. Many department stores offer low-cost or even free basic alterations with purchase. Alternately, an independent tailor can very well be your best friend. Most of them cost less than you'd think and can tailor your clothes – including your t-shirts and jeans – to fit perfectly. Just factor the price of the alterations into the cost of the clothing.

Perform a Purge on Your Closet Before Buying New

If you're the sort of person who's having a hard time putting together a cool outfit, the odds are good that you already have a closet full of regrets and bad decisions that are taking up space that could go to clothes you actually look good in. The best thing you can do is to perform a massive purge of everything in your closet. Start from the back and work your way forward. If it doesn't fit properly – if it's too big or too small – it's out. If it's labeled "relaxed fit," it goes. If you haven't worn it in months[2], it's out. If it's five years old or more... seriously consider tossing it, especially if it doesn't fit or you almost never wear it. If you got it for free at a convention, then it's time for it to go. If it looks even vaguely like Affliction or Ed Hardy... well, you might want to douse it with holy water and bury it at a crossroads, just to be sure.

Once you've pruned the deadwood in your closet, it's

2. Obvious exceptions can be made for seasonal clothing.

time to start buying new clothes. Clothing is another area where the axiom "you get what you pay for" is especially true. Skimping on the cost of clothes means you're going to get shoddier clothing. If money is tight, I recommend that you splurge strategically. A good pair of shoes and high-quality jeans are the best things to invest in if you're on a limited budget; they last longer and actually improve with age. Cheap shoes and jeans will only fall apart, meaning that you'll have to replace them more often, costing you more money in the long run. Also: women will notice your shoes and they will judge you for them.

The best way to buy new clothes is to shop strategically. One of the best things you can do is go to the larger department stores and get familiar with the brands and styles within those brands. Different brands will fit differently: a 34 waist in Gap jeans isn't necessarily going to be the same as a 34 in a pair of Naked and Famous or Diesel. Once you know which brands and styles fit you best, go online. A little time spent googling can often find you incredible deals and discounts. Don't forget to check Amazon and Zappos, by the way; you'd be amazed at how many name brand clothes they have. You may also want to consider signing up for discount clubs like Gilt or MyHabit – they have daily sales of designer clothes for up to 60% off.

Another trick: exploit the sales, especially towards the end of a season. You might have to be patient, but you can make out like a bandit with some proper pre-planning.

Start with the Basics

When you're learning how to put together cool outfits,

you want to start simply before you start trying to get very fashion forward. You wouldn't expect your first karate lesson to teach you the dim mak; you start with the basics and build a strong foundation that will form the basis of everything you learn afterwards. So it goes with style; you want the basics of a strong wardrobe before you start getting concerned with sprezzatura and trying to imitate people you see on street-fashion blogs.

So here is what's going to build the foundation of your wardrobe. You don't need to buy them all at once, but you *should* try to acquire them as quickly as possible.

Must-Have Basics:

2 pairs of straight-leg, dark indigo jeans

2 white dress shirts

several pairs of black socks

1 pair of tan or gray slacks or flat-front chinos

1 simple black belt

3-6 plain tees

2 dark ties

1 blazer

1 v-neck merino wool sweater

1 pair of good, black lace-up shoes

1 pair of sneakers (NOT athletic shoes – think Chuck Taylors, retro Adidas; shoes with simple, classic designs)

These will cover 90% of your clothing needs. Stick to basic colors, at least at first: black, gray, dark blue and white. You want to keep things as simple as possible; thus no embroidered or silkscreened designs on the blazer, no crazy studs or embossed leather on the shoes, and no "pre-worn" holes in the jeans. You want to stick to the classics; they've lasted this long for a reason.

Once you've filled out your basics, you can start

moving into accent pieces. While not as vital as the basics, these offer some more variety to your wardrobe.

Secondary Basics:

1 dark, medium weight suit

1 thin hoodie

1 slim cardigan

1 overcoat

2 scarves – one for winter, one for fall/spring

1 leather jacket

1 pair of boots (Chelsea, Chukka, etc.)

Accessories:

1 nice watch

1 pair non-sport sunglasses

OPTIONAL: Rings, necklaces, bracelets

How to Put an Outfit Together

Now that you have your basics, it's time to start learning how to put them together to build an outfit. The great thing about having these basics in these colors is that they mix and match almost effortlessly. You can combine these almost any way you can think of and have an outfit that works, dressing up or down as needed. They take the guesswork out of trying to put an outfit together; you don't have to worry about whether one piece is going to clash with your outfit or whether a particular color works with your hair and skin tone.

Here are the rules for building an outfit:

1. Your belt should match your shoes. Your socks should match your pants.
2. Consider the Destination – Are you dressing for

work, for a date, for getting a beer with friends on the weekend?

3. Consider the Weather – It should be obvious, but the weather is going to makea difference. You may look stylish as hell in your blazer, but if it's humid and you're spending any time outside, you're going to look like you've gone swimming in it. Colder weather means that you're going to layer more… but you can also express yourself with a carefully chosen scarf to go with your overcoat.

4. The last thing you put on is the first thing people notice. Pickone focus piece and build your outfit around it.

Start with something you like and want to wear: an awesome leather jacket, your favorite vintage concert tee. This is going to be the foundation of your outfit. The rest of your clothes should work around it to compliment it rather than overpowering it.

Say you've got a date for the weekend and you've made plans to go to a sushi-making class, followed by drinks afterwards. You want to have the right mix of "stylish" and comfortable, with enough flexibility that you're not going to feel underdressed but not looking like you just came from your job at Sterling Cooper either. Meanwhile, you've got this bad-ass leather bomber jacket that you've been dying to wear. You start there: your leather jacket is your focus piece. Since you want the right level of "dressy" mixed with comfort, you pick the white dress shirt, match it with dark jeans and either sneakers or boots. If you tend to go for a rocker archetype, you might want to include a thin black tie.

If you're going some place nice for dinner, start with the blazer, the v-neck sweater and a white tee shirt and expand from there – jeans and boots carry a more casual look, while slacks will look more dressy.

Don't be afraid to play with combinations to achieve specific looks. You can dress down an outfit by pairing slacks or suit pants with a sweater and sneakers. You can dress up jeans with a blazer, tie and your black lace-ups. You can take a suit and pair it with a v-neck tee and sneakers for a more informal look that's still stylish.

As much as it's tempting to go the next level and try more experimental looks, when you're starting out, simpler is better. "Cool" isn't an additive process. You can't just keep layering on accessories and assuming that each one makes you just that much cooler; you usually end up looking like you're trying too hard. This is how you end up with would-be Pick-Up Artists who dress like Russell Brand's closet just exploded all over them. Your general goal should simply be dressing a little bit nicer than the people around you. Start simply; as you develop your persona and personal style, *then* you can experiment a little and start dressing a little more extravagantly.

FINDING YOUR ARCHETYPE

Once you've got your basics down, it's time to start building your style. Style is a message. It tells the world a lot about who you are and what to expect from you. It can be hard to figure out just *what* your style should be. There are so many looks and styles out there, so many ways to be cool and desirable and…

Frankly, it can get a little overwhelming, can't it? But

the style you *want* is one that syncs up with who you are; the last thing you want to do is try to create a style that doesn't reflect your personality. Fortunately, there's a way to shortcut the development process and give you a base to start with.

Making Stereotypes Work for You

Let's take a moment to do a thought experiment. Look at yourself in the mirror. What is the first word that comes to mind that describes the person you see? Don't think too deeply about it, just pick the first word off the top of your head that describes the type of person you see in the mirror.

That word? That's your stereotype. You just made an immediate judgment about yourself based strictly on how you look. No matter how much we're taught that stereotyping others is wrong, we all do it. We make snap judgments about people within a few seconds of seeing them, and those initial judgments color how we respond at first. That guy in the stained hoodie and shredded jeans with the ratty beard and unkempt hair may well be a famous, award-winning actor, but if you saw him hanging around a street corner then your brain would immediately leap to "homeless man."[3]

Humans are built for pattern recognition. We associate certain trends or looks with particular behaviors. It's part of how we survived long enough to develop civilization, and those instincts are still with us. Our initial attraction to people is often built on those outward looks; it's a

---

3. This *actually* happened to Richard Gere. In fact, one woman actually tried to give him food and find him a place to stay for the night.

way we filter out the world. You can't tell from a glance whether that gorgeous woman with the dreadlocks is a Rhodes scholar who gives to charity and volunteers at animal shelters; you just know she's hot. We go off our initial impressions and backfill the justification for our attraction later as we get to know people.

We may want people to judge us based on who we are inside, but that can take time – time we don't always have or, frankly, *want* to spend. And so we go with our gut, basing our initial impressions on outward characteristics. Thus: stereotypes.

But that doesn't necessarily have to be a bad thing. In fact, if you play things right, you can make stereotypes work for you. We already know that people are making split-second assumptions about us based on minimal information… so why not guide those assumptions in a direction *you* choose?

Let's get back to that thought experiment for a moment.

This time, I want you to describe yourself in one or two words. I want to know who you are and who you *want* to be, distilled down to your very essence via a word or two. What are they? Writer? Parent? Player? Artist? Gamer? Musician? Joker? Biker? Goth? Businessman? Hold onto that thought. We'll come back to it.

For now, let's talk about archetypes.

The Power of Archetypes

At their core, archetypes are primal symbols, models of concepts and personas that are so deeply ingrained in our collective consciousness that when we think of a "type," we immediately picture them. When we think "movie star," we have an almost instinctual idea of what a movie star looks like, how they act and how they dress. Similarly, when we think "musician," we think of particular behaviors and idiosyncrasies based on what we assume musicians are like. We can picture them in our minds, along with all of the other ephemeral ideas and emotional responses that we associate with them as well. We think movie stars are glamorous. We think punks are rebellious and edgy. We think artists are free spirits and businessmen are conservative and restrained. We'll adjust our presumptions and our ideas about the *individual* as we get to know them, but we have this almost knee-jerk association with the archetype of what they represent.

Do you want people to assume you're glamorous and sexy? Or perhaps you want people to look at you and think that you're a little wild and on the edge? Then you guide them in that direction by means of a visual shorthand. When you consciously model yourself after a specific archetype, you cause people to associate you with those assumptions and beliefs. The more you resemble the archetype, the stronger the association. By harnessing the power of archetypes, you're able to directly influence how people see you and how they're going to respond to you. You use those archetypes to help people create the associations you want.

This brings us back to that thought experiment. Remember those words you chose. Ask yourself: is that who you *are*, or is it who you *want* to be? When you say those words, how do they make you feel? Do they resonate with you? Or do they make you feel small and ashamed? What one or two words describe the archetype of your *ideal* self?

Now that we have an idea of who you are, let's start the process of modeling your look on the outside to match that of your archetype – who you are on the inside.

Find Your Celebrity Patronus

Part of the process of modeling an archetype is knowing how to present it in the most attractive way possible. After all, when you think "writer," you could go in many different directions. On the one hand, you have Ernest Hemingway and that very classically masculine presence; on the other, you have Allen Ginsberg with his wild hair and counterculture affectations. Which of these do you find has the attractive associations you want people to connect to *you*?

It can be a little daunting at first to try to figure out the "right" way to build a style around your particular archetype. After all, you may have an idea about what "artist" looks like, but how do you arrange things so that it says "deep and creative" rather than "pretentious asshat"? For that matter, how are you supposed to build a style when you don't have a sense of style of your own?

Simple: you borrow somebody else's while you develop your own. The great news for you is that Hollywood has done most of the heavy lifting for you. Generations of directors, cinematographers, set dressers and costume designers have spent *decades* creating a visual language that presents specific archetypes in the best possible light. So as you're trying to decide what best represents *your* archetype, you are able to dip into the world of television and film to find the look that specifies the type of person you're modeling yourself after.

Hollywood has literally shaped our ideas of what the real world looks like. Lawyers watch *Law & Order, Suits* and other law dramas in order to find more effective ways to sway juries – who assume that court cases play out like the ones they see on TV. *The Godfather* trilogy single-handedly changed how the Mafia conducted itself; after the movie was released, suddenly every mob boss and made man was dressing to the nines and talking about the code of *omertà* and a culture of honor *that didn't exist before the movie.*

You can take advantage of these expectations and use them as the basis for the looks that express the archetype that represents you best. It's simply a matter of picking the roles that synch with your idea of who you are. Are you a bad boy with a golden soul like Jax Teller in *Sons of Anarchy*? Are you the live-fast-die-young-leave-a-beautiful-corpse rocker like Jim Morrison? Do you want to show the piercing soulful gaze and quiet power of Don Draper? Or perhaps you're a bit more Mod, evoking the 60s era Sean Connery as James Bond?

Even better: there are tons of resources out there – blogs, Tumblrs and Pinterest boards – devoted to helping people dress like characters from their favorite TV shows and movies. Almost two-thirds of the work has been done *for* you!

No, you probably don't look like a celebrity – most of us don't. The point isn't to look exactly like Robert Downey, Jr. or a young Michael Caine; it's to use their characters as a *base*. You're learning how they portray the attractive aspects of your archetype as you make the style your own. The more it meshes with who you are, the more you'll be able to bring your personality to it and make it a look that's uniquely *you* while still conveying the attributes you want.

Avoid Incongruity

So let's take it all back to that initial thought experiment. Remember that initial gut description? How does that match up with your chosen archetype? Odds are that it doesn't. In fact, it may be incredibly different. Your look is incongruent with who you're trying to be.

Incongruity is when there's a clash between aspects of your surroundings, between your actions and your message or, in this case, between who you *are* and how you're trying to portray yourself. Incongruity makes people uncomfortable; it makes people think "what's wrong with this picture?" and puts them on edge.

Changing your style – especially when you're making a radical departure from your old style – can be difficult. There's going to be a lot of trial and error as you try to find the look that works... and many of them simply won't be a good fit for you. Sometimes it'll be a matter of shape. If you're barrel chested and heavy-framed, you're going to have a hard time making the skin-tight leather pants of a rock god work, but while you might not be able to be Sid Vicious, you *might* make a better Henry Rollins. If you're tall and skinny, you're going to have a harder time as a biker archetype, but you might get away with other looks that still suggest "rebel" or "edgy."

Other times, however, it'll be a clash of personalities. If you're a quiet introvert, flashy styles aren't going to work as well as you might like. A more conservative personality isn't going to make a great David Bowie-esque glam rocker; you'll feel awkward and uncomfortable and that attitude will come off you in waves. But this doesn't mean that only certain personalities can be certain archetypes; there are many variations within each particular "type." F. Scott Fitzgerald and Hunter S. Thompson are both "writer" archetypes at opposite ends of the spectrum. It's simply a matter of finding the version that fits both your personality *and* the person you want to be.

THE IMPORTANCE OF BODY LANGUAGE

In Chapter 5, we talked about how vital body language can be to developing your sense of confidence. Your body language is also a critical part of how other people see you. Much like clothing, our body language is part of how we communicate who we are to the people around us. The old cliché "actions speak louder than words" is never more true than when it comes to how we carry ourselves. Learning how to master our body language is an important part of making ourselves more attractive to other people. In fact, when done right, body language can even be used to subtly flirt with people we're interested in. One critical key to being attractive is being open and approachable. Studies from Webster University have found that the people who get approached the most *aren't* the people who're the most physically attractive; they're the ones who are the most inviting and friendly.

Everything begins with a straight spine. Most of us have horrible posture. It's in no small part because of our lifestyle. We've become a desk-bound culture and we've been paying the price in back and shoulder pain. We hunch over our desks like monks illuminating manuscripts. We slump in our chairs, slouch when we walk and generally curve our bodies into unnatural shapes. It robs us of our natural height, taxes our muscles unnecessarily and, frankly, makes us look awful. Straightening out your spine will help you look taller, stronger and more confident... and as an added bonus, it'll make you *feel* better too.

So the first step is very simple: you're going to fix your posture. As I told you in Chapter 3, imagine an invisible string attached to the crown of your skull that's being tugged gently upwards. Let that string pull you up until you're standing at your *full* height. Now look in a mirror and turn until you're looking at yourself from the side. Notice where your head and chin fall in relation to your shoulders and the center of your chest; you want to have as straight a line as possible from the top of your head to your hips. Your ears, shoulders, wrists, knees and feet should all line up; you want to avoid hunching forward and curving your back.

As you're straightening your back, you *also* want to pay attention to your shoulders. Letting your shoulders curve inward is unattractive and pulls you off balance. For proper posture – not to mention looking confident – you want to pull them back. You don't want to pull them back so far that you're sticking your chest out or giving the impression that you're standing at attention. Instead, you want to form a smooth, straight line from where your neck meets your shoulder to your deltoids. This is where your shoulders *should* be when you're standing naturally. Years of working at computers and hunching over desks have trained us to roll our shoulders forward, so it's going to take a *lot* of concentration and practice before this starts to feel natural. But when it does, people will *notice*.

To help support your spine, stand with your feet directly below your shoulders and distribute your weight evenly. This gives you a strong base and helps you avoid slumping to one side or the other.

While you're at it, take deep breath, hold it for a second, and then let it out slowly. While you do so, let your muscles relax as the air flows out of you. Tension is a sign of discomfort, and if you are uncomfortable, it makes the people *around* you feel uncomfortable. People can read the tension in the way you carry yourself, in the stiffness of your movements and the set of your shoulders. Taking a moment to loosen up and let your muscles unclench will make you seem less uptight and more confident. Plus, if *you're* relaxed, *they'll* relax.

Take up Space

One of the quickest ways to make yourself more attractive is one of the simplest: take up more room. Yes, I'm serious. You can make yourself more appealing to others simply by draping your arm across the back of the couch while you're sitting, leaning against the wall with your other arm holding your drink down at your side, or spreading your legs a little wider in your chair. There's a direct correlation between somebody's perceived attractiveness and what's known as "spatial maximization" – positioning your body to expose itself more by taking up space in the room. By being willing to take up space and spread out, you're displaying a number of attractive traits. To start with: you're displaying increased confidence. Confident people are willing to own their territory and be noticed. By taking up more space, they're making themselves more visible. Unconfident people, on the other hand, fold in on themselves. They duck their heads, pull their arms and legs in tight and hunch over, as though they're trying to avoid being noticed. They're afraid of offending people with their mere presence.

The other benefit to being willing to take up space is that it forces you to open up your body. Slouching, crossing your arms across your chest and crossing your legs at the thigh are all seen as defensive postures; you're *literally* blocking people out, putting barriers in between you and them. It makes you look unfriendly and unapproachable. Someone who's taking up space on the other hand is pulling their limbs *away* from their torsos instead, adopting more open body language. It makes you seem friendlier and approachable, which in turn makes you more attractive to others.

It's worth noting though that there's a difference between "taking up space" and "sprawling." It's one thing to be willing to spread out a little. Keeping people from being able to sit down because you look like you're airing your balls out is another thing entirely, and it's the antithesis of being attractive.

Do Less

One thing men do that makes them less attractive is fidget. Squirming, shifting your weight from side to side, flapping your hands wildly while you talk, letting your eyes dart around the room when you're talking to someone, talking like a chipmunk that's discovered the joys of a triple espresso... these are all signs of nervousness and agitation in a person. It makes you look like you lack self-control or that you're desperate to get away. It makes other people feel awkward and uncomfortable and less likely to want to talk to you.

You want to learn how to do more by doing less. A level of stillness and control is seen as being cool and composed. It makes you look more at ease, both with yourself and with the people you're talking to. As with taking up space, this helps make you look more confident, and confidence – as we all know – is sexy.

So to start with, get those nervous little gestures under control. Don't continually play with your hair, adjust your clothes, drum your fingers, tap your feet, bounce your knees or do any of the other nervous gestures you may not even realize you're doing. It can take conscious effort at first – you have to be aware of the times you're being fidgety and force yourself to be still – but with time and practice, it becomes second nature. Sometimes it can help to develop habits that will force you to slow your roll. If you have a tendency to constantly shift your weight back and forth, try leaning on something; leaning up against a wall or the bar helps convey an air of nonchalance as it keeps you from swaying from side to side. If you can't keep your hands still, hook your thumbs in your pockets. When you do move, do it with precision. Don't gesticulate or flop around. You want to have a specific purpose to each gesture, even if it's just to illustrate a point.

This applies to how you speak as well. Avoid hemming and hawing when you start off with a thought; if you're unsure what to say right off the bat, pause for a second or two to collect your thoughts. Not only does this make you seem more composed, but pausing before you speak can actually make you a more persuasive and compelling speaker. You want to speak at a moderate rate. You don't want to speak like you're running an auction, but at the same time you... don't... want... to talk like... a cartoon... turtle.

Give Good Face

One of the best ways to make people feel that you're likable and approachable is to use basic body language signals as a way of telling someone that you're interested in them.

The most critical way of doing this is through eye contact. Making strong eye contact is a critical part of forming a connection with somebody; if you can't meet somebody's eyes, you're crippling your ability to build rapport with them. We all know the feeling of somebody looking through us or looking past us when we try to talk to them – it's incredibly alienating and makes us like that person less. When someone refuses to make eye contact with us, we assume that they don't like us or that they're untrustworthy. On the other hand, making direct eye contact is strong, incredibly strong. Psychologists have conducted studies that found that two people simply exchanging a mutual, unbroken gaze into each other's eyes for two minutes is enough to inspire feelings of love and passion for each other.

Obviously you're not going to be able to just go up to someone and stare at them until they go home with you; what you want to do is learn how to use the power of your gaze effectively. Making frequent eye contact prior to an approach is a classic way of building attraction. Glancing at her, letting her see you looking at her, then breaking contact by looking to the side is a strong start. Don't break contact by looking down, as that's a submissive gesture. Don't look away quickly: that makes you look like you were trying to get away with something. Look, then casually look away... then look back again and *smile*. That smile is incredibly important; not only does it signal that you like what you see, but it also lights up your face and makes you more appealing and attractive. It's a sign of friendliness and inspires others to feel warmly towards you as well.

Being attractive isn't just an individual trait or a matter of winning the genetic lottery. It's a holistic approach, blending together multiple aspects that form an appealing whole. And once you've learned how to put it all together, then it's time to start making your move.

CHAPTER 6.

HOW TO TALK TO WOMEN

STARTING CONVERSATIONS AND THE MYTH OF PICK-UP LINES

For the last four chapters, we've been laying down the prep work to get you ready to go out into the field. Now it's time to start putting everything into practice. It's time for you to get out there and start meeting women.

Of course, taking that first step – going up and trying to talk to somebody that you're attracted to – can often be the hardest. For a lot of guys, especially those who've been having issues with their dating life, very little is quite as terrifying as making that initial approach. And in fairness, it *can* be intimidating. You're effectively walking up to a total stranger and trying to get her interested in exploring the possibilities of a sexual or romantic relationship with you – how awkward is *that?* Not only is this difficult, but it can be quite risky on an emotional level. You're making yourself emotionally vulnerable and being rejected can sometimes feel like a rejection of everything about you.

But here's the thing: you're stressing yourself out over what is actually one of the most *natural* things in the world. We're just trying to get to know somebody new. But we never see it that way. We see it as the end-all, be-all of our lives. We stew in our fear and let our brains come up with a long trail of worst-case scenarios that starts with saying "hello" and ends with us on the floor and pawing at our faces as we try to wipe away the pepper spray while everybody around us points and laughs before calling the cops.

Most of the problems men face when it comes to making that initial approach is that they spend more time trying to game it out and psych themselves up than they do actually approaching. By the time they've played through it in their head a thousand times, they've spent so much mental energy on the subject that they're *exhausted.*

And it's ridiculous. When you're approaching someone, you're trying to accomplish one thing and one thing *only*: *You're trying to start a conversation with them.* Everything else is secondary.

This is why the approach is literally the *least* important part of meeting somebody. It's all just a lead up to talking to somebody and finding out whether or not there's enough to them as a person to justify your continued interest. If there is, *great!* If not, then it's no big deal; you shrug your shoulders and move on.

You don't need pick-up lines. There isn't anything you can say – up to and including "I have a twelve inch tongue and can breathe through my ears" – that will magically make women interested in you. There is no hypnotic phrase that breaks past women's "bitch shields" [1]and goes straight to their groins. There isn't some magic "alpha" demonstration of value that does the work for you. You

---

1. A PUA term for when women are cold and unreceptive in hopes that someone will get the hint and back off.

don't need "openers." The only thing they're really useful for is making it easier on you to talk to somebody. Otherwise, the words out of your mouth don't matter; it's just a pretext to a conversation.

I can tell you from experience: 99 times out of 100, they won't even remember what the first thing you said was; what they'll remember is how you made them *feel*. As long as you don't start off with something along the lines of "Your skin looks soft and supple. It would make a great leather jacket," you're golden.

Here are some of the *exact* lines I have used to start conversations that eventually lead to getting a date with a woman or having sex with her:

- "You seem like you're really cool and I wanted to meet you. Hi, my name is…"

- "What are you drawing?"

- "You're very tall! High-five!"

- "Has anyone ever told you that you look like a Bond girl?"

- "I like puppies. Your turn."

- "Holy God, please tell me you're talking about something interesting. My friends just keep talking aboutstock derivatives and I'm about to blow my brains out."

- "Can I get your opinion on something? Do you believe that men and women can be friends and still have sex?"

- "Let me ask you something: Do you agree that pirates are inherently better than ninjas?"

- "Do you know how to cook this?"

Granted, some of these are a little on the absurd side, but they all *worked*. They did what they were supposed to do: get the other person talking to me, giving me time to connect with them and hook them with my charm and wit.

You can say just about anything in order to get the approach started. You can make an observation about them or the place around you. You can ask them for an opinion on a random subject. You can make a joke based on things going on around you. You can say something absurd. Or you can just say, "I think you're interesting and I wanted to get to know you." It's all in the delivery. If you treat it like something you do every day, *they* will respond similarly.

There's only one rule: don't make her uncomfortable. Social context is the key. You can get away with being a little offbeat and goofy at a party, where the accepted social contract encourages talking to strangers. Coming up to a woman at a grocery store and saying, "You're very blonde," is going to be off-putting. However, asking her, "Hey, could you give me an opinion about something? What spices do you think would work well with this?" or "Do you know anything about $FOOD_PRODUCT?" is relevant to the situation and gets the conversation started.

Don't forget: "You seem cool and I just wanted to meet you" is almost always socially relevant.

READ HER SIGNALS (WITHOUT READING THE TEA LEAVES)

Imagine how much easier dating would be if you were able to just *know* how somebody felt about you. A question I get over and over again from men is "How do I know if a woman is interested in me?" The same question that has plagued geeky boys since junior high has an annoying tendency to follow us all the way through to adulthood, leading to grown-ass men plaguing their friends with an endless repetition of "Do you think she *likes* me, likes me? Or just likes me?" Men will mistake friendliness – or even professional politeness – for interest and end up frustrated when they get rejected. Meanwhile, one of the most common complaints you'll hear from women is about how guys never notice when she's *very clearly* trying to flirt with him.

Chalk this up to a classic difference between how men and women are socialized. Men are traditionally taught to be the aggressors, while women are taught to be passive and to subtly encourage men to make the first move. Men are taught to be straightforward, even blunt, in their dealings with others. Women, on the other hand, are taught to be indirect and non-confrontational, especially when dealing with men. Being direct often makes men uncomfortable, even *angry*. As a result, women will frequently signal interest or disinterest through body language cues, rather than overtly spelling it out.

Small wonder that we have so many problems in dating. We're functionally speaking two entirely different languages and getting frustrated when the other person doesn't understand us.

Understanding how to read women's signals isn't nearly as difficult as people think. It's a matter of learning how to recognize and interpret the signals she's giving off. Once you do, it's suddenly like playing a game on the lowest difficulty setting possible. Knowing how to read people lets you know whether someone is interested in you or not, and whether she wants you to approach her. Understanding how to interpret her signals means being able to gauge just how well an interaction with someone is going... as well as how to tell when you've fucked up. If you know how to recognize a woman's signs and body language, you'll be set to read her like a book.

Watch Her Eyes

If you want to read a woman's mind, you need to start with her eyes. A woman's eyes are more than just a place to look when we're pretending that we wouldn't rather be staring at her boobs; they're full of vital non-verbal communication.

Eye contact is incredibly intimate and powerful, which is why we get uncomfortable locking gazes with strangers. And yet, eye contact is a frequently overlooked, yet subtly potent, way of communicating interest or disinterest. If you haven't used eye contact to gauge interest, you may have been missing out on one of the most sure "come here" signals there is.

Signs That She's Interested:

The first sign – one that many women use to signal being open to an approach – is that she plays the eye-contact game. Locking gazes is an intimate act; in fact, sociologists have found that prolonged eye contact between strangers can increase feelings of passion and intimacy. Many women play the eye-contact game. They will make a point of making eye contact with someone they're interested in, then looking down and away before looking back again with a smile. Because we're instinctively attracted to movement, the act of *deliberately* breaking eye contact actually works to catch our attention. Breaking eye contact to look down is a submissive action, designed to look demure and inviting, while looking back up to re-initiate eye contact – especially through lowered lids – is a way of checking to see if you noticed. The smile that comes with it is an approach invitation. She's all but screaming, "Yes, that was intended for you, now why don't you come over here and talk to me already?"

Some women, especially particularly confident or assertive ones, will give what's known as the elevator gaze by looking up and down your entire length. It's a blatant "sizing you up" look and getting it is a sign that she likes what she sees. Similarly, if a woman is looking at your mouth a lot, then odds are she's *very* interested. One look to watch out for is the triangle-gaze, where she looks from one eye to the next, then down to your lips. That's a sign that she's actively thinking about kissing you.

The eyes are also a good way to tell whether she's engaging with you or not. If you're talking to someone who maintains eye contact or breaks and reinitiates it quickly, you can feel certain that she's actively interested in what you have to say. She doesn't want to hold eye contact *too* long, but she also doesn't want you to think she's getting bored. Slightly lowered eyelids as you talk are frequently a sign that she's actively flirting with you; it's a coy, come-hither look.

Signs That She's Not Interested:

She's actively avoiding eye-contact. Does she seem to look away as soon as she notices you looking, but *doesn't* look back? She doesn't want to talk to you. The most you can expect from her are polite but curt answers before she either tells you to go away or gets up and leaves. Similarly, if she catches you looking and looks up and away, the intended message is very clear: "Don't even bother."

While you're talking, does she seem to be looking around the room every few seconds while you talk? Either she's incredibly bored or she's looking for an acceptable way of getting out of the conversation without blatantly violating the social contract. Once you notice that she seems to be looking everywhere but at you, you can be fairly certain that she's about to see someone she needs to talk to right now – who also happens to be as far away from you as possible.

Check Her Smile

After the eyes, the next biggest signal of interest is her mouth. Just because she's smiling at you doesn't necessarily mean that she's happy or interested in you. In fact, that smile may very well be her way of hiding her *disinterest*.

Smiling is an important means of non-verbal communication that has its origins in our primate ancestry and can carry a wide variety of meanings.

Smiling is often a sign of submission and reassurance. In many cases, by smiling we are sending the signal that hey, we're not a threat, you don't have to hurt us. A smile is frequently a way of placating others, especially if they seem as though they're aggressive or angry. Baring one's teeth in a smile can also be an implied threat or dominance challenge; Southern women especially learn early on how to deliver withering insults with a faux sweet smile. Because they are socialized to not be rude, women will often smile at people they're talking to even if they don't particularly like them. A fake smile can keep up the social illusion that she's interested in what you have to say, when in reality she desperately wishes that you would be decapitated by a flying toilet seat.

Signs That She's Interested:

Her smile reaches her eyes. This is known as a Duchenne smile. A genuine smile engages not just the muscles around the mouth but the eyes as well; a real smile will cause crinkling at the corners of the eyes and cause a slight upturn of her lower eyelids.

Signs That She's Not Interested:

Her smile doesn't go past her lips. A fake smile just engages the mouth but not the rest of the face; this is occasionally known as the Botox smile for the way the rest of her face doesn't react. If that grin seems pasted on and doesn't actually reach her eyes then she's smiling out of politeness, rather than due to any actual desire.

Watch Her Body

The body is a goldmine of signals that tell you whether a woman is interested or not. The human body is incredibly expressive; we can convey emotional states, complex concepts, even sexual interest with just the position of our bodies and limbs. Women will give far more information via body language than almost any other signal, which is why you want to be on the look out for particular behaviors.

Signs That She's Interested:

Check to see if her body is "open" to you. A woman who is interested in you and who is comfortable in your presence will have more open body language. She will be sitting up straighter, orienting herself towards you and leaving her arms uncrossed. If she's *especially* interested, she may sit in a way that leaves her inner thigh exposed; when coupled with open body language, it's a very intimate signal.

Next, watch where her limbs are pointing. Humans are goal-oriented, which often translates into our body language. When we're interested in something, we often unconsciously aim ourselves at it, whether it's the buffet, a sexy stranger or a speedy exit. If she's pointing herself at you – especially with her knees and feet – she's interested in you. If she's standing, she may move one leg closer towards you.

Watch how she moves. If you find that the woman you're talking to is mirroring your actions – she takes a sip of her drink when you take one of yours, when you cross your legs and lean to one side, so does she – it's a strong signal that she likes you. We tend to like people who are similar to us. Mimicry is also a sign that the person you're talking to is paying close attention to what you have to say. The more absorbed she is in what you're saying, the more likely she is to mimic you unconsciously.

Notice if she's invading your personal space. When we're interested in someone, we tend to get closer to them. One example is the classic known as the "whisper and lean" – lowering her voice and moving in as though you're sharing a secret. Many women will encroach on your personal space in a subtle manner by using objects as stand-ins for their bodies. If you're at a bar and she leaves her glass close to you – especially if her hand lingers there as well – it's a way of subtly indicating that she's checking to see how you feel about her. If you're sitting side by side, then see where her legs are; if they're close to you (and there's enough room that you're not *forced* to be close together) then she may well be thinking of what it would feel like if the *rest* of you were in her space. A quick check is to let your leg rest against hers briefly. If she's interested, she'll leave hers there. If not, she'll pull back.

Proximity is *also* a way that women will signal that they want you to talk to them. When a woman is consistently hovering in your general vicinity for no apparent reason or making a point of brushing past you even though there's plenty of room for her to get by otherwise, she's hoping that you'll notice that she's there and will come over and talk to her.

Watch for incidental touches as well. Many women will signal interest by touching the person they're interested in, especially when you're flirting. If she's touching you frequently while she talks, or when you say something funny, then she's increasingly interested in you touching *her.* Those little affectionate punches or shoves are indications that she's hitting on you... literally. One of my favorite ways of checking for attraction is to use the high-five test. It's very simple: when she says something that impresses you or makes you laugh, you say, "That's awesome. You get a high-five." Then offer a high-five with your fingers spread. If she's interested, when she makes the high-five, her fingers will intertwine with yours and she'll clasp your hand.

Sign's That She's Not Interested:

A woman with closed body language – pointing herself away from you, crossing her arms across her chest, holding her drink or her purse across her torso, hunching in or taking up less space – is trying to tell you that she's closed off to you. These are all subtle ways of putting barriers between you and her, using her limbs as a sort of shield.

If she's orienting herself away from you, then that's an indication that she's bored or annoyed by you. She's putting herself into a position where it's easy to get up and move on. Similarly, if she's positioning herself *opposite* from you – leaning in a different direction than you, for example – then she's deliberately *avoiding* mimicry. It's a way of decreasing rapport.

Check for Fidgeting

There are two types of nervousness when it comes to dating. There's the "Oh God, I think he's going to tell me to rub the lotion on my skin" nervousness that comes from being with someone we think is creepy and the "Oh God, he's hot, do I have something in my teeth, shit, what about my breath, do I have any gum, please Jesus tell me I didn't put on my ugly underwear today" nervousness that comes from being attracted to the person you're talking to. Both women and men tend to unconsciously indulge in what's known as "preening" behavior when they're interested in somebody; these are little gestures and movements aimed at trying to groom themselves a little and presenting a better, more attractive display.

Signs That She's Interested:

One of the most common forms of preening behavior in women is playing with their hair. Tossing the hair draws attention to the face and especially the neck and shoulders – two areas that are especially sensitive during foreplay. Twirling or absentmindedly playing with her hair is an unconscious way of drawing attention to it; the unspoken intent is to reinforce her femininity and desirability. It also helps show off her hair itself, a subtle indication of health and genetic potential.

Another common sign is if she starts fussing with her clothing – straightening things out, fiddling with buttons or hems. It's a way of trying to fix her appearance because she wants you to see her at her best.

Other signs of attraction include leg crossing. Many people will repeatedly cross and uncross their legs when they start feeling anxious or nervous; being attracted to someone can make them squirm in their seat at times. Much like with watching for orientation and pointing, how she's crossing her legs can be a clue. A woman who's interested in you is more likely to point her upper leg in your direction – the better by which to show off her gams to their best advantage. It's a subtle sign, but one worth looking for.

If she starts touching herself – rubbing her hand along her thigh or touching her arm or neck, then she's very interested. These are ways of drawing attention to parts of her body and making you think about caressing her there. Other signs of attraction-based nerves involve calling attention to her mouth. Lip licking – the "my mouth is dry" kind, not the *Basic Instinct* type – is frequently a sign of interest. Excitement tends to cause our mouths to go dry. It also calls a man's eyes to her lips – another visible reminder of her femininity as well as one that prompts men to think about kissing.

Signs That She's Not Interested:

There's aroused and interested fidgeting and then there's "bundle of nervous energy" fidgeting. When she's becoming increasingly curt and seeming like she's having a hard time getting comfortable, tapping her feet or shifting her weight side to side, then she's giving signs that she's looking for a chance to get away. This is especially true if this is paired with other signs of disinterest like turning away from you or crossing her legs; these tend to be signs that you've screwed up and she's losing interest.

Watch for the Rule of Four

One thing to keep in mind is that many of the behaviors

I talk about can have multiple meanings. You don't want to just assume that someone's dying to take you home because she shifted her weight in your direction, nor do you want to assume that she's wishing you would leave because she's suddenly squirming in her seat. What might be a sign of attraction could just as easily be a random gesture. Is she preening for you when she's playing with her hair while she's talking to you, or is this just something she does when she thinks? Is she angling her body towards you because she's interested, or because she's more comfortable that way? Is she mirroring you or are you imagining it?

The problem is that guys tend to look for signals in isolation. Any *individual* signal could mean almost anything, after all. Watching for signs spread out over the course of an evening is equally unhelpful. One hair toss at the start of the conversation, then preening behavior an hour later, followed by cocking a hip towards you later still are all functionally meaningless; it might be a signal or it might be noise. The key is to look for *clusters* of signs – several indicators of interest that occur nearly *simultaneously*. Women don't give one signal at a time. In fact, by the time a man has noticed *one* signal, she's frequently given *dozens*. A smile by itself is one thing. A smile accompanied by her opening her body language, a hair toss *and* angling her knees towards you – *that's* a cluster of signs that yes, she is interested and you should proceed accordingly. Similarly, crossing her arms could be a sign that she's feeling defensive around you... or it may be her way of giving her hands something to do. Crossing her arms, coupled with angling away from you and looking around the room, on the other hand, is a sign that she's ready to go find somebody else.

When in doubt, follow what body language experts call the Rule of Four: look for at least *four* simultaneous indicators of interest instead of picking one and hoping for the best.

EMBRACE THE POWER OF CONVERSATION

I have a friend, an attractive woman slightly younger than me, who I have known almost all of our lives. She is very much in the mold of "the younger sister I never wanted," and we've always been close. So as one of her surrogate older brothers, I have frequently been in the position to watch her various relationships come and go over the years. I could always, *always* predict which guy she was going to end up dating, with 100% accuracy, right down to the guy she eventually married. It wasn't any particular psychic insight, nor was it a tendency on her part to date a specific "type."

No, every guy she ended up dating, the first thing she said about him was, "So we just had the most incredible conversation."

The ability to have a conversation – not flirting with somebody, but simple, pure conversation – is a critical part of being a more interesting, more compelling person. Even if you're made of raw sex appeal, if you can't actually *use your words*, you're going to be at a severe disadvantage in the dating scene. Being able to talk with people is how we connect with them. It's what makes the difference between feeling like you've known somebody for years and watching attraction melt like a snowball in Hell.

Find Your Real Voice

Any musician will tell you that before you start to produce music with your instrument, you have to tune it. And most of you are out of tune. Put bluntly: you're speaking wrong.

Yeah, I know. It sounds weird. You've been speaking all of your life; you've had this shit down since you were a kid, right? Well, not so much. Almost all of us have picked up bad habits over the years that prevent us from using our voices to their full potential. Consider the difference between a trained Shakespearean actor and the average man off the street: the actor has greater control in both pitch and volume. When he speaks, he know he's going to be heard and understood, even if he's directing his words to the people at the far end of the room. Meanwhile the average Joe is going to wear out his throat trying to make himself heard. The actor has a voice that commands attention, while the average guy… well, you know he's speaking, but do you really *care?*

One of the most basic keys to effective use of your voice is to learn to speak with the support of your diaphragm. If you're like 99% of the population, then you're doing most of your speaking with your upper lungs and nose and you've never even realized it. When you're speaking from your upper chest, you're not getting as much oxygen or projection as you would be from speaking from your diaphragm. If you want to learn how to speak from your diaphragm, first you have to *find* it. Lie flat on your back on the floor and inhale deeply into your stomach, not into your chest. Put your hands over your stomach and let it expand when you breathe. Feel where it pushes out against your hand. This is your diaphragm. Now make a short exhalation – a "huh" sound. Notice how your stomach tenses up when you speak? This is where you want to speak from. It takes time and practice to learn to speak from the diaphragm, but once you're aware of it, you can start training yourself to use it. Practice breathing into your diaphragm and then speaking simple sentences. "Hello. How are you? My name is Inigo Montoya. You killed my father. Prepare to die." Speak at different volumes or at different parts of the room such as close up, to the middle and to the far end of the room. You'll be amazed at how much power your voice will have and how much less effort it takes to project it.

Next, you want to find your natural pitch. You're almost certainly speaking higher than you naturally would – directing your voice through your nose rather than through your throat. The easiest way to find your natural pitch is to do what is known as the "Hum Test." Close your lips and hum a continuous tone that feels natural to you. You'll feel the difference if you're either too high or too low. As you find your pitch, hum and then start counting "one, two, three" at that pitch. You'll notice that it's actually easier on your vocal cords to speak at your natural pitch. Once again, practice saying simple sentences in this pitch until it starts to feel natural.

Reduce Fillers in Your Speech

One issue that many people have is that they put out a lot of verbal static. We have a tendency to use vocal fillers – "um," "er," "ah," "like," "basically," "actually" and other verbal placeholders – when we speak. They're a sort of conversational speedbump that buys you time to try to come up with what you want to say. They're a natural part of conversation, but they can easily overwhelm what you're actually saying; using too many of them weakens the impact of your words and makes you lose credibility. The fewer vocal fillers you include in your speech, the more intelligent and confident you will sound. You don't need to eliminate them entirely – that makes you sound mechanical and inhuman – but you *do* want to restrict their use in your natural conversational flow.

The easiest way to start eliminating them is to make yourself aware of them. Most of us use them completely unconsciously and never even realize we've said them. Use the voice memo feature on your phone or record your voice using your webcam's mic and speak for thirty seconds about any object in your room. Just ramble off the top of your head. Now play it back and count the number of fillers.

Now try again: ramble for thirty seconds about anything without planning it out and without stopping… but this time, you aren't allowed to use "like," "you know," "um" or other fillers. After you're done, play back the recording and note how many times you said "um" or "err." It'll almost certainly be more than you thought you did.

There are two ways to help eliminate fillers. The first is simply to *slow down*. The faster you talk, the more your mouth gets ahead of your brain and you realize you've lost what you were talking about. Speaking slower and more deliberately gives you the air of confidence as well as giving you more time to consider your words.

The other technique is to replace the fillers with pauses and silence instead. Silence, when used properly, can be incredibly powerful. Pauses and silence will make your speech flow smoothly and cause people to listen more intently. A pause in your speech will act as a vacuum; the person you're talking to will want to fill in that sudden empty space and they'll be more interested in what you're about to say.

Keep practicing with the recordings and you'll find that speaking slower and using more pauses will start feeling natural.

Make Eye Contact

This is another one that feels like it should be obvious, but it's a frequent stumbling block for people. Making eye contact is an incredibly important part of communication; when we don't look people in the eye, it implies that we don't trust them, that they scare us or that they simply don't *interest* us. All of these are detrimental to your goal of connecting with the other person.

At the same time, you don't want to just give somebody the hairy eyeball. An intense, unwavering stare is incredibly intimidating and most people will take it as a challenge or a threat. A good rule of thumb is to deliberately break eye contact every four to seven seconds to avoid looking like you're trying to hypnotize them. Casually look to the side for a second or two (use minimal head-movements here; you don't want to look like you've just been distracted by someone) and then re-engage.

If you have a hard time looking people in the eye, you can fake it by looking at the tip of their eyebrow or the bridge of their nose. And for God's sake, *blink*. Too many guys tend to stare at women they're talking to without blinking and it's intensely creepy.

Avoid Awkward Silence by Asking the Right Questions

There's nothing more uncomfortable than a sudden silence during a conversation. It's not necessarily a *bad* thing; in fact, some studies suggest that *every* conversation has a natural lull every seven minutes or so. They're not something to panic over. Occasionally it's good to just take a moment to think about what you were saying.

However, it's those moments when suddenly you've both suddenly run out of things to say that leaves you looking around awkwardly and wishing for something, *anything* to talk about. If you want to avoid these, you have to make sure you're not accidentally shutting the conversation down by asking close-ended questions. When you ask questions that can be answered with one or two words, you're functionally cutting off the conversation. This is why you want to avoid asking questions with "closed" answers like a simple "yes" or "no" or a recitation of facts. Using questions that hinge on variations of "to be" or "to do" encourage shorter, curt answers.

"What time is it?"

"4:30."

"Where are you from?"

"Kentucky."

Instead, you want to use more open-ended questions that not only require more than just a simple answer, but that encourage the speaker to elaborate. This is why journalists and interviewers rely on the classic questions: who, what, where, when, why and how – they prompt longer and more detailed answers. Just make sure you don't go into interview mode; nobody wants to feel like they're being interrogated by the cops or a secret agent. You can avoid the "interrogation" feeling by grounding your questions in situational observations or relating them to events in your own life. It makes them feel more immediately relevant rather than like you're fishing for information.

Remember: when you're actively listening – instead of waiting for your turn to talk – just about *anything* can be a springboard to another conversational thread. If you end up with a lull that's verging on the uncomfortable, ask another open-ended question to take it in a new direction.

Don't Hog the Conversation, but Don't Bow Out Either

Conversations are two-way streets; they only work when *both* parties are able to feel as though they're equal participants. While one of you may be doing the most talking in the beginning – especially as you're only starting to feel comfortable around one another – it's best to keep the overall ratio relatively even. It doesn't have to be exactly 50-50, but you don't want to let it drift too far to one side or the other.

It's important not to dominate the conversation, and considering that we all love to hear ourselves talk, that can be incredibly easy to do. If you realize you've been talking for a while – especially if the other person hasn't really gotten a word in edgewise – pause, acknowledge that you've been going on for a bit and ask them an open-ended question. At the same time, however, when you're being an active listener, you can end up accidentally bowing out of the conversation entirely. This isn't necessarily any better; in fact, it can make the other person feel incredibly self-conscious and awkward.

The best way to keep a conversation rolling smoothly is to treat it like a game of catch. Let the other person pass the ball to you; when they do, give it a bit of spin with your own perspective on the subject, and then pass it back. Keeping a smooth back and forth will help keep the conversation flow steady and even and enjoyable for everybody involved.

CONQUERING APPROACH ANXIETY

One of the most common afflictions that holds people back from the social life they dream of is approach anxiety: the feelings of anxiousness, fear and panic that we feel when we attempt to meet people we're attracted to. It covers the gamut from mild nervousness to full-blown panic attacks at the very thought of trying to go up to an attractive man or woman and introducing ourselves. The mere *idea* of approaching that hottie you've had your eye on for a while sends shivers down your spine. Your heart starts to pound, your mouth goes dry and your hands get clammy. You start picturing all the ways this could go wrong. In the end, you end up not doing *anything*, convincing yourself that it's just not worth it or there are plenty of *very good* reasons why you shouldn't approach her right now.

I've gone through this more times than I care to count.

It's exhausting and, in many ways, humiliating. You feel like you should be able to get past it, and when you can't, you feel like a failure. Logically, you know that the worst that can happen is that someone will tell you "no." The problem is that approach anxiety isn't logical; it's *emotional*. Approach anxiety is all about avoiding fear and conflict and how humans respond to fear stimulus. If you want to get over approach anxiety, you have to learn how to handle that fear and overcome it.

Desensitize Yourself by Practicing Approaches

One of the worst things you can do when it comes to trying to beat approach anxiety is to talk yourself out of it. It never works; you're trying to rationalize an emotion, but when your amygdala decides to have its say, logic goes right out the window. You can't out-logic fear. What you *can* do, however, is learn to reduce the fear effect through practice. Desensitization via graduated exposure is a common treatment for many types of phobias and anxiety disorders. It can work for your approach anxiety as well. What you're going to do is perform a series of very low-investment, low-risk approaches, gradually upping your game until you're starting full-blown conversations.

Start by picking a public place with a decent amount of pedestrian traffic; you don't need to be in Times Square, but you don't want to be lingering around an otherwise empty street either. A street with plenty of shops nearby, the quad on your college campus, the mall, or even a grocery store all work. Once you're there, spend a little time going up to people, giving a smile and asking them,

"Hey, do you happen to know what time it is?" When they tell you, you say, "Cool, thanks!" and keep on walking. Repeat this again with another person a little further down the road: smile, ask the time, say thank you, and walk away. Do this twenty times – a little less if you're able to do this with no hesitation or a little more if the exercise makes you uncomfortable.

Once you've gotten used to asking the time, you want to move up the engagement ladder. Now you want to ask for directions. Once again, pick a public place with plenty of foot traffic and approach someone standing around or walking towards you. Give a smile and ask them: "Hey, do you know where the Starbucks is?" Starbucks makes for an easy reference point since in any major city you're almost guaranteed to be within two blocks of one; you can name any location as long as it's something visible and well known – a 7-11, a gas station, a Wells Fargo, an Apple Store, a local landmark, whatever. If they give you directions, repeat them back, then say, "Awesome, thank you," and walk in the general direction of your destination. If they don't know, then you say, "Okay, thanks anyway," and keep walking. As with the previous exercise, practice this twenty times –more if you're still nervous.

If this feels like it's almost absurdly easy... well, that's kind of the point. It's a low-stakes approach. Most people aren't going to tell you to fuck off when you're asking for directions. You don't feel like you're asking someone to judge you on a personal level when you just want to know how to get to Mr. Noodle. These easy victories help you realize that you *can* approach people. So now you're going to make it slightly more complicated: you're going to have a mini-conversation with the people you approach.

Now you're not going to be asking for directions; you're going to be asking for *suggestions*. Don't let yourself get stressed about this; asking for advice is actually a very good way to encourage someone to like you. You're essentially telling them that you value their input and this tends to make people feel positively inclined to the person doing the asking.

Pick someone who isn't in an obvious hurry – someone who's window-shopping or wandering aimlessly – and ask them if they know a good Thai place nearby. Or if there's a cool bar around there. Whatever they say – yes, no, I don't eat Thai – you say "thanks" and explain that you're new in town and you're still trying to get to know the area. This will prompt them to talk a little more. They may ask where you came from, talk about how much they like or don't like the city or commiserate about being in a new town. Talk for a minute or two and then say, "Cool. Hey, I've got to run, but thanks for the suggestion!" and move on.

Take your time at this stage; it can be a little stressful if you have approach anxiety and you may stammer, get nervous or even trip over your own words. The more you practice this, the more natural it will feel and the smoother it will go. Again: these are very low-stakes approaches, with people you have no real interest or investment in. The worst that can happen is that someone doesn't have time to talk to you and you say, "Cool, thanks anyway," and walk on.

As you get more used to making these practice approaches, challenge yourself a little. See if you can continue the conversation for a little longer. Make small talk with the people you encounter on a daily basis. As you put more practice into talking to new people, you'll start noticing that you aren't feeling that adrenaline-dump-racing-heart panic response as much as you used to. These practice approaches are fundamentally the *same* as approaching people you're interested in; you're trying to start a conversation and possibly make a new friend.

Edit the Nightmare Scenario

Want to minimize the fear of rejection when you're approaching people you're interested in? Stop planning how you're going to get rejected in advance.

Here's an interesting fact about the human brain: our brains treat what we imagine as a real experience. When you imagine being rejected by somebody, your brain triggers the same emotional and physical impulses as though it were really happening to you. Every time you picture being rejected – one of the many aspects of approach anxiety –you're quite literally living through it. You're actually feeling that fear. No wonder you're afraid to approach somebody! You're emotionally exhausted and feeling lower than a snake's ass in a drainage ditch before you've even left your house.

But what if you could *break* that cycle? What if you could reduce the power that those imagined scenarios had over you and turn them into visions of success? What if, instead of feeling as though you've been rejected a thousand times, you felt the thrill of *success* instead?

Sound crazy? It's not. It's simply a matter of editing the nightmare scenario that plays in your mind.

Here's how you do it. I want you to think of the last time you saw someone you were attracted to. Imagine going up to them, initiating a conversation and it goes *exactly* as badly as you always thought it would. She starts pointing and laughing at you. Her friends come over and spread the word around the party and now everybody knows that you hit on somebody out of your league. She lets you know in no uncertain terms that she finds you repulsive and beneath her.

Now... you're probably feeling pretty bad right about now and wondering why I'm asking you to do this. You see, this nightmare scenario you're picturing? It only hurts you because you let it. You *invented it*. You have given it the power to harm you and you can take that power away again by making it *not real*.

So take that scenario and imagine it again, only this time, I want you to picture it in black and white as though you were watching an old film on TV. That level of abstraction – picturing it in back and white – makes it less "real"; it's not something you're living through so much as something you're observing. Now, I want you to imagine the exact same scenario *again*, only this time, everybody sounds like they've sucked down several tanks worth of helium. How ridiculous is it to hear someone reject you when they sound like a chipmunk? Now imagine it again at double speed as Yakety Sax plays in the background. Then imagine it, only this time when she's starts to reject you, her head starts inflating like a parade float. She's standing there, gesturing and telling you off while her head just swells to three times its size, bobbing in the breeze. Or perhaps this time her head *shrinks* as she's talking. Maybe she suddenly looks like a clown. Or Elmer Fudd. Or every time she opens her mouth, she spits bubbles instead. Or someone erases her body and draws in a random cartoon in its place.

The more you play with that scenario, the more absurd

you can make it, the more you're reducing its power over you. You're taking something that feels real and, bit by bit, making it something that's just too ridiculous to be afraid of. You're breaking the associations between that imagined scenario and reality and changing how your brain responds to it. Now, instead of feeling like you're being rejected, it becomes something too absurd to take seriously, robbing it of its impact.

Now, having edited that nightmare scenario so many times, I want you to imagine it going *well*. In this version, when you come up to introduce yourself, she gives you a big smile. She's charmed by you. She's hanging on your every word, laughing at all of your jokes, swatting you playfully on the arm in mock outrage and then leaving it there as you talk. She doesn't just give you her number; she's telling you that the two of you should get drinks that weekend.

Notice how much more real this new scenario feels, now that you've neutered the rejection scenario? Notice how much *better* you feel? Spend time imagining the *positive* outcomes instead of draining your emotional energy and self-esteem by living out imaginary failures over and over again. I realize this sounds very woo-woo new-agey-crystals-and-patchouli bullshit, but it works. By changing how you picture the scenario from something you dread to something you laugh at, you're changing the cycle of emotions and experiences. Negativity is a self-fulfilling prophecy after all, and when you go into an encounter assuming the worst, you're going to subconsciously sabotage yourself.

Of course, this is all great prep-work. But what do you do when you're at that party and you see somebody who looks like every dream you've ever had?

Follow the Three Second Rule

Everything I mentioned regarding imagining worst-case scenarios about approaching someone is *doubly* true for when you're out and about and you see somebody that you're dying to get to know. While it's perfectly natural to want to mentally rehearse before making your move, too often people tend to fall down the rabbit hole of worst-case scenarios that suck your motivation away, leaving fear in its place. As a result, you start coming up with all sorts of perfectly plausible reasons why you shouldn't approach her: she almost certainly has a boyfriend, she's talking to somebody, you need a drink, you need a couple more drinks, you've only just arrived and you're not quite in a social mood yet...

Before you know it, you've talked yourself out of making the approach and now you're just standing there kicking yourself because *come on* you should be able to do this, right? But no, you're still just standing there. And the longer you're stuck there, the worse it gets, because now everything is about how you're *not* approaching anyone and thus everything starts to reinforce your current stalled-out state.

So you want to keep yourself from locking up in the first place. You want to follow what's known as the Three Second Rule.

The Three Second Rule is very simple: when you see somebody you're interested in, you have three seconds *from the moment you've seen them* to make your approach. Otherwise you've waited too long and now you're going to start overthinking things and draining your motivation away. You don't wait for "the perfect moment," you don't stop to practice what you're going to say, you just roll straight in there and say hello. Yeah, you may screw up. You may say something stupid. Hell, there was a time when I literally choked – full on, coughing and unable to breathe choking – trying to approach somebody. But here's the secret: *it doesn't matter*. You don't need to be perfect; you can recover from mistakes. You just need to be approaching. The important part is that you're in motion, not getting stuck in place. Emotional momentum follows the same laws as *physical* momentum; an object at rest is going to stay at rest, while an object in motion is going to want to stay in motion. Following the Three Second Rule helps keep you in motion and making approaches instead overthinking things and stalling out.

Will you strike out? Possibly. But there is no reward without risk, and *not* approaching someone guarantees that you won't get that chance to meet them.

Fortune favors the bold, and the bold follow the Three Second Rule.

Learn How to Handle Being Rejected (by Being Rejected)

Ultimately, the best way to conquer your approach anxiety is to simply stare it down and do what you're most afraid of: get rejected. Because at the end of the day, being rejected *isn't that bad*. I should know. I have approached literally thousands of women in the span of just one year in just about every venue you can imagine. I have asked out co-workers, flirted with friends, bantered with baristas, winked at waitstaff, and hit on porn stars, low-tier celebrities, trust-fund babies, white collar professionals, club kids and just about every variation of stomach-churning "what am I thinking, they are so far out of my league" scenario you can imagine. Don't get me wrong here: I'm not saying I hooked up with all of these people. Quite the opposite, in fact. For every success I've had – whether it was getting her phone number, getting a date or taking her home – I've been rejected at least ten times. At first, it hurt. I'd leave the bar fighting back tears and carrying the tattered remains of my self-esteem back to my apartment to spend the rest of the night on Call of Duty death-matches. But if I was perfectly honest with myself, *it wasn't that bad.* Yeah, my ego took a beating, but if I could pull my head out of the self-pity party, it was really minor. The sky didn't fall, I hadn't gotten maced, I didn't get a drink thrown in my face[2], nobody was pointing and laughing and I didn't get thrown out of the bar. She said, "No, thanks," and that was it.

What, exactly, was there to be afraid of again?

Over the years, the worst rejection I've ever received was stony silence. She looked at me, then went back to talking to her friend without saying a word to me. That's *it.* And this was in South Beach, Miami – home to some of the snobbiest, stuck-up-attitude-holding, hardest-to-approach people in the world. Yeah, it wasn't fun, but it wasn't the nightmare I had imagined it would be. I have never had anyone laugh in my face. I've never had anyone demand to know why I thought I was good enough to talk to them. I have never had someone call her friends over to watch my humiliation. Whenever I got shot down, it was simple and usually fairly polite:

---

2. The one time I *did* get a drink thrown at me, I rather decidedly earned it by being a drunk and incredibly rude asshole.

"Thanks, but I'm not interested" or "Look, it's nice talking to you, but I need to get back to my friends."

Yeah, we all worry about being humiliated. But "humiliation" is what you make of it. Nobody is going to notice or care that you got rejected. Everybody else is too absorbed in their own drama to pay attention to a random stranger who isn't even talking to them.

When you get rejected, it's almost always for one of two reasons: either you need to work on your skills or you weren't compatible in the first place. Maybe she had a boyfriend. Maybe she just broke up with someone and didn't want to deal with anyone that night. Maybe she didn't like gingers or brunettes or guys whose names end in R. Maybe she was in a bad mood, maybe her chi was fucked up. All any of that means is that you wouldn't have worked out and now you're free to go approach somebody else instead. Make a note of what to work on for next time and then just *roll on*.

There's a saying in the pick-up community: the first thousand approaches don't count. You're trying something you haven't done before and you're still learning. The more you learn to handle rejection and not let it destroy you, the better able you are to get that practice in and challenge yourself. Nobody gets good without paying their dues in blood, sweat, bruises and effort. The more you challenge yourself and put yourself out there, the more you'll realize that approach anxiety is nothing that you can't handle. And when you've conquered it, you'll be amazed at how much better you get at meeting amazing women.

DON'T BE A CREEPER

One of the things that's critical to dating success is understanding how your behavior is being perceived by other people, especially the women you're interested in.

Too many guys out there – especially those who are a little less socially experienced – don't quite understand the difference between how they perceive themselves and how they're coming across to others. As far as they're concerned, they're the very model of chivalry and gentility. But the women they're talking to? They have a slightly different opinion about the matter. The more kind-hearted ladies would describe them as "intense." Or they would say, "He comes across a little strong, but he means well. You just have to get to know him." The less kindly would say it flat out: "He gives me the creeps."

It's surprisingly easy to give off the creepy vibe to women, especially if you aren't aware of what you're doing and why it makes women feel the way they do. Your friends may know you well enough to know that you don't mean to be a creeper, but you don't have the time to explain that to every woman you meet. There are a lot of people – mostly the socially inexperienced – who worry about being called "creepy" by women and having it destroy their entire lives. Because, as we all know, all women everywhere are connected to a powerful underground information sharing network, thus ensuring that anyone saddled with the "creeper" label shall never have sex again... not even with himself.

I understand the fear; most people don't want to come across as creepy and worry about accidentally ruining an interaction with someone they're attracted to. It can feel like you're walking on a tightrope over a pit of flaming, judgmental sharks who are dying to rip your nipples off. Also, you're doing so without a net. And the tightrope has been greased with all of your unused sperm and is on fire. But, like many of the emotional pitfalls and fuck-ups that come with dating, this is a matter that is entirely within your own control. Avoiding being a creeper is equal parts practical measures and self-awareness. Over the years, I've noticed some issues that correspond with people being unintentionally creepy, and working on those issues will help you avoid being a creeper.

What Is a Creeper and Why Are Women Afraid of Them?

It's important to understand just what makes someone a creeper. A lot of guys will say that a creeper is simply someone who's unattractive and has the gall to talk to a pretty woman and that handsome men aren't ever creepy. This is rather demonstrably untrue; you only have to watch movies like *American Psycho* or *Red Eye* or *Kalifornia* to see classically attractive men who are *scary as hell*. Creepy isn't a matter of looks; it's a matter of behavior. A creeper is someone who makes a woman uncomfortable or fear for her personal safety. Behavior like touching a woman when she's uninterested, pushing up against her boundaries or making inappropriate jokes all serve as potential warning signs that the person she's interacting with may represent a legitimate threat to her.

The thing that's important to remember is that men can take their physical safety for granted, especially when dealing with women. While there will always be individual exceptions, the average male is larger, stronger and heavier than the average woman. In practical terms, this means that the average man is fully capable of overpowering the average woman with relative ease... and women *are very aware of this fact*. Women have to gauge every interaction with men, especially men they don't know, on whether or not he presents a threat to her. This is the unspoken subtext for every time a guy talks to a girl, sends a Facebook friend request or asks her out. This means that they are going to be on the lookout for clues in somebody's behavior that they may be dangerous. Is he a potential rapist? Is he a potential murderer?

Because women live in a state of near-constant threat awareness, they are far more cued in to the slight clues that hint at potential danger than guys are. Because the stakes are much higher for women than they are for men, women are more sensitized to these little hints. This can occasionally lead to false positives – guys who are essentially harmless, just a little clueless or unaware how they're coming across – but when the consequences of being wrong are so high, it's safer for them to err on the side of caution.

Guys – who don't have to do this mental calculus on an almost hourly basis – are frequently unaware of this issue. They may be well-meaning, but they're often ignorant of how they're inadvertently sending all the wrong signals. In fact, because they don't live with the same omnipresent threat that women do, they're frequently offended by the idea that it's their behavior that creeps girls out; after all, *they* know that they're not a threat! Other guys fall on the other end of the spectrum – they're terrified of giving off the wrong signals and creeping women out by mistake, and end up being afraid of even *talking* to a woman lest they accidentally creep her out.

But it's actually not that hard to avoid being a creeper. What it takes is a little self-awareness and a willingness to see how other people might interpret your behavior. Once you recognize what creepy, predatory behavior looks like, you're better able to adjust yourself and avoid triggering women's Spidey-Sense.

Watch Your Body Language

Body language is one of the ways that women use to gauge men's intentions... and it's one of the ways that guys mistakenly give off the creepy vibe. Because of the way men and women are socialized, it's possible to present yourself as more aggressive or threatening than you are.

One of the first mistakes that guys make, especially when they approach women, is that they walk up to her directly and plant themselves directly in front of her. This is common behavior when men are conversing amongst themselves; we face each other directly when talking, pointing our feet, torso and face directly at the person we're talking to. To guys, this is a sign of attention, that you're engaged in communicating with the person in front of you. To women, this can be incredibly intense, almost *aggressive* –someone just planted themself in front of you and is facing you head on. It can feel like you're trying to prevent them from going somewhere. This is especially true if you're broad or tall; you may think you're being direct or confident, but you're coming across as overbearing and threatening. This is *especially* true when her back is against an obstacle like a wall or the bar or if you do the "lean" when you put one arm against the wall next to her. You've effectively trapped her with no way of leaving besides trying to push past you. And if you're standing within her personal space – usually 1 1/2 feet – then you're in a position to easily grab her.

To avoid being creepy, learn to avoid giving women the full frontal. When you approach them, approach from an angle, or even from the side. Make sure that they have plenty of room to walk away that doesn't include pushing past you. As you're speaking, angle your body slightly away from her; it's a way of giving her more room to move if she feels the need. If she's up against a wall or other obstacle, stand to her side with your back against it and address her from over your shoulder. The more comfortable a woman is with you, the more directly you can face her without causing her to instinctively reach for the pepper spray.

It's also important to be aware of physical space. There are certain zones of personal space. The outer edges are known as public space, while the closer you come, you pass through the social space, then into increasingly intimate personal space. The physically closer to someone you are, the more intimate the space. If you aren't someone who we give permission to enter our intimate space – family members, close friends, lovers – then getting that close is incredibly uncomfortable to the other person; as a result, they'll often try to re-establish a distance between the two of you, moving away until you're at "public space" levels. If you're talking to someone and they're stepping back from you, you can safely assume that you are too close. Do not make the mistake of stepping forward. This will inevitably be seen as threateningly aggressive. You've now gone from making them feel uncomfortable to making them feel pursued. And if you inadvertently back them into a wall or a corner, you will have moved them from uncomfortable to "actually fucking afraid."

It's important to realize that a person's sense of personal space is context sensitive. In a crowded bar, where intruding into somebody's intimate space is unavoidable, people will be *somewhat* more tolerant of physical closeness. However, if you're in a confined space, say, an empty elevator, then you want to give her more space in order to help her feel comfortable. Ideally, you should provide enough space that she can get past you without feeling as though you can keep her from leaving.

Yes, it can seem difficult to figure the balance between giving someone space and also being able to flirt with them. It takes practice to build up your sense of social calibration that will help you understand how to navigate between social and personal space. While you're learning, the safest option is to let the person you're talking to set the pace; the more attracted someone is to you, the closer they'll allow you to come. Give a little space at first for her comfort; when she's cool with your coming closer, she'll let you know.

You also need to be aware of touch. This can be a tricky area because touch and physical contact are incredibly important to humans. Touching, when used properly, is a critical part of flirting. However, too much touching or touching her the wrong way sends the wrong message. The wrong kind of touch can come across being aggressive or dominant, rather than flirty and fun. Leaving your hand on a girl for too long – even in a neutral place like the shoulder or middle of the arm – will read as though you're claiming possession of her... or worse, that you're going to drag her off somewhere.

Don't worry if this seems contradictory; I'll be teaching you how to use touch the *right* way in the next chapter.

Different people have different tolerance to touch; some folks are very touchy-feely, while others won't want to be touched *at all*. You want to avoid touching people in a way that makes them physically uncomfortable or tense. If you put your hand on somebody and feel them tense up, you need to pull your hand back. Do it calmly, not like you've just touched a hot stove – just with an air of "ah, sorry, didn't mean to make you uncomfortable."

As with personal space, it can take some time to learn how to calibrate yourself with regard to touching. Once again, if you're unsure, then the best option is to let *her* establish what level of physical contact is acceptable. When she wants you to touch her, she will make sure you know.

Another thing to avoid is staring. It's easy to get caught up in watching somebody, and the difference between flirty eye contact and staring can be delicate. When we're giving someone a flirty look or playing the eye contact game, our faces are softer, with genuine smiles and softer eyes. A stare, on the other hand, is a threatening look; you're watching with unblinking eyes and a set, often stern, expression. A flirty gaze says, "I think you're amazing." A stare says, "I want to lick the inside of your ribcage." To avoid accidentally looking like you're staring, you want to make sure you have a soft expression – let your eyelids droop a little and your smile reach your eyes as if you were looking at your favorite puppy. Try to avoid holding eye contact for too long. Five seconds is the upper limit before it starts to feel uncomfortable; deliberately break eye contact by looking up and away with a smile.

That smile, by the way, is important. A warm smile is frequently the difference between "I'd like to get to know you" and "I wonder how many lampshades I could make out of your skin."

Watch Your Language, Too

Just as your body language says things that you may not intend, the words that actually come out of your mouth will also affect how people see you. This is about more than just swearing… it's about the implications behind what you say and how it comes across to others. There are certain things that will seem funny to you but will be incredibly off-putting in another context. Women already have to fear for their safety on a daily basis. The last thing you need to do is remind her that, oh yes, you represent a potential threat to her. This means that there are certain jokes that you just shouldn't make. Jokes about rape, abduction, physical assault or murder are off the table. Period. Too many women have experienced physical or sexual threats and violence for you to jokingly suggest that you might kidnap or rape her.

You may think you're being funny when you walk up to girls holding a napkin and asking, "Hey, does this smell like chloroform to you?"

You aren't. You're being creepy. Now stop it.

Respect the "Soft No"

Most women are socially conditioned not to be direct, especially when men are involved. Saying "no" directly is often seen as rude or needlessly hurtful and so they have a surprisingly complex system of refusing without actually saying the words. These are known as "soft no's." A woman who isn't interested in going on a date with you, for example, will come up with multiple reasons why she can't go, which all sound like "I'd like to but..." without suggesting an alternate option. Similarly, not responding to you when you text them, message them or otherwise try to get in contact them is a "soft no"; they're hoping that you'll recognize that they're not engaging with you and will get the hint. No response *is* a response.

We all tend to recognize a "soft no" when we hear it. The problem is that often we *don't like the answer*, so we may try to rationalize an explanation that says we're not actually hearing a "no" and can continue to pursue them. This is a bad idea. When you ignore or rationalize a soft no, it tells women that you consider your desires more important than hers and will deliberately interpret her "no" in a way that favors you.

The idea of a man who's so persistent that he wears down a woman's resolve is only romantic in movies and fiction. In the real world, that sort of behavior screams, "I don't respect your boundaries." Trust me: women who *are* interested in you and want you to stick around will make a point of letting you know.

Know When to Approach and Know When to Leave

One of the worst things you can do is to hover around someone. I get that approaching women can be intimidating, especially when they're in a group. However, if you're hovering around a girl while trying to work up the nerve to talk to her, you're going to be creeping her out. Women are incredibly aware of their surroundings; they have to be. A guy who's making a point of being in her general proximity without actually approaching her or talking to her is going to be seen as acting strangely. You may be waiting for an opening. You may be waiting for her to walk away from her friends so you can approach her by herself. You may just be trying to psych yourself up to deliver your opening line. But she doesn't know that; she just knows there's some stranger hanging around the periphery like he's hoping to separate a gazelle from the herd. This is one more reason why the Three Second Rule is so important; it helps you avoid hovering around and generally seeming "off."

The other end of this is not knowing when it's time to leave. One of the keys to avoiding being creepy by accident is to follow the social cues that say it's time for you to go instead of hanging around when you're not wanted. Guys who seem like they're missing the hints that they're not wanted are inherently creepy; it carries the implication that they're less concerned with her desires than their own. Most women are socially conditioned not to give offense or hurt men's feelings and so they'll rarely break off a conversation directly. Instead they'll be looking for a socially relevant reason to leave. If the conversation is starting to die off, you don't want to try stick around desperately trying to keep things going. It's better to end the conversation early and come back later than it is to try to extend a conversation past its natural limits. Make your excuses and bow out of the conversation gracefully. Similarly, if you notice that her eyes are starting to dart around to the sides – as though she were looking around for someone – you need to realize that she's looking for someone to rescue her from you. Take the hint and say, "It's been nice talking to you, but I see someone I need to say 'hey' to," and move on.

You Can't Argue Your Way Out of Being Creepy

Many guys will get upset over the idea that they're being creepy by accident; some may actually make things *worse* by trying to explain how it's unfair for people to see them as creepy.

Cold hard truth time: you don't get to decide what's creepy to other people. You don't get to appeal somebody else's decisions. Everybody gets to set their personal limits and those are not up for debate. If someone decides that you creep them out, then you've creeped them out. Sorry. Nobody is obligated to accept why you should be the special exception to their feelings of self-preservation. You need to remember: nobody is going to give a damn where you grew up or what everybody does back home if you're creeping them out. Being from another culture isn't an excuse, and the longer you've been in the place you currently live, the lamer that reason will seem. It is incumbent on you to make allowances for the culture you're interacting with and to learn to adjust your behavior to what's socially appropriate. Being socially awkward isn't an excuse either. Not recognizing that you've tripped over a line doesn't mean that the line wasn't there in the first place.

How to Avoid Being Creepy

Hey, I get it. After reading this long list of ways that you can be creepy by accident, it can make you feel like trying to interact with women is like tap dancing through a minefield. It can make trying to get a date feel even *more* intimidating than it did before. It can seem like an almost impossible number of things to keep in mind while you're flirting with someone. And I'll be honest with you: you're *going* to screw up. Even the most socially conscious player out there will occasionally trip over his own dick. Hell, you can do *everything* right and still trip over an emotional land mine you had no way of knowing existed.

But there's a very easy trick to avoiding being creepy. When you creep someone out by accident, you apologize. Giving a little (literal) space and a sincere apology is all that it takes to turn from "potential creeper" back into "that cool guy I'm getting to know." However, you have to do it the right way. You make that apology short, simple and sincere. "Hey, I think I just may have crossed a line/ creeped you out a little. I'm sorry about that." You don't put on a production begging her forgiveness, you don't beat yourself up over it, you don't freak out and you don't try to bowl her over with how abjectly horrified you are. Despite the words, this is literally the opposite of apologizing; you're not saying you're sorry, you're making it all about your discomfort and asking her to reassure you. You also don't issue a non-apology apology that just deflects responsibility. "I'm sorry you took that the wrong way" or "I'm sorry if you were offended" really say, "Actually, *you're* the problem" and just confirms that you're being a dick.

Now here's the critical part: after having apologized, don't do it again. The whole point is to acknowledge that yes, you made a mistake but now you know better. Making the same mistake again – or other boundary-testing behavior for that matter – carries the message that you're not sorry that you made a mistake, you're sorry you got caught and you're going to try again as soon as you think you've got an opening.

It can seem intimidating, but it's much simpler than many people realize. A little social calibration mixed with a willingness to apologize when you mess up is all it takes to avoid being a creeper.

CHAPTER 7.

HOW TO BUILD ATTRACTION

WHAT IS CHEMISTRY?

Ask anyone about one of the most important parts of dating and they'll tell you: It's chemistry.

Unfortunately, nobody's able to actually explain what chemistry *is*. If you ask people to describe chemistry, you'll end up with a mix of inconclusive and unhelpful answers. "It's... you know. That spark." "That feeling." "That moment when the two of you just... click." "You just know it when you feel it."

Frankly, you'd have more success asking nerds to explain the Force – it's about as abstract and more useful.

Because people believe that chemistry is something that's simply there or isn't, it often becomes akin to predestination: "We knew it was going to work because we had incredible chemistry together." As though chemistry can only be found by random chance. We treat chemistry as though it were a binary; either two people have chemistry together or they don't.

Except... it *isn't*.

The problem is that when you're talking about

chemistry, you're ultimately talking about emotions. Simply put, most people have no idea why people who may look perfect on paper leave them cold while somebody who's the opposite of their type makes them want to rip all their clothes off right then and there. Humans are good at understanding that we feel a particular way, but we frequently have no idea *why* we feel that way. This is known as "misattribution of arousal": we process how we feel first and then assign meaning to it after the fact, retroactively deciding the "why" in a way that justifies our assumptions. When we feel our pulse racing, adrenaline pumping through our veins and our limbs are shaking, we may be afraid, we may be excited, or we may be aroused. We don't decide *which* until we look around and pick a reason. Are we standing at the edge of a cliff or are we standing next to an incredibly hot woman? The sensations are the same, but the emotions attached to it are different.

Small wonder that we keep getting the wrong ideas about how sexual and emotional chemistry work.

Now imagine if, instead of just hoping that you might feel that level of passion, you were able to consciously inspire it in other people. Imagine if you could *deliberately* create that feeling of "love at first sight" or intense sexual attraction?

You can... if you understand how chemistry works. Chemistry, put simply, is a mix of emotional rapport, intellectual engagement and sexual attraction. Each of these individually is powerful, but when you know how to put them together, the results are often *explosive*.

The key to chemistry is to remember that you need balance. There's an understandable impulse to focus all of your attention on building sexual attraction – after all, who *doesn't* want to feel like an irresistible sex-god? However, sexual attraction isn't the end-all, be-all of chemistry, nor does attraction lead to sex by itself. A woman may find someone to be sex on toast, but that doesn't necessarily mean she's going to sleep with him or her. A guy who's hot as a four-alarm fire is nice and all… but a man who's desirable *and* knows how to make her feel good, makes her feel desired and just gets her on a deep, almost primal level? *That* is a man whose clothes she'll be tearing off with her teeth. Building those emotional connections and engaging her intellectually helps push them from "maybe" to "oh hell yes." Similarly, too much attention to emotional rapport and too *little* sexual attraction leads to a platonic relationship, rather than a romantic or sexual one. Having an intense emotional connection is awesome, but without that frisson of sexuality, it's impossible to make the leap from "good friend" to "boyfriend." Keeping the proper level of sexual tension in the relationship helps spur her desire; you go from being "the guy she *wishes* she was attracted to" to "the guy she can't stop thinking about."

Each aspect of chemistry balances and enhances the other. You don't just want to get into her pants; you want to get into her *head* as well.

HOW TO FLIRT

One of the key parts to learning how to build attraction is through flirting. Unfortunately, flirting has become something of a lost art; most people aren't just bad at it, but so terrible that other people can't tell that they're flirting at all. When guys do make attempts at being more obvious in their flirting, we go about it the wrong way. If you start showering someone with compliments, you end up looking like a suck-up who's hoping to win their approval. Humor may be sexy, but if you're only telling jokes, then you end up looking like you're practicing your stand-up routine instead of having a conversation like a normal person. If you start negging or using insults as a way of either showing you're not intimidated by them or trying to make them seek your approval, all you're doing is telling her you're an asshole.

Flirting is, at its core, a way to engage, size up and generate attraction in a prospective mate. It's a way of showing someone that you're interested and prompting them to be more interested in *you* in return. It's light and it's friendly. There are many, *many* different ways to flirt and you want to find the ways that work best with your personality. Not every flirting style works well for everyone.

Show Her That You're Interested... But Not Too Interested

One of the most important parts of flirting is that the person you're flirting with *needs to know you're interested in her*. Playing it cool and pretending you're above all that actually makes you *less* attractive to her. In fact, if she thinks that you don't like her, the odds are better that she's going to move on to somebody else – after all, why spend time trying to get to know somebody who's just being aloof and uninterested?

Like I mentioned back in Chapter 5, we're instinctually attracted to people who like us. This is part of the Reward

Theory of Attraction; we're drawn to people whose presence gratifies us and makes us feel good. We all want to be liked or loved. When we think people like us, we feel special and our brains fire off dopamine that lights up our pleasure centers like the Las Vegas Strip. When a particular individual's presence in our lives brings us rewards that outweigh the potential costs, we prioritize that relationship and want it to continue.

However, you can't just love-bomb somebody and expect them to start throwing their panties at you. Going overboard with expressing your interest signals that you have a number of unattractive traits like low self-esteem or low social intelligence. Worse, it might make you seem creepy and obsessed. So you want to strike a balance; you want to be obviously showing interest, but not over the top. Let her know you like her, but give her space. After all, you want her to put in some effort as well.

You want to remember the idea of push and pull. Pull her in a bit – letting her know you're interested – and gently push her away. Give your attention to her and flirt, but then go and talk with other people. Flirt, then dial back the flirting. This principle of push and pull will tie into just about every other form of flirting you may do.

Flirt With Your Eyes

Eye contact is a critical part of how we communicate, and it can be shockingly intimate. Our eyes are one of the most expressive parts of our body, yet people are consistently underestimating their value when it comes to flirting. The eyes can be a potent source of non-verbal sexual communication; they can lend a sexual subtext without having to actually say a word.

To start with: making eye contact is a great way to signal your interest in someone. If you catch her eyes, look to the side, then back and give her a slow smile; it's a way of saying, "I like what I see." You may also want to give her an eyebrow flash when you match her eyes – it's another way of signaling interest. It's also much classier and less cheesy than giving a wink.

Using your eyes while talking to somebody is another way to flirt. You may have heard of celebrities with a "penetrating gaze" or "bedroom eyes" – a look that says they're not only seeing through you, but they're already picturing you naked and the insane things that the two of you are going to be doing later. Part of the way that this is accomplished is through the strategic use of eye contact.

Direct eye contact can be intimidating, even uncomfortable if you hold it for too long… unless you know what you're doing. As a general rule, I recommend not holding someone's eyes for longer than a few seconds. However, when you're flirting, holding someone's gaze just a little too long can work to your advantage. It's a way of taking advantage of the misattribution of arousal.

Staring into your date's eyes for a fraction longer than you would normally can cause their heart to race and cause them to feel a little light-headed. This is the beginning of the body's fear response. It's also the beginnings of sexual arousal.

Hold her stare for just a second longer than normal, then deliberately break it by looking up and away. This will prompt that rapid pulse and a certain shortness of breath. The brain starts searching around for a reason.

Is she scared? What's going on? Is there a tiger in the bushes? Failing to find something to be scared of, it settles for the next option: she's not scared, she's getting turned on.

While you're doing this, it helps to be giving her the bedroom eyes. When we're aroused – or we see something that we like – our pupils dilate. Big pupils are a sign of interest, and people will respond. Wider pupils actually make us look more attractive to others. Unfortunately, you can't directly control eye dilation, but you can create the circumstances that will cause your pupils to widen. While you're talking to someone you're interested in, look them in the eye and visualize what you want to do to them. Give a smile, let your eyelids lower slightly and just let your gaze to do the work.

You can also use the triangle gaze to inspire some dirty thoughts; look from one eye to the next, then to her lips, then back up to her eyes. It's a signal that you're thinking about kissing her... and one that will inspire similar thoughts in *her*.

Bantering, Teasing and Antagonistic Flirting

When used correctly, bantering and teasing can be powerful tools in your flirting arsenal. The problem is that many people *don't* have any idea how to do it right. In fact, many people who try teasing or bantering end up going too far and acting like an asshole instead.

Teasing is the art of telling someone you like them while saying something that seems mean in a playful way. The antagonistic aspect of teasing follows the push-pull dynamic of flirting; you're giving a compliment (the pull) while taking it back or putting up a disqualifying statement at the same time (the push).

For example: "You're the coolest person I've met... tonight, anyway," is an example of a mild tease. It's a sincere compliment – she's a cool person – with a minor disqualification at the end, a disqualification she knows isn't sincere, and one that might prompt a laugh.

"You're hilarious... it's too bad you're such a dork," is another example. You're genuinely saying that you find them funny, while calling her a dork is another minor disqualification. The word choice is important; calling someone a dork is so obviously childish that it's almost impossible to take seriously. Calling someone a loser or a snob or some other tease, on the other hand, can sound like you actually mean it. And if you say something like "You're such a bitch" instead, then you've gone past flirting into flat-out insulting them. *Not* a place you want to go.

When done *properly*, a tease invites a response or comeback rather than sullen silence. To give an example from my personal life: when I used the "You're such a dork" line with one woman I was flirting with, she responded with, "Oh, I'm the dork? I didn't realize someone wearing a Star Wars tee-shirt[1] was allowed to pass judgment on somebody else."

In the cold text, this can seem insulting, even combative; if you were to read this without any sort of descriptors, you would think these two people disliked each other. It's important that you signal that you actually like the person with your body language –smiling, giving a playful touch as you say it. You're not insulting them;

---

1. In fairness, that shirt was vintage and it was awesome.

you're trying to get them to play along. You want to convey the feeling that the two of you are in on it together, that you're having fun with him or her rather than at their expense.

The subtext of the conversation should be simple and positive. In the example I gave, I was saying, "I like you and I know you like me already, so I'm going to make you work for it a little." She was responding with, "I see what you're doing and I'm going to volley it right back to you, let's see if you can keep up."

In general, there are two ways of handling this sort of banter: you can volley it back one more time ("The girl rocking the Rachel haircut shouldn't be trying to give me fashion advice") or agree and amplify ("Hey, don't knock the shirt, the shirt gets the ladies interested. Then it's the Star Wars sheets that seal the deal").

It's important to realize that bantering can get tiresome fast – nobody wants to feel like their entire conversation is going to be a duel. Even when you're both enjoying the bantering, you should put the point-scoring aside and spend time getting to know one another. Cut the conversational thread to something serious, deliver a sincere compliment ("You know something? You really have an amazing smile") but overtly signal that the duel's over.

And remember: it's intended to be fun. Not everybody is going to be interested in banter and you shouldn't try to drag them into it if it's not their thing. It can also be easy to hurt someone's feelings by accident. If you're teasing someone and you're getting back silence or hurt looks, you've made a mistake and gone too far. Apologize and drop the topic.

One universal truth is that women *love* men who can make them laugh. Being able to make a woman laugh is like a direct pathway to the pleasure-centers of her brain. You're making her feel incredible, and that's going to make her listen longer and feel more attracted towards you.

This is the time when you want to put your sense of humor into play. The key is to make it natural. You don't want to be telling joke after joke; that's not flirting, that's putting on a performance for an audience of one. Instead what you want to do is find opportunities to inject humor into the conversation. A self-deprecating joke for example, can be an excellent way of making her laugh as well as showing that you're confident enough to laugh at yourself. Just be careful: it's very easy to go overboard and sound like you're not actually joking any more.

Another great way to make her laugh is to tell a funny story that happened to you that you witnessed. Stories can be incredibly versatile in this way – not only are you making her laugh, but it gives you an opportunity to brag a little about yourself without being obvious about it. You want to be careful about the kinds of stories you tell, though – anything involving politics or religion is going to be tricky territory until you get to know her better.

THE POWER OF TOUCH

Touch is one of the most powerful ways of flirting and building attraction. The way we touch someone communicates far more than our words do. Touch can be a way of indicating attraction or a way of building comfort. Something as simple as a hand on a shoulder can be a sign of support, conveying a message of dominance or ownership or signaling your interest in them.

It's impossible to understate how important it is to use touch when you're flirting. If someone isn't comfortable with you touching them, they're not going to be interested in sleeping with you. Touch is frequently the difference between someone seeing you as a potential lover or a platonic friend. When you understand touch and can use it properly, it can be an *incredibly* powerful tool.

Understand What Your Touch Says

Every touch carries a message, even if that message was "oops, didn't mean to do that." Touch can be subtle, and the way you touch someone can convey very different meanings, even if it's in the same place. One form of physical contact that might be acceptable – a touch of fingertips to the forearm, for example – might be completely unacceptable if the person were to use his palm. One is flirty while the other implies a level of familiarity or even implied threat.

One thing that you need to keep in mind: women frequently find that people treat their personal space as public property. Understanding how to navigate the space between welcome – even invited – and unwelcome contact is critical.

The key to understanding the message contained in your touch is to understand the intimacy ladder; different locations on the body are considered more "acceptable" or "friendly" while others are seen as being much more personal and a few will be seen as incredibly intimate.

While this will vary depending on the individual, in most Western societies, the general level of implied intimacy – from lowest to highest – goes like this:

- Upper arm
- Feet[2]
- Shoulder
- Forearm
- Back of the hand
- Upper back
- Palm
- Waist
- Lower back
- Thighs
- Hair
- Neck
- Face

I don't list breasts, crotch or butt for obvious reasons: reaching for those without a clear invitation is going to guarantee you a well-earned visit from the Slap Fairy.

How you touch someone also changes the message

2. It's worth noting that many cultures – especially Hindu and Muslim ones – see the foot as dirty or impure and touching somebody with them is a serious faux pas at best and a deliberate insult at worst. Still other people have an aversion to feet for one reason or another and touching their feet or with yours can give them the wiggins. Tread carefully.

being sent. Touching somebody with the back of your hand, for example, is considerably less intimate and more innocuous than the fingertips. Touching somebody lightly with your fingertips is going to be more flirty and intimate. Your full palm implies a much greater degree of familiarity and intimacy and – depending on where you touch her – possibly an expectation of compliance.

It's also worth noting: this is very dependent both on social context and on the individual. Everyone has their own boundaries and sense of body privacy. Some people will be cool with you touching their hair. Other people will be *very* offended if you do so without their permission. Some people will have less issue with, say, a playful ass-grab (especially between friends) than they would with a hand on the lower back. If you are unsure, it's better to keep to less-intimate forms of contact until you're getting clear signals from the other person.

How to Read Her Touch

Just as you're communicating intent through touch, so is she. The way that she responds to your touch tells you everything about how she's feeling about you. As I mentioned in Chapter 5, one of the ways you can tell someone is interested in you is through what's known as "reciprocal touching" – she touches you after you touch her. For example: as you're telling a joke or a funny story, touch her on the arm, then casually take your hand back and wait to see how she responds. If she's interested, she'll find an excuse to touch you back, most likely in the same fashion. Similarly, if your foot is pressed up against hers or your knee is up against hers as you sit together, disengage for a moment. Someone who's into you is going to want to re-establish contact quickly.

You can also gauge her interest in you by how she responds to certain touches, especially ones that are more intimate or lingering. If you put your hand on her lower back, does she relax into it? If you give the side-hug or put your arm around her shoulder, does she stand there or does she lean in towards you? The more she relaxes or conforms to you, the more interested she is. Even a basic hug can tell you how she feels. Someone who isn't interested in you sexually is going to give you the "a-frame" hug – one that's mostly shoulders, with plenty of space between your pelvis and hers. Someone who is into you is more likely to hug you around the waist or give more contact from the waist down.

One important thing to keep in mind is that her responses will also tell you when your touch is unwanted or is making her uneasy. If you put your hand on her forearm and she freezes or pulls her arm away, then you're actively making her uncomfortable. Similarly, if she tenses up when you put your hand on her back or give her a side-hug, then she's very emphatically *not* cool with you touching her like that. In the event that you've pushed too far or have accidentally tripped up on an area that she's not comfortable with you touching, then you simply disengage calmly – not like you've just put your hand on a hot stove – and say, "That seemed to make you uncomfortable. I'm sorry."

As a general rule of thumb, you want to be the person who disengages first when you've touched her in a way she's not comfortable with. Noticing that you're pushing up against a boundary and being willing to pull back is a sign that you respect her comfort levels and prioritize her feeling secure around you over your access to her body, an important trait.

How to Touch Her

Whether you're looking to hook up that night or to get a date later in the week, you want to be working your way up the intimacy ladder towards more flirty, personal forms of touch.

(Note very carefully that you're not trying to push boundaries or see what she "lets you get away with." Trying to pressure somebody to let you touch their neck or face is not the same as building mutual attraction.)

The best way to initiate a touch when you're just starting to talk to someone is in response to an emotional high point. For example, when you're telling a story, one of the best moments to touch someone briefly (three seconds or so) is during a check-in. Casually touch her on her upper arm with the back of your hand as you say, "Seriously, check this out." Another time would be when she tells you something that makes you laugh: then touch her shoulder or upper back with your fingertips.

Another way to use touch to build attraction is to use it to enhance a sense of intimacy. For instance, gently place your fingertips on her forearm as you lean in to whisper conspiratorially or share a secret. It feels much more intimate – in a good way –and reinforces the "us vs. them" feeling, framing the two of you as a conspiracy of two watching everyone else. A touch on the forearm while making a request – "Hey, I'm going to get another drink. Keep me company?" – makes her much more likely to come with you.

As you continue flirting and she's growing more comfortable with you, you want to move to more playful forms of deliberate touching. Use playful pushes or shoves when you tease her or when she tells you a joke; not only do these signal your interest in her, but they help her feel more comfortable with increasingly intimate forms of contact. It's easier to give a side-hug during an emotional high point when you're at a more touchy-feely stage of flirting than when you're still feeling each other out. You might hip-check one another as part of a joke or link arms to go get refills on your drinks.

As you progress, you'll find that your mutual touches are starting to linger longer than a casual brush of arms or a quick palm on the shoulder. This is when you can start moving to more intimate forms of touching, finding excuses to give more overtly sexual forms of touch. For example, you might take her hand for an impromptu palm-reading and trace your finger along their palm. I'm fairly extensively tattooed and frequently field questions from people I'm flirting with about whether (or how much) it hurt to be inked. If we're at the right stage, I might take their arm and lightly run my finger along the inside of their forearm or the underside of their upper arm as a way of illustrating a point about sensitivity. You might take her hand while you're showing her something on your phone or put your arm around her waist.

It can be a bit obvious, but at this stage, it's also *fun*. When you're progressing to these more intimate touches, you're already well on the way towards even greater intimacy. It's only a matter of time before one or the other of you takes the plunge and makes an obvious move. In fact, you can use touch to bring her arousal to the point of no return by building towards the perfect moment for a kiss.

One of the classic "moves" that leads towards a kiss is to move in slowly and gently brush a stray hair out of the way with your fingertips. Other touches such as a feather-soft brush of the jawline or the cheekbone can also get the heart racing. Touching someone's face is incredibly intimate, but also unbelievably arousing at the same time. Touching her lets you gauge the mood, since if she tenses up or pulls back slightly, you know you're getting the wave-off. If she's into it, however – her pupils dilate, her lips part slightly, she leans in – then not only are you golden, but your touch will be electric in all the best ways.

EMOTIONAL RAPPORT

Physical attraction is all well and good, but for true chemistry, you need more than just sexual desire. You need to engage her on an intellectual and emotional level as well. It's one thing for someone to think that you're desirable. It's another entirely when you can make her feel like she's known you for all of her life. There's nothing that screams "chemistry" quite as much as when she feels like you get her in a way that nobody else does or she has so much fun being with you that she loses all track of time.

If you can't inspire her emotions and build rapport, then you aren't going to get anywhere. Apathy is the death of desire; the least attractive people aren't the ones who she dislikes, but the ones who make her feel *bored*. You want to be the man who makes her feel on *every* level, not the one who makes her realize she's just wasted precious minutes of her life. Connecting on an intimate and personal level – exchanging information, sharing secrets – creates a powerful connection between the two of you.

Communicate Your Passion

One of the first things you should do to build attraction is to show your passion. Passion is compelling and intriguing. People who have passion in their lives have drive and certainty that other people don't, and that makes them absolutely magnetic. We are drawn to passion in others because it kindles our own emotions. When you're passionate about something, you're more energetic, you're more at ease, more full of life. Passionate people have a certainty about them and when they can talk about the things they are passionate about, it's hard not to get caught up in their emotional rhythm. That certainty is captivating; we're drawn to it because we're so used to doubt and restraint. Being willing to express yourself, to live life to the fullest is one of the most attractive behaviors there is.

My go-to example for the ability of passion to form connections is Tom Cruise. No matter whether you think he's a great actor or a couch-jumping, cult-obsessed nut job, you can't deny that he's intensely charismatic. His ability to convey his excitement for even the most mundane subjects picks you up and carries you along almost against your will. One of the best examples of the power of passion to build chemistry comes from a thirty-second clip in *Mission Impossible 3*. Ethan Hunt is a super-spy tasked with some of the most dangerous missions anyone could perform… but his day-to-day cover is that he's a traffic engineer at the Department of Transportation. When he's asked about his job, he doesn't dismiss it as boring or play it down as uninteresting. Instead, he sums it up in a way that's short, sweet and *utterly compelling:* "I study traffic patterns. You hit your brakes for a second, just tap them on the freeway, you can literally track the ripple effect of that action across a 200 mile stretch of road… because traffic has a memory. It's amazing, it's like a living organism." He has a firm gaze and a light tone, speaking with a smile, as opposed to looking down and away, shuffling his feet. In the hands of a lesser actor, this would be a moment to make the character look disconnected from the people around him. Instead, Cruise's emotion and *passion* sell it; when the two women nearby say, "I'd marry him," you *believe* it… because for just a second there, you were caught up in his spell.

Learn how to take what you're passionate about and *sell* what you love about it with confidence. Being able to bring that level of emotion, that *passion* to your dates is going to make them want to connect with you.

Use the Right Words

Words have power. Using the right words can utterly transform the way we describe things, the way we talk about ourselves or each other, and even the way we tell our stories. When we use the *right* words we can foster an immediate sense of intimacy and familiarity. By the same token, when we use the *wrong* ones, we close ourselves off and push people away… even when we didn't mean to.

When we're talking with someone, especially

somebody we like and want to like us, then we have to be careful not to use "I" or "me" too often. This may seem like an absurd idea, but the more you say "I" or "me" when you're talking to somebody, the more you're shutting them out. You're making the conversation about you, which is a common mistake; we are our own favorite subjects. If you want to bond with someone and get them to like you, the best thing you can do is encourage them to talk about themselves.

One of the ways that you can avoid seeming selfish is to use "you" more. In fact, by inserting "you" into sentences – saying, "As I was telling you" rather than "Like I was saying," for example – you're no longer monologuing. Instead, it feels like you're actively including them in the conversation, even if you're actually doing most of the talking. "You" also makes for excellent check-ins while telling stories. Using phrases like "You've been there, right?" or "You know what I mean?" helps rivet their attention. It feels like you're soliciting their opinion, which makes them feel validated.

You also want to use "we" whenever possible. "We should have another drink," "Shall we go," "We're going to get in so much trouble" and the like all support the idea of the two of you as a single unit. It subliminally links the two of you together, creating almost instant intimacy. Being able to refer back to something that's already happened while using "we" is also powerful. It's a way of reinforcing that you're *already* a couple in some ways and implies a shared history… even when you've only known each other for a half hour.

The other word you want to use whenever possible is their name. There is no word that catches our attention – or gratifies us – so much as our own name. If you can drop somebody's name into the conversation at regular intervals, it keeps their attention and makes you much more compelling and persuasive. It's a surprisingly simple, yet powerful way of creating a feeling of connection between the two of you. Giving someone a playful nickname is also another way of building rapport; it becomes something that just the two of you share. As a bonus: it also makes you that much more memorable when you text them later on...

Share Secrets

One of the strongest ways to bond with somebody is to share information about yourself. When somebody opens up to us, we feel gratified that they trust us enough to share something that (we assume) nobody else knows; we're so special that we get to know things that other people don't. Trading those secrets back and forth can create an immediate and *powerful* bond. In fact, when done right, you can end up building an incredible rapport in under half an hour.

Now, it's important to note that this doesn't mean you just start rambling about the time your parents got divorced or the first time your ex broke your heart, stole your dog and gave you the clap. There's a difference between sharing an emotional truth and radically over-sharing. Share too much too early, and you end up looking desperate for approval or that you aren't socially well calibrated. Instead, you want to start with something relatively shallow and work up to the deeper truths.

This is one of the reasons why I love to play the Question Game with women I'm flirting with. It's an excellent way to start sharing secrets and building intimacy quickly, supercharging that "getting to know you" period and leaving you feeling like you've known each other for years. Start with simple questions like "What are you passionate about?" or "What is the greatest accomplishment of your life?" and work up to deeper questions.

Just be sure to trade back and forth, secret for secret. You want this to be an equal exchange, not just one person running off at the mouth. This keeps you from sharing too much, too quickly and leaves you both feeling like you're on equal footing.

Make Her Qualify Herself

Another way to build an emotional connection is to ask her to explain why you should like her.

Yes, I realize that this seems a little Jedi Mind-Trick-y and manipulative, but there's a point to this. Stick with me for a minute.

Everybody, no matter how confident or secure they are with themselves, wonders why the person they're on a date with would be interested in them. Women especially are prone to this. A lifetime of experience has taught them that the majority of men are going to see them as potential sex objects first and potential partners second. While there will be plenty of times when women will want to find someone who's only interested in sex, it gets tedious when it feels like every guy she meets doesn't see past her boobs. A man who gets her and sees why she's awesome, on the other hand, is going to be much more attractive to her because of how rare he is.

When you're trying to build that emotional connection, you want your potential partner to know that you see and value her for more than just superficial qualities, whether it be money, looks or sexual desirability. It can be hard to shake someone out of their reservations; women have plenty of reasons to be suspicious of men's motivations, especially if they've gone out with a few assholes who thought they could manipulate their way into getting laid. So in order to show that we get them... we're going to ask for their help by asking them to explain why they're awesome. We are asking them to, essentially, qualify themselves to us.

The key to qualification is to have the right attitude. You're not telling them that they need to seek your approval and prove their worth to you. Your goal with qualification is two-fold. First: you're screening for the traits that you want in a partner; after all, if you're the outdoorsy type who likes to go hiking and mountain biking, you don't want to date a homebody who gets killer cedar-fever as soon as they set foot outside. Second: you're wanting to find out more about what makes this person awesome.

The process of qualification is simple: you ask them what makes them amazing and then you agree with them that they're amazing.

Qualifications are easy to work into the "getting to know you" stage of dates. In fact, they fit in perfectly with sharing secrets as a way of bonding. You start off with low-investment questions ("Are you adventurous?") that lead to reasons to compliment them ("Awesome, I love adventurous people because they're so exciting and into trying new things.") and then take it a bit further ("So what's the most exciting, whacked out thing you've ever done, and please don't tell me it was something lame like sneaking into a movie you didn't pay for...").

See what you did there?

Right there, you've asked them to tell you that they're cool (because they're adventurous), complimented them for being cool (because you like adventurous people), and engaged them a bit further with a challenging, flirty tease, while also showing that you find their experiences interesting. By giving a gentle tease, you're using the push-pull dynamic to keep them interested. By complimenting them on being adventurous, you're validating them – giving them approval and a bit of an ego-boost – which helps build rapport. It doesn't *matter* that they literally just told you about that part of themselves; you commenting on it short-circuits the logical part of the brain and heads straight for the emotional center.

Qualification is an incredibly versatile tool for building emotional rapport with someone. You can change the subject with another question ("What are you passionate about?" "So is $JOB something you've always wanted to be growing up, or did you want to do something else?") or take it further by making an observation about them and turning that into a qualification ("You know, I can tell from $INSERT_QUALITY_HERE that you're $INSERT_DESIRABLE_QUALITY HERE and that's really cool; I like people who are $DESIRABLE_QUALITY because...").

Just make sure that when you're qualifying someone, you keep those questions and compliments about non-physical aspects. The message you're sending someone when you use qualifications is that you understand them as a person, not just a pretty face or a lovely body.

BUILDING SEXUAL TENSION

One of the key components of chemistry is sexual tension. Not just attraction – you can find someone attractive or even be attracted to them but not feel that "spark" – but tension. Sexual tension is desire for someone that is somehow thwarted by circumstance, obstacles... or by design.

It's a facet of human nature that we want that which is denied to us. The easiest way to make someone want something is to tell them they can't have it. If you want to see someone go mad with desire for an object, hold it just outside of their reach. Like a kitten with a piece of yarn, we couldn't care less about it when it's within our grasp, but when you pull it *away* from us, suddenly it's much more enticing. When your desire for something is frustrated, you tend to want it more. Marketers know this, which is why they practice artificial scarcity; they'll tell you, "Call now, supplies are running out!" and rub their hands as people rush to buy before it disappears. Companies under-ship products to guarantee news that the hot new gadget sold out in record time.

Want to see frustrated desire in action? Check eBay the morning after a new iPhone is released; people will pay hundreds of dollars over the suggested retail price in hopes of getting a new phone *now* rather than waiting a month.

The same principle applies to dating; we want what we can't have. But you can't just dance around saying, "You can't have me" and expect to get anywhere. You have to actually build that attraction first. Before you can have tension, you need anticipation.

The Thrill of Antici...

Anticipation is all about the build-up. It's the excitement of knowing that something is coming matched with the suspense of not knowing *when* it's going to happen. It's a matter of managing expectations and subverting them. Once you know something is imminent, your attention focuses on it automatically. You're waiting for it to happen. The longer it takes, the more you want it.

Think of riding a rollercoaster. The most thrilling moments aren't the corkscrew turns or the loops and twists or the hard-banking turns. The thrill comes from the long, slow ratcheting climb up that first hill, when you *know* that drop is coming but you're not exactly sure when. Your brain starts to positively scream because it knows that you're about to drop, but the delay – the anticipation – is getting so intense that you just can't stand it, and right when you're about to explode...

...The car crests over the hill and suddenly you're in free fall, screaming with pleasure. Everything else about the coaster is part of the release that comes from all that built-up tension that leaves you happy and spent and ready to get in line to do it all over again.

Similarly, the best, most amazing kisses aren't the ones that just *happen* or the ones where you both just leap in and maul each other's faces. The most powerful kisses are the ones that you know are coming and where the air is so filled with tension that you can cut it with a knife but your heart is pounding so loud that you're amazed the neighbors aren't complaining about the noise and you're moving towards each other so tentatively, so slowly that it's all you can do not to just dive forward to cover the distance. When your lips do meet, the build-up has been so intense that release is almost like an explosion rather than a kiss.

Now imagine that rather than actually kissing, she pulls back at the last second. How badly you want that kiss *now?*

...pation

This is the key to sexual tension: the build up, the frustration, then the release. It's the game of "go away a little closer," where you pull someone in, then push them away. You build up the anticipation, then cut it off by releasing it

As counterintuitive as it may seem, that release is a critical part of building the sexual tension. Constant sexual arousal is actually *boring*; it goes from being exciting to just "how things are." You both become desensitized to the feeling, which in turn actually makes you less interested in the actual culmination of that arousal. You need more and more stimulus in order to reach the same level of excitement; by the time you actually sleep together, it's almost an anticlimax.

Releasing the tension is important because the arousal created is made even more noticeable by its sudden absence. When you've suddenly pulled back, you're effectively creating an emotional vacuum, which leads the other person to want to fill it. They've become used to that pleasurable feeling; now that it's gone, they're going to want it *back*. Pulling away, providing that release, leads to uncertainty: they don't know when or if that feeling of excitement and arousal is going to come back. By parceling the tension out, little by little, you make it that much more enticing. Those little bursts of tension keep people interested. Doling tension out in intervals makes them more invested. By adding uncertainty to the mix – never being quite sure when you're going to start building the anticipation again – they remain receptive, even *eager* for you to build it back. The uncertainty, the feeling as though you're getting closer then having it pulled away, builds the overall desire for the ultimate resolution.

How do you release? Well, there are various ways, depending on what it is you're doing.

Release Through Flirting

As I mentioned earlier, I'm a fan of playful flirting with just a hint of teasing antagonism. This style of flirting is all about the struggle for dominance and controlling the framing of the interaction. It's a question who holds the upper hand in the interaction and, by extension, the relationship. The important part of antagonistic flirting is that it's meant to be fun, a sort of verbal sparring match rather than an actual fight. Power exchange and dominance struggles can be hot; they build a tension that demands resolution. In this case, the tension is built by the sparring banter – the playful teases pushing against one another before releasing by paying a compliment. Alternately, you can pay the compliment, then take it back with a tease.

One of the greatest examples of this style of flirting is in the James Bond movie *Casino Royale*. When James

Bond and Vesper Lynd are introduced to one another on the train to Montenegro, the attraction between Lynd and Bond is electric and immediate. Within moments of meeting one another, they're striking sparks off one another with little teasing digs paired with surprising insight into each other's character before concluding with Vesper complimenting James about his perfect arse.

This is how teasing and antagonistic flirting works: a compliment followed by a tease, or a tease followed by a compliment. In both cases, they ratchet up the tension and then let it go. They're both a little combative, a little dismissive and a little playfully condescending, but they never cross the line into actual insult. It's an unspoken agreement that this is just play fighting, where any sting is taken away with the compliment.

When you put this into practice, you flirt and banter, then release by cutting the conversational thread and moving on to another topic – one unrelated to what you were just discussing and one that doesn't immediately lead to another verbal fencing match. You need to space things out to give the tension room to grow. Going from tease to tease constantly can be exhausting emotionally; you end up feeling as though you're constantly having to be on guard rather than letting yourself relax and enjoy each other's company.

Release Through Touch

I can't say this enough times: you have to get used to touching when you're trying to get better at dating. The power that touch has with building sexual tension cannot be understated. Physical contact is a key component to sexual tension; call it one of the benefits of those thousands of nerve endings we have running through our skin. Now, to be sure, you need a certain level of intimacy and comfort before you can move from casual touching to more sexually charged touch; you don't want to just reach up and stroke the neck of the woman you just met at the bar unless you're interested in wearing an amaretto sour for the rest of the night. However, as you've grown more comfortable with one another and built up that level of trust and intimacy, then touch can become one of your most powerful resources for building tension.

It's important to remember that touches intended to raise arousal and build tension should be slow and deliberate. A quick, tentative touch not only isn't appealing, it signals nervousness; your partner is going to pick up on that nervousness and even start feeling awkward herself. A deliberate touch, on the other hand, signals confidence and assurance. Confidence is sexy, after all.

You also want to vary *how* you touch her, depending on where you're planning on touching. Some areas merit a soft, gentle touch, even just a brush of the fingertips rather than the full palm or pressure. A good rule of thumb is that the softer or less exposed the skin is, the lighter the touch should be. For example, a brushing your fingers lightly against the crook of her elbow, down her forearm or at the inside of her wrist are ways of making her shiver. You might run your nails gently down her back or the back of an arm and send delicious tremors down her spine. Warm breath on the neck – perhaps accompanied by "You smell nice" – can make the difference between a chaste kiss and being grabbed by the back of your favorite head for sloppy make-outs. The hair can also be an incredibly charged area; stroking the hair, or even running your fingers through it and grasping it gently near the scalp can help charge things up.

A woman's back and hips also offer an opportunity to ratchet up the tension. A hand on the small of the back, guiding your date through the restaurant or to your car can be quite the turn-on. Contact should be firm but brief; leaving your hand there quits being sensual and becomes possessive very quickly, while that brief contact can be electric. Moving in close so that you're sharing personal space and letting the inside of your knee brush up against hers can be incredibly electric. Just be sure that she's welcoming you being that close, otherwise you're about to get a knee in an even more sensitive area.

Remember: you have to also allow for the release. Move in, make the touch – perhaps while saying something in her ear – then take a step back.

Playing Hard to Get Works

Another way of building tension and raising her attraction to you is to play hard to get. But it's not just about suddenly having last-minute plans or never returning her calls. In fact, study after study has found that being difficult to get ahold of or making people work to earn one's attention doesn't actually increase that person's desirability. Someone who's hard to get may be a challenge, but they're often not necessarily seen as being *worth* it.

However, giving the impression of being a challenge or hard to get but being *enthusiastic* about the person trying to get you increases your attractiveness immensely.

You see, the difference between playing hard to get and being hard to get but eager and interested in the person pursuing you is in the message being sent. With the former, it's simply that the person is scarce and possibly picky. With the latter, you're saying, "I'm choosy... but I've chosen *you*." Keeping them off balance initially by giving attention and building attraction infrequently and at varying intensities works to keep them from being too used to your attention. At a party, for example, you may approach a woman you're interested in and flirt with her for a while before moving on to talk to somebody else. Later on, you reengage her for a little while before moving on to other people. Then you reengage her again.

Flirting and then walking away is another form of the push and pull dynamic; you're drawing her in with your banter and releasing it by ending the interaction. That intermittent reinforcement makes you more attractive and desirable. The reward (your attention) is that much more effective because she can only get it *occasionally*, which makes her want to work that much harder to get and keep you around.

"That's All You Get for Now"

When things are going well – you're at the point of serious physical contact, up to and including kissing – then being the one to set a limit is an incredible way to ratchet up the tension immediately.

One popular gambit I've learned (and used to great success) from player friends of mine is what's known as the "almost-kiss." There are many variations of this, but the most common method is to set it up by suggesting that you try an almost-kiss. You play it off as a joke: "Okay, I like you and I'm having a good time with you, but I'm *not* quite sure how I feel about you. So I think it's time for an 'almost kiss.' Here's how it works: we lean in close – as if we were actually going to kiss – before pulling back. But you have to pinkie-swear to me that you're not going to actually kiss me, because it's just too soon. Swear?"

You lean in close as though for a kiss and hover close to their lips for a moment or two and then pull back, possibly with a dramatic flourish for comedic effect. It's a powerful way of building tension quickly; you're getting all of the build-up and none of the pay-off. That sort of frustrated desire *demands* to be released. You're building up the sexual tension then pulling back just as you're starting to get near the point of no return. It can take some practice to deliver properly; if you're not careful, the set-up is going to sound cheesy, and not in a charming way, but it's a powerful technique.

Another way form of the push-pull dynamic is to create an artificial limit. One of my favorites comes when you're at the stage of kissing someone but not quite at the point of sex. After a particularly passionate kiss, pulling yourself away and keeping a little distance between you. Give a knowing smile and say, "Okay, that's all you get for now."

It may seem counter-intuitive – if you're kissing, you would think you would want to try to move things forward, not backwards – but showing restraint, taking the tension to a crescendo and leaving it there dials the sexual tension way up. It's a powerful move... and it's better to leave them wanting more than pushing too far and risking blowing the whole thing.

Setting a limit like that is almost a direct challenge

to the woman you're pursuing, and if you've been doing your job correctly, it'll be one she won't be able to resist.

CHAPTER 8.

THE ATTRACTION PLAN

MAPPING OUT THE APPROACH

It's been said before that the world would be a happier place if dating were more like video games.

Okay, maybe I said it, back in the day. But in its own way, it makes sense.

After all, with games, you ultimately know what to expect. The nature of the medium dictates that everything happens according to specific rules. If you spend enough time paying attention, you will start to recognize certain patterns. Once you've correctly identified these patterns, you can thus formulate a way to maximize your effort in order to achieve your goal, whether it's to complete the raid, take out that bastard sniper across the map, overthrow Kefka, bring down the globe-spanning conspiracy, or find out whether another damn mushroom is about to tell you that your princess is in another castle.

The point being that if meeting and attracting women was more like a game, you could eventually find a perfect pathway to get to the end, whether it's a specific pattern or a cheat code. Enter up, up, down, down, left, right, left, right, B, A, start and you have all the chances you need to end up swimming through tail like Scrooge McDuck diving through his money bin.

This is part of what makes the Pick-Up Artist community so attractive to so many men; it provides a sense of certainty that is often absent in dating. Many pick-up schools, especially the more routine-based ones, promise sex by flow chart. Follow this pattern and everything will fall into place exactly as you want it to. Unfortunately, following routines is actually counter-productive when it comes to approaching women; not only does it make you come off like a robot, but it ultimately makes it impossible to be genuine. You're constrained by having to follow the flow chart instead of simply enjoying where the conversation goes.

However, it *does* help to have a plan.

So many of our issues with dating come from a place of fear; fear of rejection, fear of being humiliated or fear of that moment midway through talking to someone you are brain-meltingly attracted to and realizing, *Oh shit, I don't know what to say next!*

Why do we keep trying to find the "perfect moment" to approach someone we want to meet? Because we're afraid and we want to put off facing that fear. Why do we keep looking for magical openers or silver bullets that will somehow make attracting women an effortless, pushbutton affair? Because we're afraid that what we're going to screw it all up and we want 100% assurance that we can't fail.

Control – or the illusion of control – helps to assuage that fear. Treating approaching women like we're assembling furniture from Ikea (follow the steps A through Børk and don't forget your Allen wrench) gives us the feeling that it's out of our hands; there's nothing we can do to screw it up. All we need to do is not deviate from the plan.

The problem, of course, is that women aren't flat-pack furniture. Every interaction is different and each magic bullet you find is just a placebo, an illusion. Ultimately, they become a hindrance; you're not being your authentic self, you're borrowing somebody else's personality. You're not interacting with a person; you're trying to treat them like an app on your phone where repeating specific behaviors get the same results every time. Humans and interactions simply don't work like that. As a wise man once said: It is possible to commit no mistakes and still lose... that is just life.

Routines and magic bullets are ultimately useless. There's no value to canned stories and "DHV stories"[1] about your model ex-girlfriend.

There is, however, value to having a plan.

Now that you've done all of the prep work, it's time to put everything into action. Everything that you've been studying and practicing is about to come together; it's time to stop reading and start actually approaching those amazing women you wish you could meet.

THE ATTRACTION PLAN

Having a basic structure and template to follow when you're starting out gives you the flexibility to be yourself and still maintain the confidence of knowing what to say

---

1. A PUA term meaning "demonstration of higher value" – that is, stories that indicate that you're an individual with high social status.

and when you should say it. It helps you relax because you have enough of an idea of where you're going and how to get there, even if you aren't sure of the specifics. When you quit treating trying to approach a woman like trying to bring the One Ring to Mount Doom – full of twists and turns and unpleasant surprises – then you aren't as likely to have those "Oh God, NOW what do I do?" panic attacks.

Having a basic structure helps you put your focus on the areas that do you the most good – finding commonalities and building an emotional rapport – rather than on gimmicks and distractions like "demonstrations of higher value" or an overly clever opening line.

Actually making an approach can be intimidating, but it's really fairly simple. While every approach is different on an individual level, successful approaches tend to follow a pattern. You initiate the conversation, you build rapport by looking for common areas of interest and try to connect with them on an individual level, while indulging in some flirting and banter as a way of building sexual chemistry. As they become more interested in you, you work at establishing a deeper connection and reaffirm *their* interest in *you*. You check in on occasion, evaluating her interest in you. Then, as things reach their crescendo, you make your move: you get her number, you make the date or head out together on a mini-date. You may go for the kiss… or even bring her back to your place.

The great thing about the NerdLove Attraction Plan is its versatility. Once you've mastered the basics, you can shape this to fit your personality and style. Whether you're approaching party girls in bars and clubs or quiet, intense intellectuals at the coffeehouse, the underlying mechanics remain the same.

So let's walk you through the process, step by step.

Pre-Step: Establish an Artificial Time Constraint

The first step of an approach is to set up what is known as an artificial time constraint.

How many times have you been stopped by somebody who wanted to ask you a question? Maybe they're soliciting donations for a charity. Maybe they're trying to get you to come to their performance. Maybe they want you to come to their meeting so they can save your soul. Regardless of whether you're at a bar, walking down the street or at the grocery store, as soon as someone you don't know comes up and starts talking, your guard tends to go up. It doesn't really matter what they're saying, because you're already wondering how long this person's going to be bugging you. For all you know, he or she is determined to talk your ear off and now you're going to have that awkward moment when you're trying to drop hints that you have to go and they just keep missing them.

That's why when you approach someone, you want to establish an artificial time constraint: you're saying that you're not going to take up their time for very long. Knowing that there's a hard limit to how long you will be there – and knowing that you'll hit that limit soon – helps people to relax and lower their guard a little. They're more likely to listen to what you're *actually* saying, because in a worst-case scenario, you're a temporary annoyance at best.

(Of course, you and I know that they're soon going

to realize that you're someone awesome that they never knew they wanted to meet. But they don't know that yet.)

You want to introduce the artificial time constraint as quickly as possible. Either you lead with it or you follow up your opening with it. So if you were approaching a woman at a bookstore, you might say, "Hey, I'm actually about to walk out the door, but before I go…" Alternately, if you're using an indirect opening line – asking for her opinion on a book, for example – then after she answers, you might say, "Cool. I've really got to get back to my friends, but the reason I'm asking is…"

The artificial time constraint also gives you a ready excuse to leave at your convenience. If things are going well, then you can say, "Hey, I'm having a great time talking to you and I want to do this again, but I really have to go/get back to my friends/catch a cab. I'd love to see you some time, how can we make that happen?" If things aren't going well… "Hey, it's great talking to you, but I've gotta run."

Don't worry if you stay longer than you said you were going to; you can excuse it with "I'm having such a good time talking to you…" and stick around.

Step 1: The Opening

Trying to find the perfect line is where a lot of people get tripped up. Like I said before: opening is literally the simplest and least important part of an approach. All you're doing is getting the conversation started. Your excuse for coming up to them is that you want to meet them and what you say really doesn't matter as long as you have confidence – relaxed body language, a friendly smile, strong eye-contact, speaking slowly and clearly – and you transition into an actual conversational thread.

I tend to start most conversations the same way: "Hey…" or "Hey guys," to get their attention. From there, you proceed to how you want to start the conversation.

Some people are more comfortable being indirect and use a situational opening: "Hey, what's with all of the top-hats at this party? I'm suddenly feeling underdressed," or "Did you just see this crazy thing that happened outside?" Others like to ask for an opinion: "Can guys still get away with earrings?" or "Would you date a guy who's still friends with his ex?"

For people who're shy, being indirect makes things a little easier. Not only do they give you an immediate conversational topic, but they relieve the anxiety of being called out for hitting on someone, even though that's precisely what you want to do.

The potential problem with this approach is that it's very easy to get stuck. If you're shy or dealing with approach anxiety, it can feel more comfortable sticking with the conversation you already have going on instead of trying to shift gears to the next step. As a result, your interaction ends up going nowhere and you're stuck talking about nothing. You have to be willing to cut a conversational thread and move on to an actual conversation if you go indirect.

Personally, I prefer to be direct. "Hey, you seem like you're a cool person and I wanted to meet you. Hi, my name's…" or "You seem like you're cool. Are you friendly?" are almost always socially relevant. Being direct helps ensure that you have their full attention and establishes early on what your intentions are: you're interested in them and want to get to know them. If you're especially confident, you can even inject a little banter into the interaction, like: "I just wanted you to know: you are so... blocking my way to the bar" (said deadpan and followed with a big grin).

Regardless of whether you go indirect or direct, you don't want to linger on the opening; all you're trying to do is get them interested in talking to you. If you take longer than five minutes to get from asking an opinion to getting to know them, you've gotten hung up on the open and need to segue into actually talking to them.

Step 2: Start Building Rapport

No matter what sort of opening you used, you want to move quickly to an actual conversation where you can start building rapport and attraction with her. This means you want to transition from whatever you said – especially if you were indirect and were asking for an opinion on something – to getting to know her.

There are a number of ways of doing this; if you've just gone in directly, you can simply introduce yourself. If you went in asking for an opinion, then you can pivot off of what she had to say: "Oh, wait, so men and women can't be friends after they break up? I like to think that people are more complex than that. Sure, it hurts at first but if the relationship is strong..." You can ask a question that leads to a story: "Hey, have you ever done $THING? Oh, check this out..." You can use a simple phrasal transition: "Hey, you know, that reminds me... "You can make an observation about her and use that as a transition into an actual conversation.

Or you could just jump the conversational rails and start talking about something else.

Once you have the person's attention, it's time to start building interest and attraction. You want her to feel that spark, that mix of emotional engagement and sexual attraction that leaves her intrigued and wanting more. You do this by building rapport with her, finding the things you have in common while keeping a certain sense of playful fun in the interaction by flirting and injecting a little sexual tension. You want to communicate that you like her as a person but also that you're interested in her sexually. It's a fine balance; you want to develop an emotional connection with the person you're flirting with as well as a physical or sexual one.

Attraction is as much about emotions as it is about sexual chemistry. Even if somebody may think you're hot buttered sex on toast, they're not going to want to fuck you if you repulse them emotionally. In the early stages of the interaction, especially when you're starting out and earning your experience points, you want to focus on building the emotional rapport first and slowly ramp up the sexual attraction as she becomes more interested in you. Think of it in terms of ratios: 80% emotional and 20% sexual at first while slowly making them closer to 50-50 or even 40-60 by the end. As you become more socially experienced, you can experiment with finding the mix that works best for your personality and style as well as your goals.

In the early stages of building rapport, you're going to be asking a lot of questions. The trick is to not fall into interview mode; you're trying to get to know her, not interrogate her. You want to ask probing questions, ones that help get to the core of who she is as a person. Don't just stick to the surface answers, take what she has to say and follow it to the next level; get beyond the surface by trying to relate to her. One of the best ways to do this is to make statements or observations about her and what she has to say, then ask follow ups. For example:

You: "So what do you do when you're not meeting strange men at parties?"

Her: "Well, I study archeology and I play guitar."

You: "Wow, that's really cool. It must be an incredible feeling to be exploring history in such a concrete and tactile way. Bringing the past to life, trying to piece it all together and understand it in new and practical ways – that's really refreshing. Too many people seem to be stuck in the here-and-now and aren't interested in learning about what came before. Or do you just like finding ancient treasures in buried tombs?"[2]

You're taking the interaction deeper, getting into the core of a passion, relating to it and giving her feedback. You're connecting with her passion and telling her you think it's cool.

When it's *your* turn to answer questions, you want to share more than just the basics. Tell stories about yourself. You don't want to just say, "I like Black Sabbath," you want to share *why* you like Black Sabbath – without being a music snob about it. How does it make you feel? How did you get into Sabbath? What memories do you have attached to it? The more you can explain, the more commonalities you can find. She may not like heavy metal, but she may well be able to relate about finding music that speaks to her the way nothing else does.

In general, you want to guide the conversation (*guide*,

2. I know, I know, real archeology is nothing like Indiana Jones. But I used to date an archeologist and needling her with Tomb Raider jokes was way too much fun.

not force) in a direction that leads to building rapport. This means being willing to avoid small talk about work or TV – topics that she might talk about with casual friends – and focus on getting to know each other as people.

Step 2a: Break Rapport

Deliberately breaking rapport is an important part of flirting. Not only does it stimulate interest by keeping her off balance, it also establishes that you're also not a "yes man" or someone who thinks the way into a woman's pants is to pretend that you both like the exact same things. We may like people who are similar to us, but when we're exactly the same it feels phony, or worse, needy. Someone who is overly effusive in his praise or can't bring himself to disagree – or even argue – with an attractive woman is sub-communicating that he's desperate to be liked and that he's sucking up to her. This is why you want to remember the principle of the tease, the push-pull effect. You're building rapport, then deliberately breaking it, then building it again.

So be willing to disagree with her about things or even have an opposing viewpoint. Be willing to be a bit controversial… just don't be an asshole about it. Now, this isn't to say that you have to make something up in order to break rapport; you want to be authentic, not play weird dominance games. You also don't want to break rapport over serious issues or things she's especially passionate about. You don't want to tell the woman in the above example that you think archeology is stupid; you've just insulted her passion in life, after all. Keep it to small and specific issues: particular bands, books, movies, that sort of thing.

If you're doing it right, it should be glaringly obvious that you're not judging her as a person or calling her or her interests stupid. If she can't tell that you're not serious, then not only are you doing it wrong, you're being kind of an asshole. In fact, the more playful you can be, the less the disagreement will stick out as "he's a jerk" and more "okay, he's still cool."

Example:

You: Your favorite band is Mumford and Sons? It's a good thing you're fun to talk to because *man*, I dunno if we're music compatible.

Step 3: Ping Her Interest Levels

Every once in a while, you want to be able to gauge how things are going – is she into you or is she being polite and killing time until the social contract says she's allowed to leave? Periodic check-ins let you keep track of how you're doing and allow you to adjust your flirting as you go. If she's getting comfortable with you, then you're able to ramp up the sexual side of the flirting. If you detect signs that she's starting to pull back, you can adjust your approach until she's feeling better.

The signs that she's actually interested in you – as opposed to being polite – are fairly obvious if you stop to look for them. I covered many in Chapter 7, but some to look for include:

- How is she responding to you? Is she responding with interest to your questions and giving detailed answers, or is she giving short, curt responses? Is she volunteering information or is talking to her like pulling teeth? Someone who's really interested in you will give longer and more emotionally involved answers, often volunteering more personal information as a way of trying to connect with you.

- Just as importantly, is she asking you questions? Is she making a point to get to know more about you, or is she just waiting for her turn to talk?

- Watch her eyes. Is she making strong eye contact with you, or are her eyes darting around the room? Is she focusing on you or is she constantly checking her watch or her phone? These are all signs that she's looking for an excuse to get away from you. Looking around often means that she's hoping to see a friend and give a silent "SAVE ME ALREADY" sign. Checking her watch is a way of saying, "How long do I have to deal with this guy before he goes away?"

- Has her body language changed? Is she more open, facing you more directly or leaning in?

- Has her energy level dipped or spiked?

- Is she giving preening behavior – adjusting her clothes, fluffing her hair?

- Is she moving closer to you – whispering and leaning in or moving her head closer to yours? If you're sitting down somewhere, is she moving objects into your personal space?

- Touch is an important way of conveying interest. If you're touching her (and you should be) and you take your hand away, does she touch you back? I've had great success with the "side hug" – an arm across the shoulders during an emotional high point like an awesome story or being told a funny joke. Does she lean in or put her arm around you in return? These are signs that she's increasingly interested in you. Give her the high-five test; does she give you the flat-palm, or do her fingers interlock with yours?

- Is she willing to follow you someplace? One way of checking interest is to say, "Hey, I'm going to the bar. How about you come keep me company?" Someone who's interested in you will want to keep the conversation going. Someone who's not as invested in the interaction will be more likely to say, "That's okay, I'll catch up to you later."If she *does* go with you, buy her a drink, even if it's just water or soda. It's the least you can do to thank her for fighting her way to the bar with you.

Remember: watch for clusters of signs rather than individual ones. A sign by itself means little. Someone crossing her arms might be closed off to you… or she might be getting cold. Someone who's shifting her weight may be nervous and ready to leave, or she might be wearing uncomfortable shoes. Clusters of signals have more consistent meaning.

The more signs of interest you're seeing – or the more obvious they get – the better you're doing. If you're not seeing signs of interest, it's time to consider how far along you are in the interaction. If you've been talking to her for twenty minutes or longer and you're not getting much feedback from her, then it's likely that she's just not interested in you. Say your good-byes and move on. As a general rule, it's better to cut things short than to linger for too long in the conversation; in a worst-case scenario, you can always talk to her again later.

Step 4: Qualify Her

Once she's emotionally invested in talking to you, then it's time to take things a little deeper. You want to find out more about her, beyond the surface issues and more into what really makes her tick. At the same time, you want to show that you get her on a deep and personal level – that you see her for who she *really* is and what she has to offer.

Start off with a simple question: "Do you like to travel?" for example. Then you expand on it. "That's really cool; I love travelers, they're always the ones who're looking to find new adventures and take risks trying new experiences. Do you like sticking to the popular places, or do you like going a little off the beaten path?" From here you have a number of ways you can go: look for more commonalities by comparing travel stories, dig a little deeper into who they are or even take it in a flirty, sexy direction by making a tease about hooking up on vacation. You're screening for a trait you like (traveling in this case) by asking what's awesome about them, reinforcing that this makes them awesome and why (they like taking risks and trying new things) and expanding on it (What kind of traveling do you like to do? Have we been to the same places? What sort of person are you, someone who plays it safe or someone who likes a little edge?).

You should also ask more probing questions: "What are you passionate about?" "What's your most treasured memory?" "When's the last time you were *really* jealous?" "What's the craziest thing you've ever done?" "When's the last time you did something for yourself that was totally outside of your comfort zone?" These are all questions that take a greater level of investment, which is why you want to wait to ask them; after all, if she's not that into you, why would she want to tell you about her favorite memory?

It's incredibly powerful when done right; you're identifying a passion of hers, connecting to it and feeding back into it. Don't be surprised when she starts telling you that she's never told anyone about that before, or how it feels like she's known you for years. Qualification is the shortcut to a deep, emotional bond.

Step 5: Make Your Move

If things have been going well, then it's time to make your move. This is not a time to get cocky; you can do everything right and still screw up if you don't stick the landing. So you want to take care not to blow all the hard work you've put into this.

As a general rule of thumb, if the two of you have been talking and vibing for twenty minutes or so, she's going to be interested in talking to you later; it's a good time to ask for her number. A lot of guys will choke at this point, worrying about whether or not they're being too interested by asking for her number instead of hoping that she'll volunteer it. They're usually overthinking it. The script for asking is very simple: "Hey, I'm really enjoying talking to you, but I've got to go meet up with my friends and I'd like to see you again. What's the best way for me to reach you?" Short, simple and to the point; it also leaves the method of contact in her court. Some people really don't like talking on the phone and prefer to communicate over Facebook or email; pushing for a phone number from them is only going to be counterproductive.

Whenever possible, instead of just asking for her number, make *specific* plans to get together. Setting up a date for a specific day and time makes her much more likely to respond when you call or text her later. Again, just keep it simple: "I'm doing $COOL_THING on Friday and I think you'd really enjoy it. I'd love for you to come with me and check it out."

A lot of guys – especially the guys who're focusing on meeting women at bars and clubs – get caught up on getting the kiss or taking her home that night. And while getting a kiss or a make-out with someone you've just met can feel impressive... it's actually not as meaningful as you might think.

Don't get me wrong! That's not to say that kisses mean nothing, but they're highly contextual. Making out with someone at a club doesn't necessarily mean that she's going home with you that night, or even that she's really into you. She may be willing to make out with someone she met that night while the music is pounding and passions are high, but that doesn't mean that she's going to want to see him outside of the club. That being said: if that's what you want, then hey, go for it! Just don't assume it means more than she's willing to kiss you at that particular place and time.

If you're interested in going for the kiss, you want to look for signs that she's interested in being kissed... assuming she doesn't kiss you first. The classic sign is the triangle-gaze, looking from eye to lip to eye. How much space is she giving you? Someone who's interested in being kissed is going to be comfortable being up in your personal space. If you're holding her hand, give it a squeeze; if she squeezes back, she's much more likely to be interested in kissing you than if she doesn't respond.

5 GREAT PLACES TO MEET WOMEN... THAT AREN'T BARS OR CLUBS

When we talk about meeting women, we frequently talk about the bar and club scene... but that's not going to be everybody's cup of tea. It's loud, it's expensive, it's crowded, it's smoky, it's impossible to have a conversation in them. And besides, maybe the type of women you want to meet don't go to clubs. So where does a man go to meet awesome, beautiful women who *are* his type?

Well, here are five amazing places to meet women that aren't the bar or club scene.

Classes

One of the keys to becoming better with women is to be an interesting person. The best way to become interesting is to lead an active life and collect new experiences. Expose yourself to new concepts by taking some classes in subjects that've always interested you. Most colleges and universities will allow people to audit classes for a fee while others have continuing adult education programs. Even many high-end grocery stores will have classes in culinary knife skills, making sushi rolls and cooking Southwestern cuisine, for example. Taking extra classes is an excellent way to expand your horizons. Language, art history, life drawing, editing software and even learning how to play Texas hold'em all provide you with opportunities to get outside your comfort zone and try something new. Being able to meet women at the same time is a welcome bonus, isn't it?

Coffee Shops

Coffee shops are great places to meet women, especially during the daytime. Coffee shops are low-key, quiet places and most encourage lingering for hours. You'll find women studying, reading or just bored and killing time. Anyone who's at a coffee shop after the morning rush is likely to be there for a long haul, which nicely reduces any potential time constraints you may encounter when you're out meeting people. The relaxed atmosphere can play to your advantage; it's easier to start a conversation with someone who's just hanging out than someone who's clearly on their way to something. Books and sketchpads provide an instant opening for conversation, and a pleasant conversation could be precisely the sort of distraction that the women there would welcome. Another easy opening into talking to a woman: ask her to guard your laptop while you get a refill or go to the bathroom. When you come back, you say thanks and introduce yourself.

Do yourself a favor though, and focus on women who are open to being approached – they're the ones who'll seem aimless or distracted. If she's got her headphones on or she's absorbed in a book or her laptop, she's giving you the universal "Do Not Disturb" sign; leave her alone.

Amateur Sports Leagues

Just about every major city has a host of amateur sports leagues that go beyond the collegiate standbys of football and soccer. In fact, many of these leagues are dedicated to the happy regression to your childhood: kickball, dodgeball, disc golf, pool, beach volleyball, cornhole, skeeball and more. These aren't for your average musclehead ex-jocks who dream of the glory days back in high school before they realized they peaked early. The focus is on fun and socialization rather than competition.

Joining an amateur sports league is a great way to meet new people and make new friends. If you don't have enough interested friends or co-workers to field a team on your own, most leagues will help you find a team to join. Working together on a team promotes bonding and the endorphin rush that comes from exercise and victory puts everybody in a relaxed, outgoing mood... perfect for when you want to start building that chemistry. Even better, training together makes you both look good. When we anticipate spending time with people at future events, our brains automatically tend to focus on their good qualities.

Volunteer

Volunteering is an amazing way to meet women and do some good for your community in the process.

The odds are almost absurdly in your favor; surveys and studies have found women volunteer far more than men do. Going out to do community service will instantly make you stand out by virtue of being one of the few men there at all. Getting involved in politics, especially in an election year, is a great way of meeting women. Not only are you helping support your candidate, but electioneering is an incredibly emotionally charged process. You can easily get caught up in the swell of emotions; passion, after all, tends to breed passion in other areas as well. Many hookups have occurred between volunteers and staffers on the campaign trail.

Even outside of politics, there are ample opportunities for volunteers. Animal shelters are almost always desperate for help. Local theater groups, music and movie festivals, symphonies and orchestras are also ready for people to come lend a hand. Volunteering works on multiple levels: you help keep your karma positive, give back to your community, and meet women at the same time.

Bookstores

Bookstores are one of my favorite places to meet women. I am a voracious reader; bookstores are practically my second home. And when you're out trying to meet people, they're one of the best places to go. Most modern bookstores are designed to encourage lingering. They offer any number of opportunities to start conversations with women: you can ask someone to guard your laptop for a moment or ask for a recommendation for a new book. Between the magazines, the books, the music and the movies, you have an almost infinite supply of conversational topics, and the multiple sections make for easy excuses to wander around together. It's just a matter of saying, "Wait, you've never heard of Fitz and the Tantrum? Come with me, you need to hear this" and lead her over to the music section. Even better, the cafes make for a perfect mini-date on the spot; just invite her to have a cup of coffee with you. You're already right there. It's as low-investment on both of your parts as you can get.

HOW THE ATTRACTION PLAN WORKS WHEN APPROACHING GROUPS

You know what intimidates the hell out of guys trying to meet new women?

Approaching a woman who's out with her friends.

Maybe she's having a night out with the girls, maybe she's there with her guy friends, maybe it's a mixed group. Doesn't matter. You just know that if you want to talk to her, you're going to have to wade in there and face down the judgmental stares of not just one but many people. Approaching a woman by herself is intimidating enough. When she's in a group, you have to perform in front of an audience. Worse, you've just increased your risk of being shot down exponentially; now you don't have to just worry about the girl you like shooting you down, you have to worry about her friends doing it too.

But in reality, it's not *nearly* that bad. With a little insight, handling groups – whether it's on campus, at parties or at a bar – isn't that difficult. In fact, if you play your cards right, it can actually make things easier.

If you're going to be trying to meet women at parties, bars or other social gatherings, then you have to learn to approach women when they're with their friends. Women *rarely* go out alone. Whether it's at parties, work conferences or out on the town, women are almost always out in groups. More often than not, they're going to feel much more comfortable with a group of their friends than going by themselves. Going out with friends means safety in a world where women have to be on guard all the time. Having a group of friends around means that she has people to look out for her in case she drinks too much, or worse, if someone spikes her drink. It means that she has a shield in case some asshole starts bothering her and doesn't take the hint that he should go away. If things do go well with someone, then she has people who know where she went and who she went with. Having a friend or friends with her means always having a familiar face in an unfamiliar crowd.

If you don't want to drastically limit yourself in who you can approach, you *have* to learn how to handle groups. If you just hover around waiting to catch her alone then you risk coming across as being creepy. Even if you do find an opportunity when she's by herself, then there's every possibility that her friends might come over and join the conversation. If you aren't able to roll with the changes, then you make it that much harder to win her over and get her number.

The scariest part of approaching groups is that it seems to increase the chances of you being humiliated when you get shot down. If you're like me, then you can already picture them laughing at your audacity, insulting you with scathing cut-downs as everybody turns to point and laugh.

But it's like I said earlier: after having made literally thousands of approaches, I can tell you that this almost *never* happens. You have better odds of being struck by lightning than running into a collection of assholes who think that destroying your soul is the best thing that could happen that night. If you're being a cool and sociable – as opposed to acting like a sleazy pickup artist – then the worst you can really expect is a perfunctory "hey" and short, non-committal responses before they go back to talking amongst themselves.

Making the Initial Approach

This tends to be what trips people up the most. It's one thing when you're approaching a woman on her own, but having to talk to a group of people can really throw you off. The problem is that you're seeing it as a large number of people, each of whom has an (imagined) reason to shoot you down or freeze you out. Instead, you want to treat the group as a gestalt whole. Just as when you want to talk to one woman, all you're trying to do is start a conversation; the only difference is that you're starting one with the group as a whole rather than one specific person. Guys tend to think they need an excuse to start talking to a group for fear of signaling that you're interested in someone and appearing too eager. This is part of why indirect opening lines are so popular, especially in PUA communities; they're a way of pretending that you're not trying to pick up one particular person. Common ways of starting a conversation with a group using indirect methods include asking the group for an opinion on a topic: "Hey, my friends and I were arguing and we need an outsider's perspective. Who do you guys think lie more, men or women?" or "just happening" to overhear something and using it as an excuse to join them – "Hey, I couldn't help but overhear that you were talking about *Game of Thrones...*"

Another option is to simply be direct. In a social situation when mingling and socializing is expected, such as parties, school events or social mixers, it's appropriate to listen and join the conversation. Other times – especially at bars or clubs – it's easier to simply go up and introduce yourself. As with approaching an individual, "You seem cool and I wanted to meet you" is always appropriate. Ultimately, much like with approaching a person one-on-one, your opening line really doesn't matter. It's not a cheat code that automatically gets people to like you; it's just a way of getting people to talk to you in a socially acceptable way.

Whether you want to be indirect or direct, you should introduce yourself right away. So if you were to ask for an opinion, you might say, "Hey, my friends and I need an outsider's perspective..." After they give you an answer, you say, "Okay, cool. Oh, hey, I'm <your name>." Similarly, if you were being direct, you'd say, "You guys seem like you're cool and I wanted to meet you. My name's <your name>."

It's important that as you're doing this, you address the whole group. Don't focus on one person for too long; give your attention to everybody, addressing and focusing on everyone equally. If you zero in on the person you like right off the bat, you're going to trigger everybody's protective instincts and the odds are very good that they're going to close ranks and squeeze you out. Your goal should be to engage the group and get them interested in talking to you.

Establish Relationships

Once you've been accepted into the conversation, you want to ask, "So, how do you guys know each other?" It's important to establish relationships in the group because this can affect how you proceed. Are they a bunch of friends from college, or is this a bunch of co-workers out for drinks? Is that guy in the group somebody's boyfriend, somebody's brother, or a mutual friend? Having an idea who is who and how they all relate serves three purposes. First, it gives you material to transition from – you want to be able to pivot the conversation in such a way that you can talk to the person you're interested in. Second, it prompts everybody to introduce themselves to you, which goes a long way towards making them feel more comfortable; you're not strangers now, you're acquaintances. Third (and possibly most important), it helps you find out early whether any guys in the group are dating or otherwise have interest in the woman you like.

Win Their Approval

The key to being able to hit on the woman you're interested in is to get the group to approve of you. You don't have to become the life of the party or their new best friend; you just want them to think that you're a good guy. Getting their approval means that they aren't going to see you as a potential danger when you start flirting with their friend; in fact, if they like you, they're more likely to actively help you.

The easiest way to this is to start building rapport with them. You're a stranger in a group of mostly established relationships and it's easy to fall back out of the conversation and lose your emotional momentum, so you want to stay engaged. When you've established relationships, you want to transition to another topic, preferably one that will help you talk directly to the person you like. There are any number of ways to do this. You can make a statement out of a question: "I bet you're the instigator of the group." You can start telling a story about something awesome that happened to you recently and bait people into asking you questions. You can make an observation about the group that is either a legitimate observation or something so broad and generalized that it applies to most people. You want to be able to bring some value to the group – make them laugh, make them feel good, make them think – to help grease the social wheels that will make them think you're a cool guy.

As you're talking with everyone, it's important to make sure to use your body language to your advantage. You want to be in a position where you're well within the group, preferably near the center. This can feel intimidating if you're more introverted or unused to being the center of attention, but it's part of ensuring that you don't get squeezed out – either intentionally or by accident. Everybody has seen the guy on the outer edge of the group, trying to lean in and get attention. That guy looks desperate and needy, urgently trying to get the group's approval. You don't want to be that guy. You want to be in a position where you're included. As you're talking, keep your torso open and facing towards the middle and direct your conversation with eye contact; this makes you feel more inclusive.

Don't Sweat the Guys

As intimidating as a group of women can be, a mixed group – women and men – can be even more so. It's easy to think that the men are going to see you as competition for the attention of your target. In reality, most of the time, men will take their lead from you. If you roll in actively trying to pick someone up, then yes, you can expect to get clowned on. If you go in with the attitude of "I'm here to make friends," they're going to respond much more positively to you. Once you've established relationships and determined that the woman you like isn't dating anyone in the group, the best thing you can do with guys is to befriend them. Ask them their opinions, engage them in conversation… if nothing else, you can always establish a rapport based on a love of sports, money, boobs and movies. The more comfortable they are with you, the more likely they are to help you when you start showing interest in the women of the group by vouching for you as a cool guy.

Get Some Privacy

Once everybody is comfortable with you and thinks you're cool, you have more leeway to start giving more of your attention to the real reason you're there. You can focus more of your attention – and conversation – directly on her. Ideally, if things are going well, then you'll want to have time talking with her one on one, rather than in the group. You don't necessarily want to pull her away from her friends – this can come across as creepily predatory if you're not careful – but you do want to be able to have a more private conversation with her.

There are a number of ways of doing this. The easiest is to have a friend or wingman who can join the group and keep everybody else occupied while you talk with the woman you're interested in. He can also help with potential obstacles, such as jealous would-be suitors who are worried that you're going to succeed where they've failed previously.

The next easiest is to step away from the group for a moment and ask her to come with you. "Hey, I'm going to get a drink, keep me company." "Hey, I'm going to step outside to get a smoke/get away from the noise/get some fresh air, why don't you come with me?" You don't want to move her too far from her friends – staying within eyesight of the group helps keep everyone comfortable – but it allows you to have a more private conversation without the feeling that there are other people listening in. If the bar or what-not is out of easy view from where the group is standing, you may want to make a point of asking permission: "Hey, is it okay if I borrow your friend for a moment? We're going to be just over by the bar/porch/patio/smoking area." This helps reassure people that you're a cool, considerate person rather than someone trying to run off with their friend.

Just be sure to ask *her* to come with you before you ask her friends for permission to borrow her. Otherwise you end up looking like you're treating her like the property of her friends.

You can also achieve a sort of privacy via body language and positioning. Start a side conversation with the person you're interested in and as you're talking, move slightly so that the two of you are facing away from the group or that you're between her and the group. By changing your position – putting yourself between her and the group – you've effectively isolated yourselves without actually moving away from everyone else.

Get the Number, Then Get Out

No matter how well things are going, at some point you're going to have to leave the group. Unless you and she have intense physical chemistry, your best bet is to lay the groundwork for a future date and get her number rather than trying to get her to ditch her friends. Make specific plans with her and then ask her for her number. Once you have solid plans, it's time to start getting ready to make your exit. You don't want to just dash out of there; not only is it rude, but it signals that getting her number was the only thing you were interested in. Instead, rejoin the group and chat for a little while, then make your excuses to leave. "Hey, it was great meeting you guys, but I have to get back to my friends…" is an all-purpose exit line that you can use to gracefully leave the conversation and head out.

Just try not to do a little victory dance until you're out of eyesight.

I GOT HER NUMBER... NOW WHAT?

So you followed my advice, you talked to that cute girl at the coffee shop and she gave you her number. You're feeling like a million bucks, right? Clearly you're home free at this point, right?

Actually... no. In fact, getting the number is really the end of the beginning. In the days of smartphones, voicemail, caller ID and social media privacy controls, getting a woman's number – or her email or friending her on Facebook – is ultimately a meaningless trophy. Just because she didn't give you the number for the local cement processing factory doesn't mean that she's going to actually answer when you call or text her. Many women will actually give out their number as a way to get guys to leave them alone and go away; it takes no effort to ignore the call when your name pops up on her caller ID. It's also possible that she may not even remember giving you her number. If you met her in a chaotic environment like a nightclub or bar, she may vaguely remember talking to *someone*, but not any of the details. If alcohol was involved, she might have given out her number and then regretted it in the cold light of sobriety.

The best way to make sure you have a solid number – one that will lead to an actual date – is to set up definitive plans *before* getting her number. This means before you ask for her number, you want to ask her out on a date. Not to "hang out, sometime" or "get a drink soon" but an actual date at a specific time and place. Making plans together means that she'll be expecting to hear from you, rather than trying to run through her mental contacts list to remember who she's been talking to recently.

Not every interaction is going to end in date plans immediately. But if you know how to use the phone – and text messages and instant messaging – to your advantage, you can turn a weak connection into something incredibly powerful that will leave her eager to see you again.

Climb the Intimacy Ladder

When it comes to women and dating, you have to understand that there are levels of intimacy when it comes to communication. From most intimate to least, it goes:

- In Person
- Phone
- Text
- Video Chatting (including Skype and Google hangouts)
- Email
- Instant Messaging (Snapchat, What'sApp, etc.)
- Facebook

Despite feeling more personal – we live our lives online these days – social networks like Facebook are actually less intimate than other forms of contact. Many people are more willing to add someone on Facebook than to give out their phone number, and with lists and privacy controls, you can effectively wall individuals away and ensure that you never hear from them. Similarly, video-chat tends to feel less personal – being a face on a screen makes you feel disconnected from them and the odd eye-lines with web cameras makes it harder to connect with the other person.

Ideally, you want to be moving up the intimacy ladder as quickly as possible; after all, you want to see them in person. However, you may well find that you bounce around the ladder quite a bit. People will use multiple forms of communication with friends and intimates; they may communicate with the same person over texting *and* over instant messaging *and* Facebook over the course of the week. Your place on the ladder is defined by what the other person will respond to. If you spend most of your time chatting back and forth over Facebook Messenger but occasionally make phone calls, then you can usually safely assume a greater level of intimacy.

Someone responding to higher levels of intimate contact with a lower level form – she only responds to your voice mails via texts, or stops responding to texts and only talks to you via instant message – is a sign that you've screwed up along the way. If this becomes a regular pattern, then you're now in damage control. Odds are good that you're about to watch this person pull a fade-away on you. On the other hand, if the two of you have been texting back and forth and she starts to call you instead, it's a sign that she's much more interested.

Establishing Contact

The first thing you need to do after getting a woman's number is to send out a ping. You want to establish that yes, this is her number and that she's actually going to respond to you when you try to contact her.

There are a lot of "rules" out there about whether to wait one day, three days or a week to call or text after getting her number. Ignore all of those. You don't want to lose the emotional momentum you've built up. You also want to establish contact while you're still fresh in her memory instead of playing the classic, "Hey, it's Jake, we met two nights ago at The Library, I was wearing the Doctor Who shirt…. no, Jake. Jay-ay-kay-ee" conversation.

As a general rule, when you're pinging someone who's just given you her number, you want to send a text rather than a phone call. Texting is lower-investment on both your part and hers when you're just getting to know one another, and it's frequently easier for guys who get shy or nervous easily. When you're texting, you have more of a chance to collect your thoughts instead of worrying about what to say next or being afraid of sounding like a doof on the phone.

Depending on the circumstances of how you met, you usually want send a text ping within a couple of hours of getting the number, but no later than the next day. The text ping doesn't have to be terribly complex or crazy; just a little reminder of who you are. Giving a playful nickname while you're flirting can be a great way of helping her remember you; it's a call-back to how you met. One of the most reliable ways to ping someone's number is the classic "Hey $NICKNAME, do you speak text? $YOURNAME."

If I met her while out at a bar or party, I may send something along the lines of "Hey $NICKNAME, it's $YOURNAME, I'm texting you now before I forget who you are when tomorrow's hangover kicks in, so WRITE ME BACK!" or "So I have a couple hours before the consequences of my actions catch up to me, $NICKNAME so I wanted to say 'hey!'" Depending on your personality, you may want to give a teasing challenge to bait her into writing back; something with a little humor and/or intrigue works best. "Hey $NICKNAME, this question will forever decide whether we can be friends: favorite Bond girl?" Make or break questions, especially any involving a binary choice, will get good responses: cake or pie, beach or skiing, Los Angeles or Miami, New York or San Francisco, New Orleans or Austin, *Game of Thrones* or *Lord of the Rings*. No matter what her answer is, you can use it to spur some light-hearted banter.

If Only You Knew the Power of the Text Message...

The text message is a surprisingly versatile and powerful tool in the arsenal of any man who's looking for dates. Many people actually *prefer* texting to phone calls, which means you need to know how to make it work for you. You can use it to build comfort or intrigue in order to help get her excited and eager to meet with you face-to-face. You can use it to maintain a connection with a girl you've been seeing or one you're trying to see but circumstances are getting in the way. You can use it to re-establish communication with a woman when things have suddenly gone quiet, even after weeks or months of inactivity. And it can be used to bypass people's inhibitions and build momentum towards sex.

Texting is a great way to build some intrigue and initiate conversations to help keep someone's interest, and open conversations that can lead to opportunities to flirt. By using silly and attention grabbing texts, you can help keep the conversation going, which helps to build the momentum towards an in-person meeting and/or sex. These texts are short and simple; you're just giving them a quick poke, not writing *War and Peace*. Examples that I've used over time include:

- "Hey, I think I just met your evil twin."

- "You just popped into my head, so I wanted to say 'hey.' Oh, and stay out of my head."

- "I had a really weird dream about you last night. How do you feel about koalas?"

- "Hey, I just saw something awesome and it made me think of you. Text me back."

You can also use texting to ramp up the sexual tension. Because there's that level of abstraction in texting – you're words on a screen rather than a voice or a video – people are often more willing to step outside their public personas via text and adopt one that's more playful or forward because in some ways it's not as "real." Because of that abstraction, it's often possible to build more sexual tension through increasingly overt flirting or even role-play over text than it is in person. It works best as a push-pull; you're pulling in a little by expressing interest before pushing her away. Being a little impish makes the sexual aspect more acceptable; it's meant in the sense of *fun* rather than being crude or creepy.

For example:

- "You've just given me the most inappropriate thought

right now and I really don't know you well enough for that yet."

- "Stop, you're turning me on and that's not appropriate right now."
- "Oh man, what'm I going to do with you? I mean, I have an idea or two, but I don't think we're there yet."
- "Hold on, you just gave me an interesting mental image… Okay, back now."

If she responds positively, you can use these to build towards a more overtly sexual conversation. If not, then you can dial things back a little until a more opportune moment arises.

All that being said: tone can be harder to read over text, so you need to be especially aware of the other person's comfort levels; the last thing you want to do is push things in a direction she's not willing to go. The more explicit or sexual you're trying to go, the more you want to make sure the other person is on board… *especially* if you're trading photos back and forth. No sending photos of your junk unless you're explicitly invited to do so.

Making the Call

As powerful as texting can be, at some point you're going to actually have to call her.

A lot of guys get nervous calling the girl they like. Believe me, I can understand; I've been there enough times, when the adrenaline surges as you're punching the numbers and you heart pounds as the phone rings and you find yourself silently praying for a voice mail instead of a live voice on the other line. It's no wonder then that a lot of guys prefer texting to phone calls; you have time to compose a reply instead of tripping over your own tongue trying to say something witty or cool in real time and avoiding that dreaded minute-long lull punctuated by, "So... anyway..."

If you're the sort of person who gets nervous talking to someone you like on the phone, then the best thing you can do is warm up beforehand. Just as you wouldn't want to start running a 5k cold, you shouldn't call that new number without getting yourself into a relaxed headspace first. Instead of putting yourself through the stress of an awkward call, schedule a specific time in the day when you're planning to call her. Then, some time between a half-hour to an hour in advance, you call someone you do like talking to on the phone. You'll already be far more relaxed and in a talkative mood, which will help you not tense up or stumble over your words.

The other thing that you need to do is assume that you're friends already. Far too many people get nervous about calling the next day because they treat the phone call as a date audition. But think about it: she's given you her number. If you've been following my advice, you have a strong connection; she already likes you and thinks you're cool. But even if you're unsure, by acting as if you're friends already, you'll be far more relaxed and comfortable talking to her, which will also make you sound more confident.

How do you act as if you're friends already? Well, think of how you talk with your friends *now*. You let conversations run down completely random tangents without trying to wrestle them back on track. You'll talk about plans for the week (you *have* plans, right? If not, I refer you back to step 5 of the attraction plan) and this will lead right into the reason why you called: making the date. Talking about what you're doing this week will almost inevitably lead to, "So what are *you* doing this weekend?"

And that's right where you want it to go.

How to Handle Voicemail and Other Etiquette Questions

Everybody hates leaving voicemails. Everyone remembers the voicemail scene from *Swingers* because just about everyone has had that experience from one side of the phone or the other. Voicemail and unreturned calls are an inevitable part of dating, and they can provide a valuable screening service. The last thing any girl wants is some guy who will leave twenty messages on her voicemail right after getting her number, each one crazier and needier than the last.

But sometimes you're going to make that first call and she's not going to answer. So now what?

Well, in all likelihood you've been texting back and forth already, so there's no real need to stress over the first call; it's just an extension of the conversation you were already having. But regardless of whether this is your first call or your fiftieth, the answer is to keep it short and sweet. Name, quick message, "Talk to you later." If you get the voicemail on the first call, you want to follow the same pattern I recommend for a first text: nickname, a little humorous call-back to meeting, drop some intrigue as a hook and your name and number... because hey, sometimes she really did lose your number. "Hey NICKNAME, it's YOUR NAME. So I think you left your koala suit behind? I want to return it, so call me back," works. Another I've used – mostly with women I've met in clubs rather than coffee shops – is "The craziest thing happened after you left, so call me back." Yes, it's a blatant hook. Honestly, though, a little humor is going to work better than anything else. As always: if you can make her laugh, she's much more likely to call back.

Short and to the point is doubly key if you're constantly missing each other's calls. "Hey $NICKNAME, phone tag, you're it!" works far better than "Call me back, pleeeeeease."

And then there's the question of how many times to call/text/IM. People tend to overthink this and worry about the subtext of how quickly they respond or how many texts they send versus ones being returned. The basic rule is simple: continue chatting in whatever medium you're using as long as the conversation is going strong. As long as the other person is responding in equal measure to you, it's going well. If the conversation starts trailing off – you're getting increasingly short or curt answers – then call it quits and chat later. In dating as in show biz, it's better to leave them wanting more than to overstay your welcome.

When you're dealing with any sort of text medium, allow for some delay in response. Not everybody is going to be able to respond immediately and not every moment of silence is a message. Sometimes they just can't get to their damn phone.

If you're not hearing back from them, don't blow up their phone or inbox; bombarding them with texts and IMs is only going to make them even less likely to respond. One unreturned text or call gets one follow-up text (*not* a call) per day. Anything lower on the ladder gets one follow-up in the same medium as the first. Switching channels to find one they will respond to is only going to work against you.

And remember: one unreturned message could be anything. Two is uncomfortable. Three is her sending you a message: she's not interested and it's time to give up and move on.

THE ANATOMY LESSON: BREAKING DOWN A SUCCESSFUL APPROACH

So I realize at this point that I've given you a *lot* of information – how to flirt, how to talk to people, what to say and how to say it – all of this can feel like a *lot* to keep in mind all at once. It can feel almost overwhelming, like you're trying to ride a unicycle and juggle fire at the same time while doing differential calculus in your head.

It can be awkward at first because you're essentially learning a new skill. You're taking something you do instinctually – talking to people – and looking at it in new and different ways. It's the centipede's dilemma: you didn't have any problems until someone asked you whether you lead off with your left foot or your right. But with practice – and dating is a skill that takes practice – it will become as natural to you as breathing.

Meanwhile, it can help to see the process in action. So with that in mind, I want to take an approach from my dating life and break it down for you.

Now to be sure, this isn't one the most dramatic or complicated cold approaches I've ever made; in fact, it's fairly low-key and uneventful. But that is exactly why I chose it: nine times out of ten, meeting someone new isn't a matter of high drama. The theatric duel of wits involved in trying to win over the hot girl who hates you makes for great movie scenes but *doesn't actually happen in real life.* Approaching someone new is simply starting a conversation and being as charming and awesome a person as you can be.

So with that in mind, I give you the tale of the Reverse Cowgirl.

The Setup

Back in my pick-up days – before I burned out on the bar scene – I spent a lot of time hitting the bars downtown. I used to go out two, three, sometimes four nights a week with a group of friends to hit a couple of our favorite bars for some good times and bad decisions. We were a crew of guys mostly out to have fun and meet women; if we got laid, great, otherwise as long as we were enjoying ourselves, it was all good. Usually on Friday nights we would meet up at this one particular bar for a drink and to chat – what we'd been up to that week, food, TV, women… your basic male-bonding stuff – before heading off to see what the night would bring.

This particular night, I was feeling especially good. I'd just finished a major project and was looking to celebrate. I ended up downtown with an hour to kill, so I decided to hang loose at a coffeehouse in the area and chat up anyone who seemed like they might be interesting until my buddies got there.

This may seem somewhat inconsequential, but it's actually surprisingly important when it comes to meeting people. Your attitude has a lot to do with success. If you're in a good mood and with an attitude of "I'm out to enjoy myself," you're going to find that more people are interested in talking to you than if you come across as someone on a mission to get laid, or worse, someone who's sullen, sulky or otherwise in a shitty mood.

Chatting with random friendly strangers can be a good way to get into social mode – think of it as the social equivalent of stretching and doing warm-up exercises before a run – and get into a more outgoing headspace.

The Girl

I noticed April[3] within seconds of the barista handing me my latte. It was the cowboy hat that caught my attention; Austin isn't known for a preponderance of urban cowboys or western attire, so anyone wearing a cowboy hat is going to stand out by default. More interestingly, it had an Old School Americana tattoo painted on the crown. The hat alone was enough to make me want to say hello – it was legitimately the coolest hat I'd seen in quite some time. The fact that the woman wearing it was cute certainly helped.

She didn't seem to be my usual type, but she was definitely someone I'd be interested in at least talking to for a little before I left to meet my friends. As I made a quick assessment – she was sitting by herself at a two-top table in a fairly well-trafficked part of the coffeehouse, a single large coffee, looking up occasionally at the crowd, but not apparently looking for anyone – I noticed that

3. Names have been changed to protect the innocent and cover the ass of the guilty – namely, me.

she was doing quick pencil studies in a spiral-bound sketchbook.

That cinched it; I'd always had success with arty types. I was an artist myself, and I was always interested in seeing other people's work, especially sketches.

The Break-Down:

When you're approaching someone – assuming you're following the Three Second Rule – a quick look around is worth it to determine several things. In my case, I wanted to make sure I wasn't about to intrude where I wasn't wanted. Was she there by herself or with friends? Approaching one person by herself is slightly different from a group, especially when they're seated; you need to be careful not to be creepy by accident. Since she was at a small table, I didn't want to steal somebody's seat if they were ordering or in the bathroom... and I also didn't want to be interrupted by an annoyed friend (or date) if it came to that. I also wanted to gauge whether or not she was in "don't bother me mode" – seated in a corner or away from the main traffic area, eyes locked on her sketchbook, headphones on or otherwise giving off "not interested" vibes. I'd done my share of sketching-in-a-public-place-to-meet-people and I recognized the signs.[4]

If all of this sounds a little like I'm trying to say I have super-Terminator Vision or some Sherlock-esque ability to notice insane little details and deduce facts from them... well, I don't. Most of what I was doing was looking for really obvious things; by this point I had made

4. By which I mean I counted the coffee cups and hoped for the best.

(and fucked up) enough approaches to have learned what to look for via a long process of trial and error. I've lost track of how many times I ended up getting shot down because I didn't notice an engagement ring or wedding band or a second cup of coffee at the table.

The fact that she was sketching gave me an instant point of commonality: we were both artists. Even if it turned out that she (or I, for that matter) wasn't interested, I was willing to bet that I'd enjoy talking to her; I legitimately like meeting artistic people, even if I'm not hoping to get their phone number.

Ironically, I would later find out that she was actually trying to catch the eye of a guy in the corner who was also drawing. Go figure.

The Approach

I walked up to the far corner of her table. "Hey, can I see what you're drawing?" I asked. She looked up – she hadn't noticed me as I'd walked over – and I smiled. I nodded at her sketchbook. "Is it okay if I look at your sketch? I know some people don't like it when somebody stares over their shoulder when they're in the zone…"

"Sure," she said and leaned away from the sketchbook.

"Mind if I…?"

I pulled an empty chair from an adjacent table and sat perpendicular to her. "I've only got a couple minutes before I have to meet up with some folks," I said as I put my latte down. The figure work was loose and sketchy, but the clothing was surprisingly detailed. "Wow," I said, "I really like the way you do cloth. Drapery drives me fucking nuts."

"Yeah, me too," she said. " Makes me wish I was only doing underwear. Are you an artist?"

God I loved questions like that. They might as well be asking, "Hey, would you like this opportunity to show off and humblebrag a little?" I wasn't the world's greatest painter by any stretch of the imagination – in fact, I eventually quit painting and took up writing instead – but I was pretty good and I'd been in a few local gallery shows. I definitely had enough skill to come up with some visually striking pictures, especially since I was working digitally at that point. Photoshop lets you correct for many, many sins. Naturally, I made a point of having copies of my latest works on my smartphone.

"Hey, first things first. You show me yours and I'll show you mine."

She laughed.

"I'm Harris," I said.

"April," she said, shaking my hand before flipping her sketchbook back to the first page. April was studying fashion design with an eye towards interesting prints and unusual dress designs and accessories.

"That explains the hat," I said.

"Hey, don't knock the hat!" she said in mock outrage. "It's my one concession to being a Texan."

"Does it get you a lot of guys asking if you could hog-tie 'em?"[5]

"Wow, that's the best innuendo you could some up with?" she asked with a grin.

I rolled my eyes at her. "Heard it before, huh?"

She nodded.

"That's what I get for going for the low-hanging fruit."

5. Smooth, bro.

"So now I'm low-hanging fruit?"

"I notice you didn't answer my question," I replied.

"No, but you'd be amazed how many guys choke when I tell them I prefer to ride bareback."

Oh, yeah. I liked her. "You mind?"

She handed me the hat. It was a gift from her roommate, who worked in a hat store out by UT campus. I was surprised to see that it'd been hand-painted. I was impressed; I was never as good with physical media as I was with Photoshop, and I would've loved to be able to paint something like that.

I flipped the hat around and put it back on her, backwards. "Here you go. Now you can tell them you're into reverse cowgirl."

She broke into peals of surprised laughter as I pulled out my phone to show her some of my paintings. She scooted closer to me and leaned in and I put my hand on her back. "You realize I'm going to have to call you 'Cowgirl' from now on. That's totally your name to me now," I said.

"Jerk," she snorted and smacked me on the shoulder.

The Break-Down:

April was fairly intent on her sketch by this point, which meant that she wouldn't necessarily see me when I walked up. I made a point of approaching from the front at a slight angle rather than from the side or behind her for just that reason – it meant that she was much more likely to see me coming over through peripheral vision – and keeping the table between us. This way I was less likely to startle her or provoke an immediate sense of threat when I said, "Hey."

When coming up to someone who's seated, it's important to sit down as soon as possible; otherwise you loom over them, which can creep them out. It also carries the context that you're seeking their approval and attention. Think of it in the context of a boss and employee: the boss is seated at his desk while the employee is standing nervously in front of him. The seated person is in the comfortable position while you're standing; the body language and position sets you up as being the one seeking the other's approval. Sitting down puts you at an equal level.

Mentioning that I only had a few minutes also helped put her at her ease; it meant that if I was a creep or a jackass, she was only going to have to put up with me for a short amount of time before I had to get up and leave... and if I didn't, she had a built in escape clause. An icy, "Didn't you say you had somewhere to be?" is a good way of telling people to fuck off when they've worn out their welcome. If we were having a good time, I could either elect to stay and keep the emotional momentum going, or leave on an emotional high-note and call later... assuming I got her number.

I was genuinely interested in looking at her sketches, which made talking to her easier. I wasn't giving the "I'm here to pick you up" vibe; I was just a guy who was interested in talking about something we clearly had in common. Having my own work readily at hand via the smartphone meant that we could compare notes and I could brag a little as well as back up my claims. I've known lots of guys who claim to be photographers or DJs but have never touched a camera or a turntable in their lives.

Her response to my (admittedly lame) joke about the hat gave me a good indication that she was interested in flirting. She called attention to it without shutting me down or telling me that it was inappropriate. Coming back with a more overtly sexual reference also gave me a good indication of her sense of humor and what level of edginess I could get away with, as seen in her response to the "reverse cowgirl" joke. If she hadn't made a similar joke back to me, I probably would have kept things dialed back a little until I had a better sense of how interested she was. As it was, when she leaned in to look at my phone – as opposed to taking it from me and flipping through it on her own – I knew she was getting into me. I had good reason to assume that she would be cool with my touching her.

Giving her a cute nickname is a good way of not only keeping a shorthand of who she was if I got her number (you'd be surprised at how quickly names can blur) but also of cementing me in her mind. If I called her up and said, "Hey, Cowgirl, this is Harry…" she'd be much more likely to remember me – and the fun she had with me – than if I said, "Hey, this is Harry, I don't know if you remember me but I talked to you about your sketches…"

The Close

As much fun as I was having talking to April, I really wasn't kidding when I said that I only had a few minutes before I had to meet my friends. We were vibing and I was definitely interested in her, but I already had plans and I didn't feel right just blowing them off. I also didn't know April well enough to invite her to come with me on what was ostensibly a guys' night. Plus, with her sketchbooks and coffee, she seemed fairly well settled in for the immediate future. I pulled one of my business cards out of my wallet – I was proud of these as they were heavy, glossy stock with one of my paintings on one side and my contact information on the other – and handed it to her.

"Hey, I have to go," I said, "but my website with all my art's on here. Let me know what you think!"

I left the coffeehouse and headed to the bar. I was still in a good mood – I'd met a cute girl, I was warmed up and ready to party like a rockstar with my buds – all in all a net positive from my perspective. I assumed that this was going to be the last I'd hear from her.

The Break-Down:

At the time, I could have stuck around; there was definite attraction there, and we were having a fun time. The logistics of the situation – being in a coffee shop with a big bag of art supplies – meant that I probably wouldn't have been able to turn this into an instant date by hopping to one of the bars near by, but we could have spent more time hanging out at the coffeehouse.

As it was, leaving her with my card was a mistake; it often comes off as a passive-aggressive move and puts all of the pressure of making contact on her. I would've done better to say, "Hey, I'm having a great time talking to you and I'd really like to see you again. Let me get your number and I'll call you tomorrow," and handed her my phone to have her punch her number in. That way, depending on how the night went, I would be able to send a ping text – "Hey, do you speak text?" or "This bar is lame, what are you up to?" – and keep the emotional momentum going. I'm a big believer in texting the same night I meet the person rather than waiting some arbitrary amount of time for fear of showing too much interest. Texting is a great way to keep flirting with someone, even bringing some sexual tension to the conversation; played right, it's possible to turn getting a number into a make-out session that same night.

Still, I needn't have worried...

Epilogue

A week later, as I was coming out of a movie, I had a voicemail waiting for me on my phone.

"Hey, this is April... you know, Reverse Cowgirl? I was wondering if you were doing anything this weekend..."

We ended up dating for four months.

CHAPTER 9.

DATING FOR DUMMIES

THE RULES OF DATING

There was a time when dating was simpler; courtship was a very structured and ritualized affair where everybody's roles were clearly and carefully delineated. Guys were supposed to do X, girls would do Y and a chaperone would try to keep them from doing XXX in the parlor when nobody was looking. Everybody knew what was expected of them and pretended to be happy as long as you were willing to ignore the rampant inherent sexism, the commodification of women and the sex-negative attitudes of the time.

So here we are in the 21st century, when gender-roles have shifted and strides towards sexual equality have been made, and yet outmoded ideas regarding dating cling like barnacles, clouding the waters and leaving everyone frustrated and confused as to just how to do this whole "dating" thing. Attempts by well-meaning souls – both conservative and progressive – to codify dating into sets of ironclad "rules" have only served to leave us even *more* confused.

Are women supposed to ask men out, or does making the first move mean she's a hussy? How many times a week are you supposed to see someone you're dating? And are you dating if you haven't had the exclusivity talk? If he buys the lobster thermidor, does that mean he's guaranteed a handie afterwards, or should you hold out for after-dinner champagne too? Is someone who goes on dates strictly for the meals a prostitute or a clever person subverting the dominant patriarchal paradigm and saving some money to boot?

It's enough to make a guy want to give up on the whole dating thing all together and just try to lead a lifestyle of nothing but shallow sexual encounters with women.

Do yourself a favor: toss all the crap about dating out the window. Here are the new rules to keep in mind to make dating simpler, more equitable and easier all around.

Rule One: What You Are Entitled to on a Date

Men are entitled to basic politeness.

Women are entitled to basic politeness and *safety*.

Everything else in a date, up to and including a good time, is *optional*. There is no rule of reciprocation where spending X dollars gets you Y in exchange. The only thing that is mandatory on a date is that both people are polite and reasonable, and that a woman can expect to have her boundaries respected without worrying that her date represents a danger to her, either socially or physically.

Rule Two: The One Who Asks, Pays

This is very simple: whoever asked the other out on a date pays for that date, regardless of gender. The other party then pays for the *next* date. After a certain number of dates (usually between four and six, or after sex, whichever comes first), it is appropriate to assume that you will be splitting the costs (subject to each party's financial standing) unless otherwise specified by both parties.

Other arrangements – splitting the check, one party paying for drinks while the other pays for dinner or alternating paying for rounds of drinks – may be negotiated prior but with the understanding that this does not necessarily establish a permanent arrangement.

Rule Three: Have Sex When You Both Feel Like It

The old standard of "no sex before the third date" – or its stricter cousin, "no sex before commitment" – are based around the commodity model of female sexuality that women who "give it up" too quickly devalue themselves, while a woman who guards her virtue tighter than Fort Knox is a prize above rubies. The idea behind this is that since guys are only interested in sex, having sex "too soon" (and what is considered "too soon" for sex is an arbitrary number with no basis in reality) means they won't respect the woman and will ditch her as soon as they get what they want.

In practice, this is saying "women have no value outside of their sexuality, therefore they have to trap a man into commitment in order to get a relationship."

This attitude towards women and women's sexuality is

profoundly sexist and insulting and – in case you needed more than that – makes it even harder for people to get laid. No woman wants to get shamed for not following somebody else's bullshit standards. Someone who's more open and understanding of women's sexuality and who doesn't judge or denigrate women for their sexual choices is someone who is *infinitely more attractive* because he's demonstrating that he's a grown-ass man.

Sex should happen when *both* parties are comfortable, willing and consenting – whether that's on the first date or the tenth. If you're not willing to wait, then admit it and move on to someone who is moving at your speed.

Rule Four: You Are Not in an Exclusive Relationship Until You've Had the Talk

Too many people get caught up in the game of "are we a couple?" causing needless confusion and heartache. While any two people's definitions of what consists of a relationship may vary, no single individual gets to declare exclusivity. Until both parties have had the Exclusivity Talk and have explicitly agreed, neither is bound by expectations of monogamy. While this does not insulate against the possibility of hurt feelings, it *does* mean that both parties should manage their expectations accordingly, rather than dealing with the fallout that comes with finding your partner doesn't feel the same way.

Dating is one of those skills that we all *think* we've mastered but keep getting wrong. We have a lot of wrong ideas about what makes for a good date that we've absorbed from well-meaning friends and family members and decades of pop-culture exposure. Worse, most of the time we don't even ask people on dates. We ask people to "hang out," turning every interaction into Schrödinger's Date where it's both a date *and* a platonic get-together and nobody knows until some poor bastard goes for the good-night kiss.

When it comes to dating, there's a definite right and wrong way to go about it.

The first mistake that people make is that dates are not interviews. The last thing you want when you go out with someone for the first time is to sit across from them and interrogate each other with the same "getting-to-know-you" questions that you've both been asked on every *other* date you've ever been on.

(The obvious exception is in the world of online dating. Meeting for coffee is less of a date and more of a pre-date audition. You're both vetting one another to ensure that not only do you have chemistry together in the real world, but also that your prospective date isn't gauging how many lampshades they can make out of your skin.)

The second mistake that people make is picking dates where you can't actually talk or interact with your date. This is why the classic dinner-and-a-movie date is a *horrible* idea – it's following up an interview with two hours of sitting in silence next to a relative stranger.

Instead, you want to plot out the ideal first date. An

ideal date is one where you're able to talk and interact with one another without falling into the audition frame. You want to focus on three things: fun, conversation and a hint of sexual tension. You want your date to go home thinking about what a great guy she just hung out with and how much fun it would be to see him again.

Exciting Always Beats Pleasant

Remember how I've mentioned the psychological quirk known as "the misattribution of arousal" before? A first date is the *perfect* time to put this into play.

You want to do things that are *stimulating*, rather than relaxing. Exciting beats pleasant when it comes to attraction; the more you engage with one another, the more attraction you build. One of the best ways to encourage this stimulation is to go on what I call an "activity" or "action" date where you're active and moving, rather than sitting around. Playing pool makes a better first date than going for coffee; not only are you actively engaging with one another, but that sense of competition helps get your blood flowing. The friendly smack-talk segues nicely into banter and flirting and that helps build the sexual tension. There are opportunities to get close as you help each other with your form, to tease one another as they're carefully lining up that game-winning shot and, of course, the thrill of winning.

An ideal date is one that gets your heart rates up. Anything that causes arousal in your central nervous system also causes sexual arousal. Going for a hike, taking a walk together through the park, riding bikes together, going paddle-boarding… all of these get your heart racing, stimulating those feelings of attraction and arousal.

Unusual first dates also help make those dates more memorable and entertaining. Everybody – and I mean *everybody* – has done dinner and a movie. But how many people have raced go-karts on an outdoor track for a first date? Instead of trying to impress her by spending money on a fancy dinner, you could learn to *make* that fancy dinner with a sushi-making class. Novelty makes you more memorable and more desirable. New experiences produce dopamine, which stimulates the pleasure centers of your brain... and your date will associate those feelings of pleasure with being with *you*.

A Date Is About the Two of You

Another mistake that people make is that they bring other people to their date.

Hold on, let me explain.

We live in an increasingly connected and distracting society. Every day there are more disturbances and interruptions that we have to tune out, especially if you're spending every waking moment wed to your email, Facebook and Twitter. Unfortunately, I've lost track of how many dates I've seen where someone put their smartphone on the table; they inevitably lose track of the conversation as they stop to check every time the notification chime rings.

You are allowed to check your phone in case of an *actual* emergency – your house is on fire, a family member is in the hospital, etc. Most smartphones have a Do Not Disturb function that silences all incoming notifications and only allows certain numbers to ring through. If someone isn't about to literally die without your immediate attention, then when you're on a date, you abide by movie theater rules and keep your phone silent, dark and in your pocket.

Keeping your date about the two of you also means avoiding the other myriad distractions that exist. Many bars and restaurants have televisions, which can be a continual distraction and annoyance; it's often hard to ignore the constant flickering light and movement in the corner of your eye. Ideally, you want to pick a venue that doesn't have these distractions. However, if you find yourself at a place with televisions, turn your back to them. Get them completely out of your field of vision. I have seen far too many people get caught up on the TV behind their date rather than on the person sitting directly across from them. You want to give your date your *full* attention. The only time you should be focusing on other people is if you're both people-watching.

Let's Do the Time-Warp Again

One of the best things you can do on a date is to visit multiple venues in one evening. In fact, many of the best dates involve going to three or more locations. For example, you might meet up for a quick drink before going to play mini-golf, then going to this incredible Ethiopian place for dinner, then perhaps a walk down to this food truck that does *amazing* deserts. If you're going to a museum or art gallery, go to a wine bar to relax and talk, then perhaps dinner at a local cafe.

Why would you want to go to all of these places instead

of just picking an awesome bar and hanging around until the staff chases you out? Because changing venues actually affects how we perceive time. Chalk it up to a psychological quirk known as "event boundaries." By changing your location, you've effectively caused your brain to see that the time spent in one venue as a separate activity and it gets filed away. When you've changed venues two or three times, you *feel* like you've known each other longer than the few hours you've actually spent in each other's company. This helps make you feel closer and more in tune with one another, even though you've really only just met.

Go Easy on the Booze

First dates and booze go together like giant robots and Japanese schoolchildren: they seem like a natural pairing but in reality have a tendency to do more damage than you could believe. I realize many dates focus around getting drinks, and it makes sense – alcohol is a social lubricant and helps relax you when you're nervous. The problem is that it's very easy to lose track, especially when you're both having a good time.

It's not uncommon to get that first drink to soothe your nerves before your date arrives. Then a second one to help get you both in a more social mood and ease you both into relaxed familiarity. But then that third drink seems to get lost on the way to your stomach, which necessitates a fourth as a search party and suddenly the line between "pleasant buzz" and "removing a much-needed mental filter" evaporates into nothingness. The last thing you want to do is trip over your own dick because you didn't realize that maybe you shouldn't have made that clever "edgy" joke about her panties and your bedpost.

It also doesn't help that there's a certain social contract that strongly suggests that we keep drink parity with our dates. The last thing you want to do is accidentally come across like you're trying to ply your date with booze.

By all means, have a beer or a whiskey or two on your date. Just mix it up with a soda or water after your second. Keeping a level head makes it *much* easier to read her signs and show her just how charming a sonofabitch you can be.

Get That Next Date

All good things come to an end, and that includes dates. When the date is winding down, there are inevitably two unspoken questions in a man's mind and neither of them are what you think they are.

The first, of course, is "when should you call?"

As a rule of thumb, I recommend a text sometime after noon the next day to let your date know what an awesome time you had and that you want to see them again. Be clear on your interest; you don't do yourself any favors by trying to pretend that you're too cool to care. It's not showing interest that makes a person appear needy, it's the way in which you express it. Saying, "I'd love to see you again," is charming. Badgering her or blowing up her voice mail with five or six "Please please please go out with me!" messages isn't.

This leads nicely into the other question: "How do you get that next date?"

Ideally, the two of you have had such a good time that you've already talked about the next time you're going to see each other. However, that doesn't always happen... so it becomes incumbent upon you to make that next date happen. One useful technique – especially if you're feeling somewhat bashful about coming right out and asking – is to seed the idea of the next date while you're on your first.

During your date, you will almost inevitably find the opportunity to talk about a future event that you're looking forward to: a band playing in town, a gallery opening, a street fair... anything fun that is occurring in the near future. Talk it up, explain why you're so excited for it, then let it drop and move on to another topic. Towards the end of the night – or when you call or text her the next day – bring it up again, except as an invitation. Say: "Hey, listen, I'm having a great time with you, and I'd like to see you again. I'm going to $FUN_THING next week, and it'd be great if you came too. I think you'd really enjoy it."

It's relatively low-pressure and doesn't feel like it was dropped out of the blue – you have some pretext for bringing it up. It also establishes that a) you have a life, b) that you're not waiting with sandwiches by the phone for her to call you back, and c) that fun event would be even more fun if he or she were there.

The important part of getting the next date, however, is to *not stress yourself out about it*. If you're focusing about the next time you're going to see someone, you're not going to be able to enjoy the time you're spending with them now. Focus on having fun and being in the moment; if you two are having a great time, then the next date will take care of itself.

FIVE AMAZING FIRST DATES

You already know that dinner and a movie is out and the coffee house date is more of a pre-date interview than an actual date. You want to wow her with something that's memorable and different. Something that's going to absolutely knock her socks off, something that's going to set you apart from every other guy she's ever been out with... preferably without costing you an arm and a leg.

So instead of asking her out "for drinks" or "to get dinner some time," invite her on one of *these* dates instead.

Go to a Comedy Club/Improv Event

Women love somebody who can make them laugh. You may not be the funniest guy in the world, but that doesn't mean you can't borrow someone else's sense of humor for a little while. It doesn't matter if it's Chris Hardwick making her laugh instead of you; you're the one who made it happen, and she's going to associate those good feelings with *you*.

Plus, comedy is having a renaissance right now – you can see some amazing up-and-coming comedians at your local club before they become headliners and play sold-out theaters. Just do some research in advance. Some comedians' material may not mesh with your date's sense of humor and their style may make things uncomfortable. The last thing you want is for the two of you to become the focus of Lisa Lampanelli's set that night...[1]

1. This has actually happened to me before.

Go Bowling

Don't let the stereotype of middle-aged men in polyester shirts and stinking rental shoes deter you; bowling actually makes for a great first date. Many bowling alleys are actively courting the young and hip with impressive bars and live DJs. Bowling is an excellent example of an active date – the physical exertion gets the heart rate up, which increases arousal, while the competitiveness allows for some playful banter and smack-talk. Being good is actually optional; if you both suck, it's easy to laugh at how badly you're both doing. If one of you is better than the other, there's an opportunity to use it as a flirty teaching moment. Want to make things even more interesting? Add a small wager to the game. It could be as simple as who pays for the drinks all the way up to something a little more spicy if the chemistry's right.

Go (Indoor) Rock Climbing

There's nothing quite like the *hint* of danger to increase arousal... especially when you're safe as houses. Indoor rock climbing lets you have the excitement and adventure of mountaineering without the dizzying heights and danger of, y'know, falling to your death. Plus, if neither if you have ever climbed before, most rock gyms have private lessons, equipment rentals and marked routes for every skill level from never-ever to "half mountain-goat."

You have the thrill of adventure and the hint of danger to get your heart pumping and your adrenaline surging even as you're safely roped into your safety harness. You get to cheer each other on as you both compete to complete increasingly difficult climbing routes or see who can make it farther or higher. Just be aware that rock climbing is physically demanding, especially for newbies; an hour is going to leave you both exhausted.

Take Dance Lessons (Together)

Want a date that encourages – even *requires* – getting in your date's personal space and putting your hands all over her? Then you want to go dancing! What if you not only have two left feet, but they were put on backwards? What if you're allergic to Iggy Azealea, cigarette smoke, impossibly loud music, overpriced drinks and Pitbull remixes?

That's why you and your date want find a dance class! Almost every dance school has open classes or social dance parties. Actual skill level and experience are irrelevant; in fact, most of these will be focused on teaching you the basics and working your way up from there. The atmosphere is open and friendly with a focus on *fun*. Ever wanted to learn to salsa? Waltz? Swing? Bring your date and let it be an adventure for the two of you.

Go to the Zoo

Want to enjoy the wonder and beauty of nature without necessarily having to struggle over boulders and check each other for ticks afterwards? Want to melt your date's heart with painfully adorable baby animals? Go to the zoo! Zoos are easy-going, relaxed dates with romance practically built right in. It's natural to hold hands as you're walking around or lean up against one another as you watch the animals frolic. You never have to worry about running out of things to talk about, since the animals are *right there*.

Many zoos offer classes and behind-the-scenes tours, even occasional hands-on events with the animals themselves. Even more have actually started offering date night events, with an opportunity to explore the grounds after hours following a catered romantic dinner.

And did I mention the baby animals?

WHEN TO KISS HER

"When should you go for the kiss?" is possibly the most stress-inducing question for guys, whether they're trying to pick up a hottie at the bar or they're on a date. It's an area where everyone feels some sort of anxiety because there are just so many unknowns. When do you kiss her? How should you kiss her? Do you ask first or just go for it? When's the perfect moment? What do you do if she gives you the cheek?

Here's the thing, though: your date has probably spent just as much time thinking about how the night is going to end as you have, if not more. Trust me, she is feeling every moment of anxiety and confusion because she wants it to go right as much as you do.

But I'm here to help you cut through all of the anxiety and confusion and know not only how to kiss with confidence, but to pick the perfect moment and deliver the kiss that knocks her socks off whether you're at the bar or standing on her front porch.

Should You Go for the Kiss on the First Date?

As far as I'm concerned: yes. Whether to kiss on the first date or not is often a matter of contentious debate and personal preference. Some people resolutely won't while others have no problem going straight back to your place if the date goes well enough. In my opinion, not going for the kiss is riskier; if you don't, you run the risk of inadvertently signaling that you're not attracted to your date after all, especially if you haven't made it 100% clear that you're on a *date.*

As with everything in dating, it's all in how you approach the subject. Your date is going to be taking her cues from you. If you make it weird, they'll treat it like it's weird. If you treat everything like it's no big deal, *they'll* treat it like it's no big deal.

So let's cover the important points, shall we?

There Is No Such Thing as the Perfect Moment

One of the first things you have to understand is that there is no such thing as the perfect moment. At the same time, *any* moment can be the perfect moment. The good-night kiss at the end of the date is practically ritual by now, but it's by no means the *only* time you can kiss her. If you end up waiting for the perfect moment, you're going to be waiting forever.

Pop culture has drilled the idea that first kiss has to be "perfect" and at "the perfect moment" into our heads. But the funny thing about those "perfect moments" is that they magically become the perfect moment after the fact. We love stories, and we'll quite cheerfully rewrite our memories to support the narrative we want to see. Even if your first kiss was in the middle of a crowded bar where some ugly sweaty dude was flirting with your date five minutes before, it will end up being the perfect moment as your brain rewrites the scenario so that *everything* was leading up to that moment. Did you close your eyes too early and get her nose instead of her lips? She'll be telling her friends how adorable the mistake was and how sweet the moment ended up being because of your little slip.

The perfect moment is the moment you make. The only wrong moment is if you kiss her when she doesn't want to be kissed. And how do you avoid that?

Well, I'm glad you asked.

How to Tell When She's Ready to Be Kissed

Women have a number of tells when they want you to kiss them. Just as watching her signs will tell you whether she's interested, paying attention to a woman's body language will let you know when she's ready for you to make her move. Remember: any sign by itself doesn't necessarily mean anything. You want to watch for *clusters* of signs.

Watch Her Body Language

How does she respond to you physically? Is she leaning in to catch every word? Is she staying close to you, even hugging your arm and snuggling up to you as you're walking together? Is she making a point to close the gap between personal space (approximately two to four feet) to intimate space (around eighteen inches or so)? The more she puts herself in intimate space, the more interested she is.

Is She Touching You?

How much touching is she doing? An occasional touch on a "safe" spot like your arm is a neutral sign. On the other hand, an intentional, lingering touch such as pressing her thigh up against yours while you're sitting together, or letting her hand rest on your forearm is a sign of interest.

If you hug her, are you getting the A-Frame hug – all upper body, with no hips – or the full body? The former is platonic; the latter is an interest in more. If she's lingering on the hug, then she's waiting for you to take the next step.

Is She Touching Herself?

A woman interested in being touched will perform what's known as "autoerotic" touching – touching herself in places she'd like *you* to. Is she gently stroking her neck or collarbone, or even near the tops of her breasts? She's trying to draw your attention and make you think about what it'd be like to touch her there... starting with your lips.

Is She Licking Her Lips?

If she's interested in being kissed, she's going to be calling attention to her mouth. She may touch her mouth and lips with her fingertips or a prop like a straw. Alternately, she may bite her lip or lick them, especially if she's within your intimate space.

Watch For the Triangle Gaze

This is one of the best, surest signs out there for when someone's interested in being kissed. She will perform what's known as the triangle gaze: looking from one eye to the other, then down to your lips, then back up to your eyes. She's waiting to see how you react. Giving *her* the triangle gaze is also a good way to make her think of being kissed.

Should You Ask, or Just Go For It?

This is a tricky subject. If you ask five different women whether they prefer to be asked or not, you'll get six different answers. Some people feel that asking ruins the moment, while others absolutely prefer having someone asking first. Some find that asking can be incredibly sweet and romantic, while others find it off-putting.

Now, I've conducted some incredibly informal and utterly unscientific polls via the Dr. NerdLove Facebook page; out of the respondents, the majority either favored just making a move or not having a particular preference, while those who preferred to be asked *strongly* preferred to be asked.

What does this mean for you in practice? Well, if you're getting the signals, then go for it. However, if you feel it's safer, then ask or at least make your intentions known. Sometimes it's better to make a statement – "I've been thinking about kissing you for the last ten minutes" –

than to ask if you can kiss her. Regardless, if you ask, wait for her "yes" before you make your move.

How to Kiss Her

When it comes to a first kiss – whether you're picking up a stranger or on a date with your crush – slow and sensual is much better than trying to dive in and maul her face. There are few things sexier than anticipation and the build-up to a first kiss can positively electrifying. Plus, it gives her plenty of time to respond; if she doesn't want you to kiss her, she's got ample time to give you the cheek or to wave you off.

Start with a gesture: brushing her hair away from her face or a light finger on the underside of her jaw. Lean in slowly, enough to let tension build but not so slowly that she wonders what the hell you're doing, and let your lips brush up against hers before giving her the full kiss. Let the kiss linger, but be the first to pull back slightly; you want tension to build, but not so much that she becomes uncomfortable. Trust me, if she wants you to kiss her again, she will let you know in no uncertain terms.

Also: no tongue. Period. Not on the first kiss.

If she flinches when you brush her hair away, tenses up or turns and gives you the cheek when you move in, don't panic. Pull back, give a sheepish smile and say, "Sorry about that, I guess I read the moment wrong," and *let it go*. This doesn't mean that everything's ruined or that she doesn't like you; it just means that she doesn't want to be kissed right now. Acting like a grown-ass man and taking a wave-off with good humor can mean the difference between "not right now" and "never."

But as nervous as you might be, keep something in mind: this isn't rocket science and your date isn't the Voynich Manuscript. She's made a point of dressing up to look nice for you and has been spending most of her evening with you. She's been laughing at your jokes, enjoying your company and hasn't been checking her phone for the "emergency" text or eyeing the clock. She's having a good time. She's really starting to like you.

So get over there and kiss her already!

DEALING WITH FLAKES

There's an unfortunate truth when it comes to dating that sometimes people are going to flake on you. It's incredibly frustrating; you're getting excited as the big day comes and then the night before (or even worse, on the day of) you get the dreaded text: "Hey, turns out I can't make it today. Maybe some other time." Suddenly, you're left all dressed up with nowhere to go, feeling your ego (and your half-chub) deflating like a leaky pool toy. Any subsequent texts get noncommittal answers and your voicemails aren't being returned.

Flakes can be maddening because they feel so unfair and arbitrary. It's social blue-balls, relationship cockblocking. You felt like you were doing everything right and then it comes out of absolutely nowhere.

So why do women flake, and what can you do about it?

When a woman flakes out on your date, it's for a very simple reason: she's not that into you.

She may have been having a good time with you in the moment, but ultimately, she's just not feeling that spark she needs that pushes her from "well, that was fun," to "that was fun and I want to see this guy again!" Other times, it's that she *was* interested but changed her mind. One of the most common reasons for this is that you've accidentally turned her off through unattractive or needy behavior. I've seen plenty of guys – myself included – who've managed to snatch defeat from the jaws of victory because they came across as whiny or needy over Facebook or via text. Once you've chased someone off through unattractive behavior, the only thing you can do is chalk it up to a learning opportunity and not make the same mistake next time.

The other common cause is the loss of emotional momentum.

The excitement and rush of a positive in-person interaction is heady, but it can wear off quickly if you don't do anything to maintain it. Like a car running out of gas, you go from speeding along to sputtering to a halt if you don't manage things carefully. Leaving with vague promises to "hang out later" or to "talk sometime" won't help maintain the excitement or emotional connection that you just spent the last X number of minutes/hours building. Similarly, going for long periods of time without contact will cause the momentum to diminish. As the momentum fades, she stops picturing you as the awesome guy she was really interested in and you become just another guy she vaguely remembers giving her number to.

How to Detect an Incoming Flake

Despite feeling like it came out of nowhere, women very rarely flake out or stand someone up without warning. When you look back at your previous conversations that lead up to the flake, there are almost always signs that a flake was coming.

The most common sign is a variation on the old classic: "Call me the day of." This is something that you'll hear most often when you're trying to arrange a date, especially if you've made a nebulous offer to "hang out" rather than making firm plans. When someone tells you this, she's telling you that she's waiting to see if she gets a better offer. If nothing else comes along, then maybe she'll go out on you. *Maybe.* But probably not. By saying, "Call me the day of," she is letting you know that you are – at best – her second choice.

Another sign of an impending flake is if she's less than enthusiastic about seeing you, even if she'd agreed to go out with you in the first place, especially if she may or may not have other plans that day. She may remember that she had already made plans with someone, but she's not sure if they're still on or not. This becomes a case of Schrödinger's Date. You're kept in a state of quantum uncertainty, where your date is simultaneously on and off and you have no idea which until the waveforms collapse... usually right before you're supposed to get together, leaving you stuck at the coffee shop with only cold lattes and the pitying, knowing glances from the staff for company.

A variation on this is if she remembers that she has plans but doesn't offer to reschedule for a specific day. Someone who's interested in seeing you will make a point of trying to find a time when you two can get together. Someone who's going to flake on you will simply suggest getting together "some other time" on some vague day in the distant future.

Of course, the most soul-crushing sign of an impending flake is if you're rapidly dropping down the Communication Intimacy Ladder from Chapter 7. If she's started returning your phone calls with texts and your texts with IMs and those replies are getting increasingly terse, then the odds are high that she's suddenly not going to be able to meet you for dinner on Saturday.

If you *do* catch an impending flake, or get blind-sided by one, there's only one way to respond:

"It's No Big Deal."

There's no profit in getting upset or calling her out for flaking; she doesn't care enough about you to go on a date with you, so why should she care if you get mad at her? You're not in a position of moral authority. You're not her boyfriend, her friend or a family member; you're just some guy she met once. Getting angry and freaking out at her only makes you look immature and childish at best. It's better to just accept things with grace and move on. Yes, it's disappointing, but let's be real here: you dodged a bullet. After all, why would you want to date someone who thinks it's okay to flake out at the last minute?

Preventing Flakes

Unfortunately, it's not really possible to reverse a flake once someone's decided that they're not interested in going out with you. Once you've gotten signs that they're planning on flaking out on you, you're officially in damage-control mode; nine times out of ten, all that's left to do is make alternate plans with someone else. Very rarely, you can get some interest back by preemptively flaking on them as soon as you see the signs. You essentially attempt to flip the script by canceling on them, reframing the situation as if they were pursuing you. Occasionally this sort of mind game is enough to reignite some interest.

But you have to ask yourself: *why would you want to go out with someone who isn't eager to go out with you?*

Trying to reverse a flake isn't worth the effort. Instead, the best thing you can do is prevent the flake from happening in the first place by making sure that she's excited to see you.

To start with: make concrete plans. Don't ask if you can "hang out some time" or "get together later"; invite her to a specific date at a specific time. Make definitive statements of intent: you want to see her, not just that you'd "like to" or "it'd be nice if…" Having the balls to be open and say, "Yes, I like you" in a confident and self-assured way can be incredibly powerful and attractive. If she suggests rescheduling without a specific time in mind, have one ready instead… especially with the implication of an artificial time constraint.

For example:

Her: Yeah, it just doesn't look like it can work today. Maybe we get together later?

You: Sounds great. Let's meet up at The Nomad tomorrow at 9:30. I can't stay long though. I told some friends I'd meet them later.

Do you have other plans? No, not really. However, not only are you demonstrating that you aren't planning on sitting at home alone if she can't come, but the artificial time constraint means that she's more likely to accept; it reassures her that if she does agree to see you, it's not going to be taking up too much of her time. If the two of you are having a good time, there's no need to actually leave; you'd much rather spend time with her, no? Otherwise… well, you're probably better off writing the date off anyway.

All told, though, women flaking on you is a sign that you're not building enough attraction before you ask them out on a date. If you want to prevent flakes, then work harder in the beginning and keep that excitement and interest high.

SURVIVING DATING DISASTERS

One of the chief sources of stress when it comes to actually going on that big date with the woman you've had a crush on is the fear of everything going wrong. Just as you may have imagined all of the ways that the approach might backfire on you, now you can see all the ways your perfect date could be ruined.

Over the years, I have gone on more dates than I can reasonably count. As a result, I have dealt with just about every single dating fuck-up that you can imagine from the mundane[2] to the downright bizarre.[3] With time, experience and multiple affronts to my dignity, I've learned how to be ready for almost any dating emergency that you're likely to encounter, and how to roll with the ones that you aren't.

You just have to embrace your inner Batman.

Stick with me here.

In a world filled with super-powered aliens, maniacal robots and gods made flesh, the Batman stands alone: an ordinary man with no super powers who triumphs through strength of will, years of training... and being prepared for damn near everything. There is no scenario he has not gamed out well in advance, and he's kitted himself out with the necessary equipment to handle the most common events.

You can learn from this. By anticipating the most likely problems and taking the time to do your prep work in advance, you can easily avoid or mitigate some of the worst-case dating scenarios and turn a date heading for disaster into a night to remember.

Unexpected Medical Issues

Let me tell you a story of a dating nightmare I experienced.

Back in my bad old days, I'd had a massive crush on a girl I met in college. Through sheer luck, she'd agreed to go out on a date with me: the typical dinner and a movie. I made the mistake of visiting a "classy" restaurant that had a... fairly shaky relationship with my digestive tract, shall we say. Eating there on more than one occasion had

2. Car trouble, credit cards being declined, ill-timed gastric distress...
3. Chasing a coke dealer all over Austin...

turned into a sort of lower-intestinal Russian roulette, and this time I'd pulled the trigger on the wrong chamber.

During an attempt at cheesy romance, my date and I took a spin on a carousel in front of the movie theater. In the middle of the ride, with less than a minute before the movie was due to start, I started to feel a rather distinctive disturbance in the Force. With no time to explain, I hopped off the moving carousel and walked as quickly – but gingerly – as possible to the nearest men's room, a good five-minute stagger away.

Needless to say, this was not one of my finest hours. But it taught me a very good lesson: keep an emergency kit within easy access at all times. This will become your dating utility belt.

(Note: PLEASE don't carry any of this in a pouch on your belt. In fact, keep your belt as free from accessories as humanly possible.)

Over the years, I've had dates that came close to ruin through digestive issues, unforeseen allergies and the occasional minor injury. As a result, I keep several key components of my dating emergency kit stashed either on my person or in my car.

In my kit, I carry:

- Anti-diarrhea tablets
- Ibuprofen
- At least two decongestants
- A bottle of Benadryl tablets
- Altoids
- Condoms

More often than not, your medical emergencies will tend to be annoying or potentially embarrassing. They will also tend to revolve around food, drink or airborne allergens. Benadryl has long been my go-to antihistamine for allergic reactions, ranging from bug bites to moderate food allergies, while a decent decongestant can help get past sudden sneezing fits, watery eyes and clogged nasal passages.

Altoids are, perhaps, the most versatile component of your kit. The mint oil helps to calm nausea and upset stomachs, handy if something starts to make you queasy. In the event that you or your date actually *do* have to puke, the mints help get the taste (and scent) of vomit from your mouth. It also will help if either of you make the mistake of eating something with garlic or onions over the course of your date and ease those first-kiss anxieties.

Your Plans Fall Through

There's an old saying: "Man plans and the gods laugh." This is especially true when it comes to dating. No matter how carefully you've planned your night out, things can and will go wrong – often at the worst possible moment. The train will be late. It will start pouring rain. Traffic will be insane or you run out of gas and you'll miss your movie or the play that you'd been planning on seeing. The restaurant will lose your reservation. The Will Call box will lose your tickets. The band you were planning on seeing will cancel because its lead singer has been found in a hotel room in Bangkok… when they were supposed to be playing in Milwaukee. Your credit card gets declined. The list goes on and on.

Obviously, your dream date is ruined, right?

Well... not so much. Not if you have the right combination of advance planning and technology.

Ideally, before you even go on your date, you should have a contingency plan just in case. Most cities have free alternative weekly papers that carry listings of goings-on for the week. Not only should you be scanning these for date possibilities, but you should keep some of them in mind on the off chance that something goes wrong and you find yourself scrambling for a plan B.

But even if you didn't manage to plan in advance, your smartphone can be your savior. Batman has Oracle, you have Siri or Google Now... not to mention Yelp, OpenTable, UrbanSpoon, TabbedOut, Fandango and a host other apps at your fingertips. Didn't make the movie on time? Get tickets to another showing. If you're in a larger city, apps like ThrillCall can help you find live music in your area as well as help you get tickets. Lost your reservation? Use apps like Yelp and OpenTable to find another restaurant nearby and guarantee that a cozy table for two will be waiting for you by the time you get there. Got locked out of your car? Time to call for Uber or Lyft.

In addition, don't forget to take advantage of help from unexpected places. Some credit cards offer perks including concierge-like service that can help snag last minute tickets or reservations that you might not get on your own.

The key is to be flexible. Yes, it sucks that you may not have gotten into the club where your favorite band was playing, but being able to switch gears as necessary with minimum drama can make all the difference between calling it quits and saving your special night out.

Also, to avoid the potential embarrassment of being caught short on cash – or having your card declined – be sure to have a stash of emergency cash in your car. $100 hidden under a seat or in your glove compartment can pull your ass out of a surprising number of fires.

Curse Your Body's Sudden Yet Inevitable Betrayal

Sometimes the worst emergencies are the ones that happen before you even leave the house. Fate, after all, has a strong sense of irony; naturally this means that your body has decided to relive all the worst parts puberty, right before you meet up with your dream girl. Fortunately, a little creative application of common household goods can get you ready at a moment's notice.

Acne:

There's nothing to make you feel like a teenager again like a sudden visit from the acne fairy. It might be your stress level, changes in humidity, even your hair products... but ultimately the cause doesn't matter because you have a date in two hours and you're dealing with a giant zit in the middle of your face. *Do not squeeze it.* Even if you do manage to drain it, you're going to leave it inflamed and swollen. Your best bet – especially if you're short on time – is to hit the medicine drawer. Any anti-rash cream with 1% hydrocortisone will reduce the swelling and redness; it won't get rid of the zit entirely, but it will go a long way to making it far less noticeable. If you're already on the go or don't have access to Cortaid, you should swing by the nearest convenience store and grab some ibuprofen liquid-gels. Break one open and apply just a little of the gel to the break out. The ibuprofen will reduce the swelling and redness almost immediately.

Another possibility: borrow a tip from women and use a little bit of concealer to cover up the errant zit. Believe it or not, *many* women wish men would learn to do this...

Razor burn:

If you have sensitive skin, you may find that daily shaving turns your face red and itchy with more cuts than a club DJ – just the look you're going for when you're meeting with your crush. Most aftershaves and lotions won't help; the majority have alcohol as an active ingredient, which only makes the issue worse. Instead, grab a handful of ice cubes. They'll soothe your irritated skin and help shrink the micro-cuts, letting them heal up quickly.

Your Breath:

Sure, you may have brushed your teeth, but you're still convinced that your breath could stun a yak at forty paces. To fix this, don't just brush your teeth: run your toothbrush over your tongue – that's where most of the bacteria that gives you bad breath tends to hang out. Rinse your brush in mouthwash and give your tongue a gentle scrub. Just be careful not to trigger your gag reflex.

Another option: take a quick shot of vodka. No, I'm not kidding. Vodka doesn't have a scent, and the alcohol content will help kill bacteria and freshen your breath, so go ahead and take a swig and swirl it around your mouth. Just don't get a flavored vodka – the sugar will actually make things worse.

You Stink:

Maybe you're a smoker. Maybe you have humidity issues in your apartment and your clothes are musty. Or maybe you just didn't have time to stop for a shower after work. No matter the reason, smelling bad is going to kill sex dead, and trying to cover up your BO with cologne is only going to make your date's eyes water from that instead. You have a couple of options here.

First, if you're headed out the door and you notice your clothes smell funky or reek of cigarettes, use an old theater trick: pour some vodka in a spray bottle and give your clothes a good misting. This will cut the nasty smells drastically if it doesn't eliminate them altogether.

Next, get some antibiotic wet-wipes and dart into the bathroom for a quick cat-bath. Use these under your armpits to get rid of the bacteria that's making you smell worse than a thing that smells bad, then reapply some deodorant. While you're at it, keep some dryer sheets in the trunk of your car. Not only will it help your car smell better, but you can use them to freshen up your clothes; give your smoke-scented shirt a quick rub-down.

Another option: pop some of those Altoids I told you to keep on hand. The peppermint oil will go through your system and actually exit through your pores as it breaks down. It's not a quick fix, but it can definitely help over the course of an evening.

You Embarrassed Yourself

Even the smoothest player will do make an ass of himself at the worst possible moment. Your joke may come off wrong. You may accidentally step on an emotional land mine that you didn't know was there. You may spill your drink on yourself, drop your entree, dance like a goon or otherwise fuck up and now you can feel your cool points draining down your leg and forming a puddle around your shoes. How do you get out of this one?

Apologize

Never underestimate the value of a sincere apology. If you have managed to somehow upset your date by acting like an ass, making a poorly timed joke or otherwise accidentally causing offense... apologize. Even if you feel that you didn't do anything wrong: apologize. Even if you feel that you're in the right or that you shouldn't be blamed for something you couldn't have foreseen: apologize. This is not the time for appropriating blame or rationalizing why you couldn't possibly be at fault and that she's wrong for being mad at you. You cannot argue someone into not being upset. Apologize simply and sincerely, then let the matter drop. Switch subjects – even if you have to be obvious about it – and move on.

Call Out the Awkward

The easiest way to kill an awkward moment is to call out the awkwardness. You both know it happened and you both feel weird about it. Trying to pretend that nothing happened only makes the moment worse. Far better to directly acknowledge that yes, that was a bit of a boner on your part. Nothing eases tension like pointing out the elephant in the room and allowing the both of you to laugh about it and move on.

Play It Off

Everybody can make an ass of themselves at one time or another. The trick is how you *respond* to it. You can panic and get upset about how stupid you've just made yourself look... or you can just laugh it off and move on. This isn't to say that you should ignore it entirely – then you look oblivious, which just makes it worse. Make a quick joke – "Hey, this shirt needed a splash of color anyway" – and let it go. Your date will be taking her cues from you; if you get upset, she's going to feel squirmy and uncomfortable. If you can laugh it off, she won't feel embarrassed by proxy... and you will have earned cool points by being able to handle an otherwise awkward moment.

It doesn't take much to turn a bad date into an awesome one. A little preparation and keeping you cool will help you get through just about any dating emergency you'll encounter.

CHAPTER 10.

I GOT HER HOME... NOW WHAT? A GUIDE TO WHAT COMES NEXT

BRINGING HER HOME

After all your practice and all that time in the field, it seems as though things are about to *finally* pay off for you.

Maybe you're on your third date with the cute girl from the bookstore. Maybe it's late into your first date with the woman you met on OKCupid after spending a week flirting with each other. Maybe it's a spontaneous thing: you met her at your friend's Halloween party and the two of you couldn't keep your hands off each other. Maybe you met at a coffeehouse and hit it off and she invited you back to her place to watch videos.

However you got there, the important detail is that there's a girl. In your pad. On your couch. Surely at this point it's all over bar the squishy noises and passionate moaning, right?

Nope.

Just because you're within reach of home plate doesn't mean that you still can't be tagged out if you make the wrong move. It doesn't take much to turn a sure thing into nothing and you're left alone with a raging sense of frustration.

Someone being willing to come home with you doesn't mean that sex is guaranteed. It doesn't even mean that you're necessarily going to get *any* action out of this. All it means is that the possibility is there... and if you don't handle things the right way, that possible "yes" is going to be come a definite "no." Too many guys focus on the end goal – getting laid – without pausing to think about the bigger picture. Sex isn't just about getting your dick wet; it's about creating an incredible experience for both of you... and that's not going to happen if you're just focused on what *you* want.

This is why you want to embrace the art of seduction. Just because it seems like sex is inevitable, it doesn't meant that you can take it for granted. It's even more important to be that sexy, awesome guy she's been getting to know. You want to build that sexual tension to its boiling point, when you're both so far past the point of no return that you can't even imagine trying to stop. A man who can bring that level of desire to a woman is someone who's never going to lack for company. You don't want to be the story of a wasted evening; you want to be the guy that she can't stop bragging about to her friends.

Now that she's come home with you, it's time to make things even *hotter*.

BACHELOR PAD OR FORTRESS OF SOLITUDE?

The first step in seduction starts long before she ever came near your front door. In fact, it starts long before you even made plans to meet up with her that night. It starts with making sure your place isn't going to make sex disappear before it ever has a chance to happen. Whether you're in the dorm, live with roommates or have an apartment that's all your own, your bachelor pad can and will destroy any chances you have of getting laid.

When your girl gets through the door and sees the post-collegiate wasteland that is your apartment with the Naruto wall-scrolls and the massive Battle of Hoth diorama you have lovingly built out of LEGO sets and balls of cotton, her vagina will give the scream of ultimate despair and she will suddenly remember an urgent appointment she has early in the morning and she's really got to go…like, thirty minutes ago.

Your pad should not be a nerd Fortress of Solitude (emphasis on "solitude").

Your home is a reflection of who you are. It's your home base, the place where you can be who you are. And we're going to change the shit out of it.

Decorate Like a Man, Not a Man-Child

Too many guys decorate their place like they still live in the dorms. The walls are festooned with tacked-up posters and pin-ups while the furniture is a mishmash of curb-rescued broken down couches, cinderblock-and-plywood tables, improvised shelves and beanbag chairs, all focused around a home-theater system that probably cost more than the GDP of a small country. That massive HDTV may be awesome to play Call of Duty on and the sound system may well blow women's clothes clean off, but it's *not* going to distract her from the sad state that is the rest of your living quarters.

You're a grown-ass man. It's time to start living like one. This means having *real* furniture and a design sense that aspires to more than "man-cave." You want to start by taking stock of everything on your walls. Unframed posters held up by blu-tack, anime scrolls, dartboards and neon signs all scream that you haven't progressed past college. Similarly, if your house is decorated in wall-to-wall Nerd with action figures, statues and dioramas, you want to dial it all back severely. You want to show that you're classy and refined, with a sense of style and taste.

So strip everything back to the bare walls and start planning a Stalinist purge of your belongings. You don't need to get rid of all of your gear, but you *do* want to pare it back to the best of the best. Once you've pruned out the deadwood from your collection, get it organized and put away. Hit up the Container Store, get some organizational kits and boxes and store them neatly in a spare closet. Having everything organized instead of a jumbled mess not only means you have a more efficient use of space, but it makes it easier to find things when you want them.

Now that you've primed the canvas that is your walls, it's time to decorate. Framed and matted photos and gallery-wrapped canvases all send a message that you're someone with a sense of class. Movie posters are also a great way to let your geek flag fly with some serious style. A James Bond poster thumbtacked to the wall isn't attractive... but that same poster in Italian in a simple frame is *art.* You can also get geek and style points by collecting artist-edition posters from art collectives like Nakatomi Plaza and Mondo Press. Just remember: a simple matte and frame turns almost any poster into a classy work of art.

Similarly, you want to dial back the toys and action figures – keep some out, but treat them as display pieces. Some of the more complex LEGO models can make excellent display pieces when positioned and mounted. The Architecture collection looks especially snazzy when it's treated like an objet d'art instead of a toy.

While you're at it, get an understated and simple display case for your CDs, Blu-rays and video games – you want them organized and neat so that your date can browse through them with ease. And for God's sake, weed out the porn. I don't care how kinky or open-minded a woman may claim to be, porn out in the open is going to be an instant turn-off. Anyway, this is the 21st goddamn century; you shouldn't be buying porn DVDs anymore. That's what YouPorn, RedTube, and a password-protected file marked "Tax Statements 2001-2011" is for.

Next, clean up your furniture. Ideally you have decent furniture to start with, but even if you're working with thrift-shop specials, you can at least make them more attractive. Grab some throw pillows for the couch. Yes. Throw pillows. Find a couple in colors and patterns that compliment your raggedy-ass couch, arrange them to cover up the worst of the stains and marvel at how it transforms into something a woman may actually want to spend some time on. An attractive throw rug can also add some much-needed color to a room and help divide up the space.

While you're moving things around, you'll want to adjust the flow of the rooms. You want your apartment to be set up to make seduction that much easier. You want her sitting on the couch next to you rather than in the chair across the room from you, after all. Move the chairs and ottomans to the edges of the living room and orient them *away* from the center. Sitting there will feel awkward and exclusionary. You want to have some things that you can do together set up within easy reach of the couch; photo books, coffee table collections of famous art, puzzles... anything that you can work on together.

Don't be afraid to read style magazines or design blogs for ideas on how to display your gear; a little creativity turns a nerd's den into a hot bachelor pad.

Clean, Clean, Clean

It really can't be emphasized enough: most young men's lairs could double as biology experiments devoted to uplifting cockroach colonies into the next stage of evolution. You should not only know that you have a floor because all your empty beer cans haven't fallen through to the apartment below you, and there is nothing less appealing to a woman than the pervasive scent of mold and rotting pizza. A clean home is a home where sex can happen. A messy, disorganized one is going to make her feel like invisible bugs are crawling all over her skin. This means you're going to have to do some deep, deep cleaning. Flipping the cushions over and shoving everything under the bed isn't going to cut it.

It can seem like a daunting task at first – especially if it's been a while since your last deep cleaning – but you can make it much easier by simply attacking everything in stages. Take a trip to Target to get supplies. You want fresh bags in the vacuum cleaner, Swiffers, garbage bags, spray bottles, white vinegar, lemons or limes, baking soda, sponge cloths, chamois, newspaper, vanilla extract and cheap vodka.

Yes. Vodka. Don't worry, I'll get to that in a moment.

Start with bulk trash removal. Gather up all of your garbage, sort it into trash versus recyclables, bag it all and haul it to the dumpster. Clearing out the obvious garbage and clutter will make it feel like you've accomplished a miracle, which will make the *rest* of the cleaning seem that much less daunting.

Next, pick up and organize your belongings. Don't just let things pile up; everything you own should have a designated home where it can be neatly arranged and organized. Don't just try to dump it all in drawers and closets, either – make sure it's all carefully arranged in a place that makes logical sense. This has greater benefits besides a clean apartment – taming the clutter around your living area actually makes you feel calmer and more in control.

Following that, you should vacuum and dust. Vacuum every single cloth surface in your place. This includes your couch, chairs, curtains and the bed. Flip over the cushions, vacuum the undersides, fluff them back up and move them around to help keep the wear patterns even. Use Swiffers on every hard surface that isn't electronic equipment (there are specific dusting cloths you'll want to use for those).

Next comes sterilization. Don't get hung up on cleansers and powders; white distilled vinegar is the only cleaning solution you need. Pour it into a spray bottle and use it like Lysol. You want to use newspaper to wipe down and dry your mirrors and windows, and the sponge cloths on all of the other surfaces. Spend *extra* time cleaning your kitchen, the toilets, the bathtub and shower. These are the areas where women will judge you the most harshly. As nice as the rest of your place may be, a disgusting bathroom can mean the difference between making out on the couch or two hours of watching a movie you hate followed by a firm handshake goodnight.

Finally, deodorize; fill a spray bottle with the vodka and give every funky-smelling piece of upholstery and clothing in the house a light misting. Vodka is an incredible odor-killer and will get funky mildew and cigarette smells out of just about *anything* without leaving weird chemical perfumes behind. Open the box of baking soda and shove it in the fridge. Pour a teaspoon of vanilla extract into a quart of water, then boil on the stovetop until it's evaporated.

Now stare in wonder at an apartment that doesn't make you afraid to wander around barefoot.

Make It Woman-Friendly

Now that you've given yourself a strong base, it's time to add the minor details that will make women want to spend time with you.

To start with: upgrade your towels and linens. If you want a woman to stay the night, you want your place to be as inviting as possible. Having luxurious bedding will make her think that much more about what it's going to feel like to slide between those sheets naked. You want cotton sheets with as high a thread-count as you can afford – the higher thread-count, the more amazing those sheets will feel. Ideally, look for Egyptian or Pima cotton sheets, although you can expect to pay luxury prices for them. A simple duvet will class up the bed nicely as well.

You also should show that you are capable of caring for a living thing, besides bedbugs, cockroaches and mold, anyway. A little greenery can make an apartment seem much more alive, as well as suggesting you have a caring, nurturing side. You want maximum plant for minimum effort, so look into succulents and cacti. They make excellent bachelor pad plants: they're cheap, require minimal care, look amazing and – importantly – are almost impossible to kill. Your date doesn't need to know that all you do is give them water once a week.

Stock the fridge with care; you want to have more in your cabinets and fridge than last week's Chinese take-out, three beers and some mayo. You want her to see that you're a grown-ass man, not that you eat like you've never heard of diabetes or home cooking. Get a bottle of white wine, milk, salad fixings, eggs, fruit and cheese. Not only does this send the message that you know your way around the kitchen, but that you're also prepared to make breakfast in the morning.[1]

Finally, consider some candles. You want votives and block candles rather than tea-lights and tapers; these convey a more masculine air instead of reading as "my last girlfriend left these behind." Don't go hog-wild at Yankee Candle; just get some that are subtly scented. Malin Goetz has many that aren't overly perfumed or "girly," while DL & Company have candles that also serve as classy decorations.

Not only do they help class up any apartment and make it smell nice, there's nothing quite like candlelight to help set the mood.

---

1. Just make sure you're actually know *how* to make breakfast beyond cold cereal. Otherwise, that's just false advertising.

THE IMPORTANCE OF ENTHUSIASTIC CONSENT (OR: WHY YOU SHOULD GET A YES INSTEAD OF AVOIDING A NO)

When it comes to sex, nothing – and I mean *nothing* – is more important than the concept of consent.

Unfortunately, whenever the topic comes up, we tend to focus on the negative: "no means no" and so forth. Don't get me wrong; respecting a "no" is incredibly important. The lack of a definite "no" doesn't automatically equal consent. You want to do more than just avoid a direct refusal. Instead, you want affirmative, enthusiastic consent.

It's not just about not getting an obvious "no." It's about getting a definitive "yes."

The Standard of Enthusiastic Consent

All too often, when the subject of consent focuses on "no means no," you find people – well-meaning people, to be sure – who end up confused. When we say that "no means no" and someone doesn't give a definitive no, what does that mean? If someone is raising objections – she hasn't taken a shower, she's on her period, she's not feeling well or "we shouldn't" – but doesn't say the words "no" or "stop" or "don't," does that mean the same thing? What about if she gives in, half-heartedly participating? Doesn't that mean that she ultimately consented?

The focus on "no" puts the burden on women to rein in the libidos of men, who supposedly can't control themselves. In many ways, this puts women at a disadvantage. Women are often socialized to be nondirect for fear of causing offense; many women are frequently uncomfortable with being up front and saying, "No, I don't want this." They may try to use what's known as a "soft" no as a way to give the wave-off without actually saying the words.

Similarly, alcohol also has a way of making it hard to give a definite "no," or to recognize one, for that matter. Booze doesn't create emotions where they don't exist. Someone who doesn't like you isn't going to magically fall in love after enough beers. What it *does* do is lower one's capacity for rational thought and decision making. A person may not want to have sex with someone, but enough booze can make them more likely to give in to pressure or otherwise ignore their own misgivings.

A focus on "no" also makes many men worry about misreading signals; how can you be sure she really does want to sleep with you instead of just giving in because you've pushed and pushed at her? Is she going home with you because she's really into you, or because she's had too many drinks and is having a hard time refusing?

However, when you switch to the idea of affirmative or enthusiastic consent – focusing on getting an unambiguous "YES" instead of stopping at "no" – it changes the equation entirely.

The Difference Between "...yes" and "YES!!!"

Enthusiastic consent is incredibly simple. At its core, it's simply making absolutely sure that the person you want to have sex with wants to have sex with *you*. Instead of listening for a no, you want your partner to be giving you clear and unambiguous signals that she wants to bang like a screen door in a hurricane. It's the difference between her saying, "Dear God I want you so badly," versus a half-hearted "Yeah… I guess, whatever," when she really means "no."

The focus on an unambiguous yes (or a "give me your cock" or "I want you to eat me out right now" – you get the idea) cuts out any confusion around the idea of whether somebody is consenting. It's hard to misunderstand your partner when she's telling you, "Please fuck me," after all. Enthusiastic, affirmative consent cuts through any vagueness or uncertainty. Someone who's giving objections without saying "no" is not giving consent. A partner who is simply not resisting but otherwise not saying anything is not giving enthusiastic consent; they're just giving in.

I want to put a special note on the word enthusiastic because, frankly, not every "yes" is equal. In fact, there are many times when "yes" still means "no." I've seen many discussions on the ways of turning a "no" into a "yes," even when their partner doesn't mean it. There are people who will suggest that a woman's first couple of "no's" don't count, and you should push past them. There are others who will tell you that phrases like "we're not having sex tonight" are meant to be a test, a challenge of "let's see if you change my mind," rather than an explicit statement that she does not want to have sex with you tonight. Some will talk about making it about what she "owes" him – he bought dinner/rented the movie/paid for the plane tickets and now she's required to pay him back with sex. Others will rely on guilt: "I guess I thought you really loved me…" or emotional threats like "if you don't, I'll find someone who will."

A "yes" gained through coercive methods – however

innocuous they may seem –does not count. This runs counter to the entire idea of affirmative, enthusiastic consent. It's not a true, enthusiastic "yes"; it's just a way of manipulating someone so that, once again, you're just avoiding a "no."

Similarly, a "yes" under the influence of alcohol is not a *real* "yes." A "yes" after a night of drinking *could* mean that she really wants to bone... or it could be she doesn't but she's giving in, even though she doesn't really want to. Like I said earlier: booze doesn't make emotions appear from nowhere, it just lowers inhibitions and impairs decision making. Someone who *genuinely* wants to have sex with you while drunk will *still* want to have sex with you when she's sober. It costs you absolutely nothing to wait until she's sobered up.

Someone who *doesn't* want to have sex with you but will anyway is someone you shouldn't be having sex with in the first place.

Rule of thumb: too drunk to drive is too drunk to consent.

Consent Isn't a Binary Decision

One of the things to keep in mind is that consent isn't binary: "yes" isn't all-encompassing, nor does it mean that it's always on or always off. Consent is a sliding scale; it can be dialed forward or backwards. Just because someone's given consent to sex doesn't mean that they can't change their mind and withdraw it at any time... even in the middle of penetration. If one person decides that they're no longer in the mood or that they're not comfortable with what you're doing, then they're permitted to withdraw their consent, without protest from the other partner. When someone changes their mind, then sex stops.

But here's the thing: consent is granular. Just because someone may not consent to one activity doesn't mean that they don't want to do other things. A person can decide that he or she is no longer willing to have penis-in-vagina sex, but be perfectly happy (again: enthusiastic, not just offering to keep the other person from getting angry or upset) to have oral sex, give a handjob or indulge in some mutual masturbation and general fooling around. The important part, though, is what it says: that you respect and are invested enough in your partner – even if it's a one-night stand – that you want their full and eager participation. It's about two people who want to have fun together, rather than one partner doing whatever it takes to get what they want as cheaply as possible.

Enthusiastic Consent Is Hot

One of the misunderstandings that people frequently have around enthusiastic consent is the idea is that it's inconvenient, or worse, unsexy. They think of it as having to ask for permission for every step along the way: "May I kiss you?" "May I unhook your bra?" "May I touch your breasts?"

That's not what enthusiastic consent is about.

Enthusiastic consent is all about *desire*. It's about knowing without a doubt that your partner is as eager to get into your pants as you are to get into hers. It's about her attacking your face and the way she's trying to pull your clothes off. It's about her grinding on your lap and taking your hands and putting them all over her body. It's about dirty talk; grabbing your lover by the back of the head and growling, "I want you now." It's about the way she grabs you and slides you into her and the sharp gasps she makes when you touch her just right. It's about saying all the nasty, dirty things you want to do to them and hearing, "Oh GOD yes…" It's them telling you, "Yes, keep doing it like that!" or "Here, touch me here!"

Enthusiastic consent means actively communicating with your partner, which is the key to *really good* sex. You have to be willing and able to talk about what you want and what you don't want. It means paying attention to each other's pleasure, taking ownership of your sexuality and knowing what the other really wants.

There aren't any mixed messages when it comes to enthusiastic consent. In a world where an explicit, enthusiastic "yes" is the threshold of consent, you know damn good and well that your partner is *really excited* to be having sex with you.

And isn't that what we all want?

THE SWEET SCIENCE OF SEDUCTION

Just because she's come back to your place doesn't mean that it's on. Sex is definitely a possibility; by coming home with you (or taking you back to her place), she's showing that she's putting a lot of trust in you. But that doesn't mean that you can just assume that it's inevitable and there's nothing left to do but wait until the clothes come flying off. She may just be looking for some making out on the couch before going home, or once she's there decide that she'd rather just go home.

We know that you want it to happen.

Now you need to make sure she wants it, too.

You need to know how to seduce her.

Here's the thing when it comes to women and sex: women are as interested in sex as men are but they're socialized to be more cautious about having it, because all too often, it's just not worth it. The guys are rarely as skilled as they pretend to be (or just think they are) and are often interested only in their own pleasure. A seducer, on the other hand, is someone who knows what turns women on and how to raise the sexual tension to the breaking point. He knows how to bring her to the boiling point and not just get her willing, but *enthusiastically* willing.

You Don't "Get Lucky," You Get Together

I can't stand the phrase "get lucky." It implies that sex is something that "just happens" to you. This attitude is counterproductive. Sex isn't something that "just happens" or something you have to bargain for or coerce. Sex isn't an exchange, it's a *collaboration*. It's a jam session between partners, each bringing something to the table that adds up to an even greater whole. Seduction is a process of mutual pleasure, not just the process of "What do I have to do to get what I want from you?"

There's a distinct pleasure gap between men and women when it comes to sex – especially during casual hook-ups and one-night stands. One study from the Kinsey Institute at Indiana University[2] found that while

2. Incidentally, this study has the distinction of being the only scientific paper to cite Katy Perry's "TGIF"...

82% of men surveyed had a positive emotional reaction after a hook up, only 53% of women did. Women were also only half as likely to orgasm during a casual hook up as they would be in a committed relationship. Meanwhile, a similar study from New York University found that only 40% of women had orgasms during a hook up as opposed to 82% of men.

Small wonder why many women are less interested in hooking up with somebody. If the sex isn't going to be any good, then what's the point?

The attitude of taking a collaborative approach to sex, where you're concerned about *mutual* pleasure and fulfillment, is key to being a successful seducer. The more you keep her pleasure – not to mention her comfort and her boundaries – in mind, the more she will be interested in actually sleeping with you.

Be Prepared

It takes surprisingly little to disrupt the mood when it comes to sex. A successful seducer should always be prepared for as many contingencies as he can so as to make the process as smooth and effortless as possible. The more prepared you are, the fewer obstacles you will encounter that will end up disrupting the possibility of having sex.

Whether you're out and about doing cold approaches or going out on a date, you should be prepared for the possibility of getting laid. To start with, you want to bring some form of breath freshener and condoms with you whenever you go out. Yes, you may not *expect* anything to happen, but it's far better to have them and not need them than to need them and not have them. Should everything go well, you can't rely on other people to have protection.

You should also make sure that your pad is prepared. At the *very* least, you want clean sheets on the bed, fresh towels in the bathroom and a relatively clean and orderly place. If you want to go the extra mile, give everything a thorough cleaning. Take out the trash, give the bathroom a scrub-down, arrange interesting books on the coffee table, maybe even put a drop of vanilla extract on the lamps.

Make sure that you're stocked for possible contingencies as well. Having some fresh fruit in the fridge – especially ones that you can feed to one another like grapes or strawberries – is always a good idea. Make sure your liquor cabinet is prepared, so you can offer your guest a drink; you want at least a good bottle of red wine, a bottle of white wine, vodka, whiskey and gin, as well as some mixers. You want to keep condoms and a water-based lubricant in your nightstand by your bed so you can find them in the dark without too much trouble. Make sure you have some basic breakfast options as well, such as cereal, coffee and eggs. If she's going to spend the night, you should be enough of a gentleman to offer her breakfast in the morning.

Set the Mood

Atmosphere counts when it comes to seduction, so make sure you're creating the right mood. You want to create a feeling of comfort and intimacy with the right hint of naughtiness – it's just the two of you taking advantage of being off in a world of your own.

When you're setting the mood, it's almost impossible to go wrong with a little romance. Dim the lights and light some candles instead. Have a playlist of mood-appropriate music ready to go – music that works best at a low volume. Keep things soft and intimate, encouraging that the two of you get closer together. Let your initial touches – touching her hair or brushing your hand on her arm or skin – be soft and gentle.

Remember: no matter how nervous you might be, you want to project an air of calm assuredness. Whether this is your first time or your fortieth, you will be setting the tone for the evening. By coming home with you, she's choosing to make herself vulnerable to you; she's going to be especially alert and responsive to the emotional cues you're giving off. If you're jittery and uncomfortable, she'll feel jittery and uncomfortable and then you'll be lucky to have a handshake goodnight. Instead, you need to convey that having a girl over to your place is the most natural thing in the world. That air of confidence and ease will help relax her. That's not to say that you're nonchalant – you're excited for her to be here – but you're calm and relaxed.

Take It Slow

One rookie mistake that people make is to try to rush the seduction process and get to the bedroom[3] as quickly as possible. This is great if the two of you are already passionately mauling each other's faces before you can even get your key in the lock – go ahead and just carry her straight to bed. If not, however, then you need to be

3. ...or the couch, or the floor...

willing to take your time. If you push too hard, too fast then you risk pushing her beyond her comfort zone; at that point, she'll be making a beeline for the door, no matter how much she wanted to sleep with you before then.

Instead, you want to let the moment build. Anticipation is the key to sexual tension, after all; the more you allow the tension to build, the more amazing the payoff will finally be. So start slowly – gentle, closed-mouthed kisses and feather-soft touches along her skin, then let the kisses get a little firmer before parting your lips slightly. Pull back and breathe, watching her and drinking her in with your eyes. Let your seduction be a tease; it's not a question so much of whether it's going to happen but *when*, building her passion and arousal until she feels like she's about to explode.

Switch between different types of stimulation so that she doesn't get too used to any one sensation. As you kiss her, run your fingers down her back or along her sides. Trace your fingertips along the insides of her thighs or her forearms. Women are more than just lips, nipples and vaginas, so don't just focus your attention on them. Instead, find her *other* erogenous zones, the ones that aren't so obvious. Don't just kiss her lips; kiss her neck, her earlobes and the crook of her elbow. When you caress or kiss her breasts, don't focus just on her nipples; run your fingers over the tops of her breasts or use your lips and teeth on the underside. As you make out, don't just rush to penetrate her with your fingers; instead use your hand or your thighs to provide steady but firm pressure on her pubic mound. Let each progression of intimacy build on the last, bringing her close to her peak before pulling back and moving to another, keeping her teetering on the edge until she begs you. The more you build the tension and the arousal, it will start to feed itself, snowballing to the point of no return as you take her hand and lead her to the bedroom.

Check In With Her

The key to seduction is mutual arousal and pleasure. However, while men have been socialized to advocate for their own pleasure, women frequently have *not* for fear of being seen as slutty. This is why one of the keys to a successful seduction is communication. No two people get off the same way and when it's your first time together, it's going to be a learning experience all around.

The difference between some guy and a masterful lover is to care about *her* pleasure. The average man won't make the effort; after all, they're practically strangers. The master seducer, on the other hand, will make a point of connecting with his lovers and drawing out what makes them shiver and quake with pleasure. As things progress, check in with her: ask her, "How does that feel?" and *listen* to her responses. You also want to pay attention to her non-verbal cues – if something you do makes her gasp and tilt her pelvis towards you, that's a sign of "keep doing that until further notice" while something that makes her tense up and pull away means you should try something different.

Just as important: if she says, "Keep doing that" or "Just like that," then don't start to change things up. I realize it should go without saying, but I've lost track of how many women I've known who've complained about guys who would immediately shift to something else after being told what to do.

Remember, an open mind and a willingness to listen and follow directions – whether those directions are increased moans of pleasure or physically guiding your head or hands – trumps any lack of experience you may have. When a woman is telling you what she likes, it's not a criticism of your skill; she's telling you, "Do this and it will feel amazing." And that's what you want.

Know When to Stop

One of the most important parts of seduction is knowing when you've reached her boundaries

In the heat of the moment, it can be hard to want to tap the brakes, especially when you're not hearing an explicit "stop." In fact, a "We should probably stop" can sound an awful lot like "Convince me I don't want to stop." And to be fair: sometimes that's exactly what she was saying. However, there are more times when that "probably" means "I want to stop but I don't want to upset you." Women are often socialized to be indirect and less assertive than men and will at times frame a refusal or a request to stop or slow down as something other than a direct "no." It's critically important that you be willing to respect it.

If you reach a point that she objects to, up to and including being inside her, then you need to stop and take a step back to something she was okay with… and you must be completely cool with this. I cannot emphasize this enough: you are always absolutely fine with pulling back or coming to a full halt if need be. If she wants to stop, you are absolutely okay with it. You don't argue, whine, wheedle or ask why. Nobody has ever argued or debated their way into a woman's pants, and trying to do so just makes you look pathetic. The only acceptable response is, "I understand." You can try again a little later. She will let you know through her words and actions when it's okay to continue and when it isn't... so assume that it isn't unless otherwise stated.

If she *does* want to stop, then don't pull away or remove any sense of intimacy. You aren't trying to shame or pressure her into sex by freezing her out; you're trying to make her comfortable. Pulling away or freezing her out – refusing to talk to her or touch her – is more than a supreme dick move; it's coercive, it's manipulative and it's an attempt to play upon her insecurities in order to get what you want. You should be completely clear that you aren't frustrated; yes, you want to have sex with her, but it's more important that she feels safe and comfortable with you. So you're dialing things back to make her comfortable. When she's ready to try again, she will let you know. When she does, then progress slowly to where she wanted you to stop before. If she wants you to stop again, you stop again.

Yes, it can be difficult, especially when it feels like the finish line is within reach. Yeah, blue-balls hurt. If you're so horny that you can't think straight, slip off to the bathroom and rub one out so you can calm the hell down.

Remember: there is no reason to feel frustrated. If things have gotten to this point, then she will sleep with you eventually. Pushing her boundaries only guarantees that she won't want to see you again. Ever.

Stick the Landing

Just because you've slept together doesn't mean that the seduction's over. One area where men inevitably make a mistake is worrying about how to handle the aftermath. You may have gotten your rocks off, but that doesn't mean that all that's left is to kick her out of your place. All that does is guarantee that not only will you never see her again, but she'll make sure all of her friends and friends-of-friends know what a jerk you were.

Instead, even if this was a one-time hook-up, you want to handle the post-coital denouement like a gentleman.

To start with, shut up and savor the afterglow. You don't want to leap out of bed as though you desperately need to wash her off your skin. Take some time to cuddle and savor the moment. There's nothing quite as gratifying after amazing sex to hear your partner take a deep breath and say, "...Wow." Give a little time before taking off to the bathroom. While you're at it, offer her a warm towel or some water – it's just polite.

At this point, you will run into the tricky question of "is she going to stay the night?" Just about everyone worries about the implications of staying over: Is the other person going to get too attached? Are they going to think that *you're* getting too attached? Do you really want them to see what you look like first thing in the morning? Can you really handle the possibility of morning breath?

The best thing to do is to offer her the option of staying, especially if she seems like she's not sure whether she should go. Not everyone is going to want to stay; plenty of women would rather just go sleep in their own beds, same as men. Giving her the opportunity to stay makes the entire wind-down far less awkward, even if she *does* decide to leave.

Regardless of whether she stays or goes, you owe her a call the next day. Not a text. Not an email or a voice-mail. You shared bodily fluids, you want to actually speak to her and let her know that you had a great time. When you do call, only say, "We should do this again" or something similar if you *actually* intend to see her again. If not, just leave it at "thank you" and having enjoyed seeing her. The last thing either of you want to do is the awkward dance of "did she/he really mean that, or were they being polite?"

The better you can manage the morning after, the more success you will have in the future.

THE MOST COMMON SEXUAL MISHAPS – AND HOW TO RECOVER FROM THEM

Murphy's Law states that anything that can go wrong, will go wrong... usually at the worst possible moment. This is never more true than during sex, when any mistake can feel like an absolute disaster. Maybe you say something wrong or maybe you can't quite perform the way you were hoping to.

Don't panic. Just because you run into some calamities doesn't mean that you can't recover from them. In fact, when you know *how* to recover, you can even make sex better than ever.

5) You Came Too Quickly

Every man worries about his sexual stamina. Never mind the fact that the average length of sex – from penetration to orgasm – is around five to seven minutes. Sexual endurance is the number one anxiety that men have about sex, beating out STDs, pregnancy and penis size. No man wants to be known as a two-pump chump and years of porn have given us the idea that *real* men can go for hours before ejaculating.

So what do you do if your hang-time isn't where you wish it were?

Step One: Calm down. Every guy has times when they cum a lot faster than they would have liked. Getting upset isn't going to help you and will only make things awkward for the both of you. She's going to take her lead from you; if you treat it like it's no big deal, she will too.

Step Two: Give a self-deprecating laugh, tell your partner that she had you really turned on and you just couldn't hold back. Then go down on her. As long as you have two hands, a tongue and a can-do attitude, you can still give her amazing orgasms.

Step Three: Deal with the problem afterwards.

Premature ejaculation – defined as when a man ejaculates sooner than he or his partner would prefer – can have a multitude of causes ranging from simple anxiety to hypersensitivity and extreme arousal. There are a number of ways of lasting longer. The simplest is to practice Kegel exercises; the pubococcygeus muscles, which control the flow during urination, are the same ones that control ejaculation during orgasm. Strengthening your PC muscles by contracting them and releasing them repeatedly is a simple way of controlling one's orgasm.

You can also change up your sexual practices. Some sexual positions change the level of friction or the muscle tension that makes it easier to last longer; positions that require you to support your own weight will create tension in your pubic muscles that will make it more likely to orgasm quickly. You may also want to employ the classic stop-start method; when you feel the orgasm starting to build, stop thrusting for a few moments while letting the sensation fade before restarting. It can be almost torturous for guys to do this – once you feel that familiar tingle, you want to pound away as hard as you can – but a little discipline will bring desirable results.

And remember: when in doubt, rub one out. Masturbating a couple hours before sex can help you last longer.

4) The Mood Gets Ruined

No matter how much you prepare, sometimes things won't just go wrong, they will go embarrassingly wrong. Boner-killer wrong. You call her by the wrong name... and she catches you. Her dog leaps onto the bed. You let loose the loudest, nastiest fart you have ever known while she's going down on you. She reveals that she's a squirter... without warning you first. Your leg starts to cramp up just as you're about to show her why the girls back home called you "Mr. Crazy Straw."

What was going to be a momentous night of passion is now reduced to the two of you awkwardly looking at each other while you feel the atmosphere – and your erection – deflating into nothingness. How do you salvage things before she decides that it's time to go home and never call you again?

Laugh it off. Seriously.

Treat the situation like it's a scene in a romantic comedy, embrace the absurdity, make a joke and laugh it off. It only has to be serious and awkward if you both want it to be. The best thing you can do is defuse the interruption by making it into something silly. Laughter will lighten the mood, relax the both of you and transform what could have been the end of the evening into a temporary break until the two of you are ready to resume again.

Almost any interruption or mood-breaker can be laughed off, but some *are* going to be harder than others. If you called her by the wrong name, you'd better be ready to follow up quickly. If she calls you on it, it's time to insist that her name really is "Jesse." Or "Martha." Or "Bambi." Pretend to be confused and give her a different name every time she says something, then demand to know who the hell she is and why she's been calling herself "Sarah" all this time.

If she buys your bluff, then understand that I will never *ever* play poker with you.

3) Your Sexual Techniques Are Incompatible

Everyone has their routines when it comes to sex. Years of repetition and accommodating partners teach us to keep certain techniques as part of our standard repertoire. Every woman you've known has *loved* your mastery of the Swirly-Go-Round, the Transylvanian Twist, even the occasional Rusty Venture… until you run across the first partner who not only did not expect that particular move but is actively repulsed by it.

Maybe it was just the fact that it was a surprise. Maybe you crossed a line of what she is and isn't willing to try. Maybe you accidentally hit a trigger that you didn't know was there.

Regardless of how it happened, the only thing to do is stop and apologize right then and there. Sex requires trust above and beyond anything else and no woman will be willing to keep you as a partner if she thinks for a moment that she can't trust you to respect her boundaries. Tell her that you were caught up in the moment and didn't realize that what you were doing was going to upset her and that the last thing you want to do is make her uncomfortable or try to do something she wouldn't like.

You may have to accept that you're not having sex again that night. That's *fine*. Take this without complaint. Let the moment pass, and for fuck's sake, don't do it again. If you *do* get the green light to continue, keep your technique to strict vanilla unless otherwise asked and discuss matters later, when you're both fully clothed.

2) The Condom Broke

Things have been going great, but at some point, you realize the condom's no longer intact. In the heat of the moment, the condom either broke or slipped off entirely... and now you're faced with the awkward moment of telling your partner and dealing with the resultant anxiety that comes with it.

Ideally, you want to keep this from happening in the first place. Make sure that the condoms you're using fit properly. This is no time for pretending that you need Magnums when you actually need a snugger fit. A condom that's too big is going to slip off during sex, while a condom that's too small is more likely to rupture or tear. A condom should fit securely at the base of the penis and not slide off easily; depending on the style, there could be a variable amount of give or material at the head, but it should NOT be nearly skin tight.

Next, make sure that you put the condom on properly. Pinch the tip of the condom to prevent air bubbles while unrolling it towards the base of your penis; trapped air will cause the condom to rupture during sex.

During sex, take a moment or two to surreptitiously check the state of the condom. Reach a hand down and feel at the base of your penis and see if the condom's still there. Pull out, take a quick glance to make sure that it's in once piece and get back to bangin'.

If the condom does break or fall off, don't panic. What you need to do depends on several factors. If you notice this before you orgasm, simply stop, make sure that there aren't bits of the condom left in your partner, put on a new one and continue onward.

If you don't realize that the condom failed until after orgasm, then you need to inform your partner immediately. Your next steps depend on whether she is on a secondary form of birth control such as the pill or an IUD. If she is, all is most likely well.

If she isn't... well, it's time for Plan B. Literally. Plan

B – also known as the Morning After Pill – is available over the counter at most pharmacies. Make sure to call in advance to ensure they have it in stock and head over immediately.

By the by: You're accompanying her to the CVS because you're a goddamn human. If you think that you're sending her off on her own, then you need to understand that karma is going to ensure that you will never have sex again including with yourself.

1) You Can't Get It Up

Erectile dysfunction is a nightmare for men. There's nothing that makes you feel like less of a man than being unable to produce a rock-hard boner at a moment's notice. But as the joke goes, the difference between concern and panic is the second time you can't get it up for the first time. While the occasional inappropriately limp penis happens to every man over time, the instant that it happens to you sets off a downward spiral as you begin to imagine that your days of sex have come to an end.

The key to dealing with an unfortunate and occasional bout of flaccid meat is to not panic. An inability to get hard could have any number of causes ranging from alcohol consumption, side effects from medication, allergic reactions, or the capricious whims of a cruel and uncaring god. Sometimes it happens and it's not a big deal. You know what never goes limp? Your fingers and tongue. Shrug your shoulders, give your best Han Solo smirk and proceed to give her the greatest oral sex of her life. She'll love you for it.

CHAPTER 11.

DATING PITFALLS

DON'T FALL VICTIM TO ONE OF THE CLASSIC BLUNDERS

This is the big one.

See, now that you've made it this far, the last thing you want to do is fall victim to a classic dating blunder. The most famous one is believing that women owe you anything, but less well known is this: *never* put up with shitty behavior just because sex is on the line!

In all seriousness, by the time you've made it to this part of the book, you've come unbelievably far. But as far as you've come, it doesn't mean that you can't still find yourself getting caught up in some of the most common dating pitfalls out there. Even after I started my personal transformation, I still found myself losing ground when I let myself get stuck chasing after an ex-girlfriend for months. I made myself miserable – and worse, set my personal progress back – because I couldn't bring myself to admit what everybody else knew to be true: there will always be people who aren't going to like you the way that you like them. The sooner you're willing to accept this and move on, the happier you will be, and the better you will do socially.

I had to learn this the hard way. Hopefully, you can learn from my mistakes and avoid the heartache and misery that I went through.

Don't let yourself fall into these particular pitfalls.

BLUNDER #1: NOT ENFORCING YOUR BOUNDARIES

When I look back at my bad old days, one of the things I remember most is how I would put up with horrible behavior from people because I was desperately afraid that they would stop liking me. In fact, I let my first serious girlfriend literally drag me away from my friends because she decided she didn't like me spending time with them instead of her.

In fact, that phrase – "I let her" – defined the majority of our relationship.

At first, I hadn't noticed how she was treating me; I was so amazed that I was having sex at all that she could've set a basket of kittens on fire and I would've found a reason why it was okay. But once the honeymoon period ended, our relationship became a matter of constant fighting, jealousy, guilt trips and having to justify myself on an almost daily basis. Our life was constantly dramatic – something was always going on in her life that required my full attention at all times. The only plans we could have were ones she approved of, because I was only allowed so much personal time every week. Every disagreement we had – down to things as mundane as what to rent at the video store – was a potential relationship-ending event.

It was constant waves of highs and lows; when it was good, it felt like we were the only people in the world, and did I mention I was having sex? This was a new and amazing world to me. But when it was low, it was crisis after crisis and drama after drama. I deliberately avoided amazing opportunities to travel and see the world because I couldn't possibly leave her behind. I spent less and less time with my family because she insisted that they were poisoning me against her.

I was willing to put up with this behavior from her because, quite frankly, I didn't think I could do any better. If I put up even a hint of resistance, she would hold our relationship hostage. If things were especially bad, she would make dire pronouncements about how she didn't know what she would do without me. And so, I would stay... and the bad behavior would continue.

The Value of Boundaries

Stop me if any of this sounds familiar to you:

- You can't spend time with your friends without your girlfriend because she gets jealous if you have a life outside of your relationship.

- Your friend is constantly pushing you to do things you aren't comfortable with. If you resist, they get angry or passive aggressive, badgering you until you give in.

- Arguments with your girlfriend never stay on topic; any disagreement immediately turns into a litany of the ways you've wronged her and often only end because of threats to break up with you or to go sleep with someone else.

- The woman you met is willing to make plans but continually flakes at the last minute.

- Your family member continually brushes off your concerns as "unimportant" or tells you that you're being silly or irrational.

- Your relationship is in a constant state of drama; either things are amazing or there's a new source of conflict.

- You keep passing on opportunities that you would otherwise take because you don't want to disappoint or upset a friend, family member, or romantic partner.

- You have a friend, a family member, or a partner who is an emotional vampire; you can't talk with them without feeling bad about yourself and having your energy sucked away.

- Your girlfriend requires constant reassurance and assistance from you. Not a day goes by that she doesn't have a new crisis in which you need to intervene.

If you said yes to any of these, you likely have issues with maintaining strong boundaries. These situations are often a sign of having poor boundaries, the result of a mix of low self-esteem and an unwillingness to take a stand for yourself.

This isn't uncommon. In fact, many people who are socially inexperienced – geeks and nerds especially – will have encountered all of these and more over the course of their relationships. Many people assume that these are just par for the course when it comes to relationships, whether platonic, romantic, or familial.

By being unwilling to maintain strong boundaries, you

inevitably end up in emotionally-shredding, toxic relationships. Having poor boundaries attracts drama queens, emotional manipulators and toxic people into your life, all eager to take advantage of you.

However, by taking responsibility for yourself and refusing to play along with other people's emotional manipulation, not only will you find that you're a happier, healthier person but the quality of your relationships will improve immensely.

Shirking Responsibility and White Knight Syndrome

It's easy to end up with weak boundaries when you don't believe in your own worth. It's hard to stand up to someone you presumably care about, especially when you believe that this is your only chance at love or sex. When it feels like your relationship is constantly on the razor's edge of falling apart – and that it'll be all your fault when it does – you often will feel like you can't draw a line in the sand and say, "No. I will not tolerate this."

It becomes an ugly, self-perpetuating cycle. You already feel that you don't have the right to stand up for yourself, and you feel even *worse* when you admit that you're letting other people walk all over you. It's very easy to feel that you've "earned" their mistreatment; after all, if you were cooler or a better person, you would be able to push back.

Unfortunately, this feeling of worthlessness often leads to unhealthy relationships. One of the most common examples of sacrificing your values and taking responsibility for other peoples' emotions comes in what's known as White Knight syndrome – the desire to "save" a woman in order to prove that you're worthy of being loved.

White Knights are attracted to "endangered" women – usually women with emotional issues or ones who have histories of abuse, trauma or addiction issues. Would-be saviors frequently have an overly idealized and romanticized vision of the women they focus on and see them as impossibly pure and good. Similarly, White Knights see themselves as having only the purest of motivations, hoping to "save" women out of a sense of heroic altruism and expecting no reward other than the deed itself.

They are, of course, lying to themselves. By "rescuing" these women, they're hoping to be rewarded with sex at the very least, if not a relationship. Deep down, the White Knight trades on "fixing" problems for others because they believe that they have *nothing else about them* that makes them worthy of being loved. They rely on the social contract of reciprocation – salvation for love – rather than their own inherent worth. This frequently leaves them stuck in a relationship with an emotional vampire who drains the life out of them as they struggle to try to manage *her* life as well as their own.

Her fears and constant need for reassurance can be alluring at first; after all, the White Knight loves to be needed and being able to assuage her fears will make him feel strong. Over time, however, that need becomes increasingly unreasonable and unmanageable; she goes from needing reassurance to requiring his presence at all hours.

Other unstable women might take advantage of his need to please and fear of abandonment by using it to excuse their own bad behavior. It's his fault she made a scene while they were at the gallery show because he was being overbearing, or not attentive enough to her needs. It's *his* fault that she cheated on him because he abandoned her when she most needed him, so she had to find someone else to take his place. The manipulator uses his neediness to saddle him with responsibilities that aren't rightfully his and then makes him feel guilty for things that he wasn't liable for in the first place.

Saying No to Bullies, Drama Queens and Emotional Games

People who have poor boundaries and low self-esteem are typically easy prey for abusers. One of the most common signs of a predatory, abusive personality is the testing of boundaries: trying to push someone further and further out of their comfort zone, using a cycle of rewards and punishments in order to manipulate someone into being willing to knuckle under. Many women have had boyfriends who continually pushed the envelope of what they were comfortable with – demanding nude photos or trying to bully them into sex they didn't want to have. Many men have had a girlfriend who would use guilt and emotional manipulation to pressure them into doing whatever she wanted, no matter how they may have felt about it.

People like this *thrive* on those who don't have the confidence and the self-worth to stand their ground and push back.

Of course, there are a multitude of ways that people will try to trade on the poor boundaries of others. Almost everyone has had that one toxic friend who would steamroll over others in order to get their own way, using the social contract of obligation to push others into doing what he or she wanted. Or perhaps they had the friend who would get pissed at them for disagreeing in public, or the two-faced smilers who are pleasant to people's faces but have no problem cutting them down when their back is turned.

How many times have you had someone – a friend, a lover, a family member – pull a guilt-trip on you? "Oh, you're the only one who could do this for me, everybody else just ignores me. You're the only person who cares about me," for example, or the ever-classic, "If you really cared, you'd do this simple thing for me." They are trying to use guilt as their tool to pressure you into taking on their responsibilities. How many people have said, "How can you not do V when I've done X, Y and Z for you?" – even when you didn't want them to do these things? They are trading on reciprocity, making you feel obligated to them because they've done something for you.

These are people trying to exploit your poor boundaries. So are the friends and lovers who will try to drag you into their drama – who have a never-ending list of complaints and grievances that they expect you to take responsibility for. They are the ones who throw childish tantrums and yell at you, who try to hold you hostage to their whims with threats – threats of cheating on you, threats of breaking up with you, even threats of self-harm in order to keep you in line.

But the only way they can control you is if you *let* them. You have the power to stop them, if you would only reach out and take it. It takes two to play their games… but only one to bring the games to a grinding halt.

Take a Stand

It's one thing if you're willingly making a sacrifice for someone because you care about them and you want to make them happy. That is part of being a good partner in a relationship. However, it's another entirely when you're being made to feel *obligated* to do it or when you're only acting in a particular manner because you're afraid of the consequences. Sometimes you need to face those consequences in order to establish your boundaries.

It can be incredibly difficult to establish your boundaries at first, to say to someone, "No, I'm not going to let you guilt me into doing something you *know* I don't want to do," or to tell somebody that they're treating you badly and you won't put up with it. There's a tremendous amount of social pressure to give in; people who play emotional games are masters at using the social contract against you.

But at the same time, once you take that power back – when you establish that you're not going to play games – it makes you so much stronger. It's not a get-out-of-consequences free card; you have to be willing to face the consequences of refusing to let others use you. This may mean having to deal with the ensuing drama. It may mean ending the relationship. But all of that is worth it when you realize how liberating it is when you no longer allow people to manipulate or push you into accepting responsibilities that aren't yours.

I had a girlfriend who insisted on talking to me on the phone for hours at a time every day, no matter what else I might have planned. If I didn't clear my schedule for her, she would make my life miserable until I begged her forgiveness. She had trust issues, she would tell me, so it was on me to reassure her every day that things were just fine. And I would give in because I didn't want to deal with the drama if I said "no." What I should have done instead is simply put my foot down. I should have started by offering a compromise – we'll schedule calls and talk from this time to that time each day – and kept to the schedule. If she pressured me to talk longer than I wanted to or fit into my plans, then it would be time to say, "No. You know I have other plans, which is why we set this schedule. I want you to respect my wishes and my plans."

Would there be a fight? Quite possibly. But being willing to face the other person's push-back is a critical part of maintaining boundaries. And if that person continues to push against your boundaries despite your clear wishes, they've made it clear that this is not someone you want to be in a relationship with. And therein lies the benefit of strong boundaries: the better you are at maintaining them, the less often you will end up dealing with manipulative users and toxic partners.

Yes, making that first step – being willing to take a stand and accept the consequences of doing so – is difficult, but establishing boundaries will bolster your self-esteem and confidence. It will feel empowering to realize that you not only have a choice, but that you can and will decide what you are and are not responsible for. Just as poor boundaries can be self-reinforcing, so too can having strong ones. By drawing that line in the sand and saying that you will not be pushed past it, you're eliminating neediness from your life; you're saying that you're not so desperate for affection that you're willing to allow others to treat you like a doormat just so that they'll like you.

And that is incredibly attractive.

BLUNDER #2: DEVELOPING A CASE OF ONEITIS

One of the hardest lessons to learn when it comes to building your new dating life is the acceptance that not everyone is going to like you, not in the way you want them to. This isn't a bad thing; once you realize that some people aren't going to want you back, you're free to find the women who will. However, there will almost inevitably be one of those times where you don't want to find someone else... because who else could possibly measure up to *her*? So rather than spending your time going out and meeting one of the millions of amazing women who are out there, you spend all of your time focused on *her* – your one true obsession. You feel as though she's your one chance at love, and nobody else in the world could mean as much to you as she did.

You're suffering from Oneitis – an unrequited crush on someone that borders on obsession. She may be an ex-girlfriend that you haven't been able to get over, even though it's been months – or even *years* – since you broke up. She may be the woman that you've always had a thing for, but who just stubbornly, rudely, never returned your feelings. She may have given you the Let's Just Be Friends speech, or you may never even have made your move in the first place... but you can't stop thinking about her.

Oneitis is a pernicious affliction. It doesn't feel like anything is wrong; in fact, it frequently feels amazing. In its earliest stages, Oneitis feels almost exactly like the honeymoon period of a new relationship. Everything they do is fascinating and you just can't stop staring at them when you think they aren't looking. You do surreptitious deep-breathing exercises in their vicinity just so that you can properly appreciate how good they smell. The way the sunlight glints in their hair is hypnotic. They are, for all intents and purposes, *perfect.*

If they're your ex, then your past relationship becomes the benchmark for all relationships. It may have had its problems, sure (obviously – she dumped you) but when you were together it was just *right* and how could you possibly let go of something that amazing? Surely a love like that is worth fighting for?

Except... it's not. Oneitis is a self-limiting belief, a manifestation of a scarcity mentality and one that makes you miserable. Living with Oneitis is an invitation for continual heartbreak; your dearest fantasies of being together will continually break against the rocks of reality. Instead, you'll watch her date and fall in love with other men and feel as though your soul is being ripped from your body over and over again. You will waste months, potentially even *years,* of your life that you will never get back – time that you could have used to find other women to be happy with.

Recognizing the Symptoms of Oneitis

Part of the problem with Oneitis is that it's often difficult to self-diagnose. After all, it doesn't feel like anything is wrong; this person is so amazing, so perfect for you that it can seem only natural that you think about them all the time. So when you find yourself getting hung up over one person, it's worth asking yourself some questions:

Are you spending all your energy trying to figure out how to win them over?

People with Oneitis will go to unbelievable lengths in order to chase their crush. Many will involve some variation of the Platonic Friend Backdoor Maneuver, deliberately putting themselves in the Friend Zone in hopes that they can slowly worm their way into the woman's affections. This is especially true if the victim of Oneitis used to date his crush. He will frequently lie about being over her and insist that he's completely cool with her wanting to date other people. Of course, his *true* goal is to stay close to her, in hopes of wearing her down and getting her back.

Others will try more esoteric methods of winning the love of their crush. Many members of the pick-up community got their start due to Oneitis, hoping to find the perfect mix of pre-scripted routines and emotional progression models that would move them from Platonic Friend to Lover. Still more will take inspiration from romantic comedies and make increasingly grand (and ultimately, embarrassing) romantic gestures ranging from ordering thousands of dollars in flowers to purchasing romantic getaways for the two of them in the hopes that material demonstrations of their love might work where dogged patience and wishful thinking have failed.

Do you obsess over her to the point of neglecting other women?

Men suffering from Oneitis frequently elevate their feelings from "obsessive crush" to "an epic love to last the ages." Oneitis can be especially pernicious because it mythologizes the relationship. Many people afflicted with Oneitis will romanticize their own pain; to them, their unrequited love becomes something to be celebrated. In their minds, they have become the hero of their own tragic love story instead of a curious footnote in someone else's relationship. A man with Oneitis isn't just a guy who can't let go. He's someone tormented by fate and if he can only hold on for long enough, then true love will win in the end.

As a result, they never see other women as potential romantic partners. There is no room in their hearts for anyone other than The One; to admit that they feel attraction for anyone else would be tantamount to admitting that their love isn't true. Occasionally, someone with Oneitis will attempt to date someone else – sometimes in order to make the object of their infatuation jealous, other times because it's better than being lonely. All too often, this ends up being profoundly cruel to their prospective girlfriends; a man with Oneitis is rarely dating in good faith. She's merely there to keep him occupied, and he will throw her over at the merest *hint* that he stands a chance with his One.

Does your crush not have any flaws?

When someone has Oneitis, they tend to overlook the multitude of flaws that every human has. They're not in love with the individual so much as their fantasy of her. In their mind, she can do no wrong. She's so singularly amazing that cartoon birds do her hair when she gets up in the morning and even her farts smell of cotton candy. They are perfectly compatible... or at least they would be if only she would realize it. Her sole flaw is that she refuses to love him back.

This symptom is especially bad in sufferers who have been dumped by their crushes. These poor men feel as though their one chance at love has been ruined and that they will never be happy again. They will frequently self-edit their relationship, remaining willfully ignorant of all of the bad parts and changing the high points to glorious fantasies usually only seen by Disney heroines.

Because their crush has been elevated to such levels of perfection, no other woman can possibly compare in the mind of a Oneitis patient. To this end they miss out on other opportunities for sex and romantic relationships with people who are not only better for them, but who might actually love them back.

Do you read meaning into everything she does?

Men with Oneitis are so determined to convince themselves that their crush is starting to fall for them that they will assign meaning to everything that their crush does. Does she twirl her hair while she's talking to you? This means something. Did she agree to go to an impromptu dinner with you? That means something. Did she leave her hand on your shoulder for just a microsecond longer than she normally would? Clearly it's a sign that she's weakening! This quickly becomes a self-inflicted case of apophenia, desperately seeing patterns and significance where none exists. Ultimately, *everything* that she does will be seen as proof that he is making progress. Incremental progress, to be sure, but progress nonetheless.

These little clues that they see in every movement, choice of words and life choices are part of the self-justification that Oneitis victims use to maintain the fantasy. Deep down, people with Oneitis understand that they have no chance. But rather than face up to that harsh reality, they prefer the comforting fantasy that with a little more patience, a little more effort, they can still make that magical fairy tale ending happen. The fantasy of success is, to them, better than the potential reality of rejection that comes with pursuing somebody new.

How to Cure Oneitis

Oneitis has a fairly simple cure, although it's not an easy one: the sufferer has to make the conscious decision to give up. Not to *pretend* to give up, in hopes of fulfilling an "it will happen when you stop looking," but to actually quit. He has to let go of his crush and admit that it's just not going to happen.

It's the finality of that statement that frequently makes it so difficult to get over a case of Oneitis. It can feel like an utter betrayal of one's self, an admission that your love wasn't strong enough or true enough to withstand the trials of outrageous fortune. It can feel as though you're giving up your *one* chance at finding love, because no other woman could possibly be so right. But what makes it especially difficult is that in the end, you have to willingly cut yourself off from your crush.

In many ways, recovering from Oneitis is like trying to break an addiction – and the only way to do that is to go cold turkey. It's a painful but necessary step for recovery. You can never recover from an addiction if you continually throw yourself into temptation's way. Oneitis is never going to fade if you continually torture yourself by Facebook stalking your crush. Staying away from them – eliminating all forms of contact, down to blocking them on social media if necessary – is critical. It's incredibly easy to lie to yourself, to say, "No, I'm totally over her" when in reality, you'd fall for her again in a heartbeat. It's like the alcoholic who insists that one drink wouldn't hurt.

Removing her from your life is what keeps you from relapsing.

During the early days of cutting yourself off from your crush, you want to keep as busy as possible. There's no cure for heartbreak quite like work; this is the time to throw yourself into a period of self-improvement. Go to the gym and get lost in the sensation of your body as you run on the treadmill or vent your frustrations by pounding out more reps on the bench press. Pursue new hobbies and interests, take classes… do anything that will not only distract you but leave you a better person in the end.

And while you do so, look around. Notice how many amazing women there are out there. To quote Tim Minchin's song "If I Didn't Have You": "…your love is one in a million/you couldn't buy it at any price/but of the 9 point 9 9 9 hundred thousand other loves/statistically some of them would be equally nice." The more you notice those other women, the more you *pursue* them, the quicker your Oneitis will fade. You'll be trading in a fantasy for a reality, one that's better than a dream that could never come true.

BLUNDER #3: YOU'VE BEEN TRAPPED IN THE FRIEND ZONE

If there's one dating pitfall that is universally dreaded by men, it's the Friend Zone. It's the dating equivalent of The Bermuda Triangle. It is the Phantom Zone of love. It is the Chateau D'if of l'amour. Every man has heard of it, and almost every man has experienced it.

It's generally accepted wisdom that women automatically classify guys as either Boyfriend or Just Friends, and never the two shall meet. The idea of guys crossing from "Just Friends" to "Boyfriend" is almost exclusively the domain of bad comedies.[1] People who have actually made the leap are like the Loch Ness Monster – everybody's heard of it, almost nobody's seen it, and everyone's pretty sure the people who say they have are lying.

Except they're not. Because the people who've escaped the Friend Zone know a secret that other men don't.

The Friend Zone Doesn't Exist

This is one of the hardest truths to accept: there is no such thing as the Friend Zone. When you're hearing "I just want to be friends," "You're like a brother to me," "I like you but..." or the equally dreaded, "It would ruin our friendship," you're not being thrown in the Friend Zone. What you're actually hearing is the cumulation of a lifetime of social pressure telling women that they can't risk being direct for fear of offending someone. They're

1. ...Starscream.

trying to let you down easy. The words may be "You're just such a good friend to me," but the intended meaning behind it is "I don't want to sleep with you."

That's it. There's no grand conspiracy. There's no "ladder" where men can only be friends or lovers but never both. It's just a case of insufficient attraction. Everything else is about how you react to it.

Now, this doesn't mean that when you've gotten the dreaded "Let's Just Be Friends" speech that you're doomed to a sexless existence. In fact, if you've been following the advice from this book, you should never encounter the Friend Zone[2] ever again. But before this can happen, you have to understand just *why* people hear that LJBF comment.

The Many Forms of "Let's Just Be Friends"

There are a number of ways that someone ends up hearing that their crush has no interest in sleeping with them. Sometimes this happens because they pushed too hard, too fast and ended up ruining the chance of a sexual attraction building naturally. Sometimes, this is intended as a brush-off – the one giving the LJBF speech is hoping that the person on the receiving end will take the hint and leave. Other times, they are being entirely honest and they really *would* prefer to be friends. They may think that sex ruins friendships or they may be interested in somebody else. But then you run into other issues. For example:

---

2. Yes, I know I just said it doesn't exist. We'll be using the term for the sake of simplicity and ease of reference.

The Big Lie from a Nice Guy™

This is what happens when someone is in a platonic relationship under false pretenses. Also known as the Platonic Best Friend Backdoor, the person hearing this has been pretending to be a woman's friend in hopes that he can eventually weasel his way into her heart and/or panties over time. It's the move by men who fear rejection more than being a dishonest prick and would rather submit themselves to the Friend Zone than risk losing the fantasy. This is fundamentally dishonest and a complete dick move; the pretender is trading on his crush's willingness to believe him when he insists that he doesn't have ulterior motives in trying to be friends with her. Ironically, the men who find themselves in this form of the Friend Zone have the hardest time recognizing the harm they're doing – both to themselves and to the women that they claim to care about.

The Mistaken Intentions

Occasionally someone will hear the LJBF speech because they were too shy or afraid of rejection to actually make it *obvious* that they were interested in someone romantically. More often than not, they made an approach, but didn't make it clear from the jump that they were interested in a *date*, not just hanging out as friends… and as a result, ended up being considered as a friend rather than a potential romantic partner. This is why when you're approaching women, it's important to be clear instead of hoping to coast by on ambiguity until you feel more secure on admitting that you like them romantically or sexually, rather than as a friend.

The Genuine Friend

Occasionally, you can get hit by a sudden case of the tingly-pants for someone who is legitimately your friend out of goddamn nowhere. You may suddenly realize that your childhood friend is actually really hot. Sometimes it's a case of a crush striking out of the clear blue sky and making things complicated. Occasionally it's a matter of feelings that have been simmering undetected coming to the surface; after all, it's clear you have *emotional* chemistry at the very least. Is it so strange to think that perhaps there's some *physical* attraction there as well?

Unfortunately, this scenario can be one of the most pernicious and hardest to avoid as it often seems to come on suddenly and out of nowhere. It is also one of the hardest to escape from; since these tend to occur in long-standing friendships, it can be difficult to reframe the situation.

In any of these scenarios, the best way to not get stuck in the Friend Zone is to avoid it in the first place by making your intentions clear from the start.

Understand the Difference Between Friends and Lovers

The key to avoiding being in the Friend Zone is to recognize that the way you behave is going to affect how others see you. If you act like a friend, people are going to see you as a potential friend. If you want to be a potential lover, you have to act like one.

A lot of guys are hesitant to put themselves out there in an obvious manner. They're afraid of being rejected, so they play the plausible deniability game, where any tentative move towards showing interest can easily be passed off as friendship with nervous laughter and stammering. Other times, they go overboard in trying to generate the emotional chemistry and neglect the physical side of things. Cold hard truth time: every relationship, no matter how fairy-tale romantic it may be, has a core of sexual attraction. If you want to be a potential lover, you *have* to be willing to make things sexual. This doesn't mean that you have to act like a sleazeball who's only interested in getting her into bed, but you *do* have to be willing to flirt, touch and generally make it clear that while you may love her for her mind, you *want* her for her ass. Light, flirty, sexual humor and a willingness to break the touch barrier are keys towards establishing that yes, this *is* (potentially) a sex thing.

You also have to avoid acting like her new BFF. Don't get me wrong; I'm not saying that you shouldn't be friends. In fact, a strong friendship is key to a strong relationship. But at the same time, behavior that is appropriate in close friends does not read the same when it gets mapped onto a potential lover. Being constantly available, hanging out all the time (in non-romantic contexts) and talking at all hours can be great... but it doesn't send the "lover" vibe. This is one of those times when it's all too easy to make it seem like you have no sexual or romantic interest in the other person, which will make them consider your interest as platonic and respond to you accordingly.

But that's how you avoid the Friend Zone. What do you do if you're *already* friends and you want to be more?

Hit the Cosmic Reset Button

One of the reasons why it's hard to shift from being a friend to a lover is because we have very firm ideas about other people. We tend to have mental associations with people in our lives, a form of emotional shorthand that describes how we relate to them. These associations will filter how we see them and interpret their actions and behaviors; everything people say or do is seen through the prism of that relationship. This is why you often hear, "Oh man, it'd be like making out with my brother!" when asking women about hooking up with certain male friends. The lack of sexual attraction is a key part of their mental image.

If you want to break that association, then you have to essentially break their mental image of you. You have to hit the cosmic reset button that gives you the opportunity to redefine your status quo, allowing for the potential of sexual and romantic attraction.

One of the easiest ways to do this is to change your look and style. If one of your friends has ever made a sudden change to their wardrobe or hairstyle – one that seems out of character for them – then you've felt that cognitive dissonance in action. You know that it's your friend, but they've moved so far out of your expectation that you're forced to look at them in a new light. Sometimes the changes work – they feel natural and help emphasize your friend's good points – and sometimes they don't... but either way, your mental image is shaken.

Back in my bad old days I didn't exactly know how to dress or how to carry myself. Everything about me screamed "LOW SELF-ESTEEM!" My style was "whatever is (mostly) clean and is comfortable." My archetype was "Reclusive Nerd." This was my default for decade, and this was the image that was locked into the heads of my friends, especially the ones I had an interest in.

When my friends saw me few years later, they were astounded. I had made a complete transformation – I'd lost weight and taken up weight training. I had learned to appreciate stylish, well-fitting clothes. I had a hairstyle that wasn't the SuperCuts Discount Special and I had much more confidence, even a certain level of swagger. I was no longer "that nice guy I've known for years" – I was almost a stranger. They had to re-learn who I was and this gave me the opportunity to re-define our relationship.

Now, this is not to say that you have to completely re-invent yourself; in fact, you might be surprised by the response you get on some small changes to your look. Better fitting clothes and a new, more flattering hairstyle can work wonders. If you wear glasses, consider contacts. If you have facial hair, shave it off or adopt a style that works better with your face. The more striking the change, the more it shakes up the person's mental image of you.

Just keep in mind: the longer you've known your crush – and the closer you are with them – the harder it can be to shake that mental image of you. I'd been friends with mine for close to a decade or longer before they stopped seeing me as "just a friend," and part of what assisted my transformation in their minds was not seeing them for a few years.

Just as with avoiding getting the LJBF speech, you want to build attraction. It's important that she see you – and know that you see *her* – as a sexual being.

At the same time, you can't just start telling her that you think she's hot and you totally want to screw. Doing so is going to make her think you're only her friend because you've been trying to get in her panties from the beginning. You want to acknowledge your attraction to her, but that you love being her friend too. You're not friends with her because you've been harboring this secret desire for years, you're friends with her because she's awesome. The fact that she's awesome is also why you are attracted to her.

Part of why people can feel uneasy when their friends admit to being attracted to them is that they worry that this is going to affect their friendship, and with good reason. One of the worst things you can do if you want to try to move from friend to lover is to make your friendship a referendum on "But *whyyyyy* won't you date me?" Not only is that unfair to do to a friend, but it's a very good way to destroy a friendship. All you're going to do is make her profoundly uncomfortable and wish the two of you could go back to *before* you made your little confession, *especially* if she just doesn't like you that way. Instead, you want her to understand that you like her... but that it's not a big deal.

The attitude you want to convey – even when you're flirting with her – is "I like you. I want to get together with you, but it's totally cool if you don't feel the same way. I think you're amazing and value you as a friend, and even if nothing happens, I'm *still* cool with being your friend. That's not going to change." Flirt, but be uninvested in the outcome; flirt just because it's fun to flirt. If it makes her uncomfortable, then lay off the flirting. Not putting her on the defensive about how she does or doesn't feel and showing that you recognize and respect her boundaries is going to make her that much more comfortable with you and the way you feel about her. After all, if she's not comfortable with you, her feelings aren't going to change.

Date Other People

When you're trying to make the jump from friend to lover, it's important to still be dating other people casually.

Yes, it seems counterintuitive, but it works.

To start with, the last thing you want is to end up with a case of Oneitis. Dating other people will keep you from spending all your time whining about the Friend Zone and annoying all of your friends about how unfair it all is. It also helps keep you grounded in the realities of relationships instead of getting caught up in the fantasies about what dating your friend could be like. It's also important to be reminded that not only are there other awesome women out there, but they find you attractive too. This will boost your confidence and self-esteem and you will ultimately be less invested in your non-relationship in the Friend Zone.

It also will help her realize that you're serious about not letting it affect your friendship. Yes, you're attracted to her, but you're not pining away. And she'll notice that clearly you have something going for you if all of these other women find you attractive. Maybe, *maybe* she will get just a little jealous that these women are getting the attention that used to be hers and hers alone. But if not, it's still no big deal.

Ultimately it's a win-win situation; on the one hand, you win your friend's heart. On the other, you may have been shot down by your friend, but you're still dating awesome women.

Friendship Is Not the Consolation Prize

Now here's the part you probably don't want to hear: sometimes you can't get out of the Friend Zone.

Some people just aren't going to like you the way you want them to, no matter what you do. You can do everything right to try to make the jump, but it still may never happen. The chemistry just may not be there. She may have met someone who she clicks with in ways you don't. She may be attracted to you, but really does worry about ruining the friendship. Ultimately, the reasons don't matter; it comes down to how she feels and, sadly, she doesn't feel that way about you.

But here's what you need to remember: friendship is *not* the consolation prize. It's not the lesser offer. A woman offering you friendship isn't the end of the world or horrifically undesirable, and to be perfectly honest, it's incredibly insulting to treat it that way. You're telling her – in no uncertain terms – that you see talking with her and spending time with her to be a chore that's only worth it if it leads to sex.

If you only like someone when you think there's a chance that they're going to touch your penis but resent them when they won't... well, we've pretty much figured out *why* they don't like you that much.

Now, just because someone wants to be friends doesn't mean that you're obligated to take them up on it, especially if you don't think you can let go of your attraction enough to be a legitimate friend to them. But if you can, it's frequently worth it. Presumably the things that made her an awesome person still make her an awesome person, even when sex is off the table. And let's face it: couldn't you use more awesome people in your life?

And look at it another way: just because they don't want to date you doesn't mean that they don't know people who will. If you can handle rejection with grace and be a real friend to her – as opposed to hanging around just because you hope she's going to change her mind – then you're showing that you're an awesome guy. And she's going to be sure to tell her friends how awesome you are.

Just because it didn't work out with one person doesn't mean that it's the end of the world.

In fact, it could be the start of something *amazing*.

CHAPTER 12.

AFTER COMPLETION

A NEW BEGINNING

There is a saying my father taught me: the only things we value are the things we fight for. And he was right.

My personal transformation wasn't easy; in fact most of the time, it was pants-shittingly intimidating. I was forcing myself so far outside of what I thought was my comfort zone that I would come home at night and start crying. I was forcing myself do things that I thought were literally *impossible* for me and then do it all again the next night. I worried that I couldn't change, then I worried that I couldn't possibly be good enough. I lost track of how many nights I couldn't sleep because I was so caught up in my anxieties that all the improvement I'd made was just illusion and I was still the same old loser I'd always been.

I spent years trying to become someone else only to realize I couldn't stand that person and then tried to unlearn being him. I spent thousands of hours practicing, trying to find out what worked through trial and error and why. I'd take one step forward and then end up taking five more back. I lost months of progress by letting myself get caught up in a nasty case of Oneitis over an ex-girlfriend, even when *I knew better*. I got my heart broken more times than I could count by total strangers. Some nights were the best nights of my life. Some were easily the worst and I wondered if there was any point to *anything*.

And you know what? I don't think I would trade it for the world. For all the heartache and the confusion and the tears, it lead me to who I am today – and I am happier and more satisfied than I've ever been.

Now I want to help *you* get to that place too.

This book is the product of all the mistakes I made over the years and all the things I had to learn the hard way. This is all the information I wish *I'd* had when I was first starting out. You've got an amazing adventure ahead of you and this will help you get there a lot faster than I did.

Before I leave you to the challenge of becoming your new, *best* self, I want to share something with you. I have a tattoo on my forearm, the 63rd Hexagram from the I-Ching. It symbolizes the concept "After Completion"[1]; it means that the moment you think you've mastered something, that's the moment you realize you're only *beginning* to learn. You haven't finished; you're merely at a point of equilibrium, the well-deserved rest before you advance to the next level of mastery.

Just getting a girlfriend or a lover isn't the end; it's the *beginning*. Relationships, whether romantic or platonic, purely sexual or completely chaste, don't exist without work or effort. Similarly, working to improve yourself and building your new life doesn't stop just because you've reached your goals. There will always be more to

---

1. The fact that it's also the mark of the Arashikage ninja clan from GI Joe is completely irrelevant.

learn, more to work on, more to strive for and more to improve.

And it will be *amazing.*

It *will* be hard. It's going to take practice and effort. You're *going* to fuck up. You're going to make mistakes. It's going to be incredibly frustrating and you'll wonder if there's any point to it all.

I didn't say that it would be easy.

But it will be *worth it.*

Good luck.

FURTHER RESOURCES

There will always be more to learn and more ways to grow as you continue to build your new life and become the person you've always wanted to be. Visit Paging Dr. NerdLove for more of the latest and most up-to-date information on dating, relationships and self-improvement.

Twitter: @DrNerdLove

Facebook.com/DrNerdlove

ABOUT THE AUTHOR

Harris O'Malley is a dating coach who provides geek dating advice at his blog Paging Dr. NerdLove as well as Kotaku and Thought Catalog.

He and his work have been featured on Buzzfeed, The Good Man Project, The Daily Dot, Think Progress, Lifehacker, Wired, The Huffington Post, Sex Nerd Sandra, Sex With Timaree, Daily Life, Slate, New York Magazine, The Austin-American Statesman, The Guardian, The Washington Post, MTV's Guy Code, Boing Boing and The Harvard Business Journal and many others. Paging Dr. NerdLove has been named one of the top 10 geek dating blogs by DatingAdvice.com.

He lives in Austin, Texas.

Printed in Great Britain
by Amazon